ROUTLEDGE LIBRARY EDITIONS:
FINANCIAL MARKETS

Volume 17

THE ECONOMIC ORGANISATION OF A FINANCIAL SYSTEM

THE ECONOMIC ORGANISATION OF A FINANCIAL SYSTEM

EDWIN H. NEAVE

LONDON AND NEW YORK

First published in 1991 by Routledge

This edition first published in 2018
by Routledge
2 Park Square, Milton Park, Abingdon, Oxon OX14 4RN

and by Routledge
711 Third Avenue, New York, NY 10017

Routledge is an imprint of the Taylor & Francis Group, an informa business

© Edwin H. Neave, 1991

All rights reserved. No part of this book may be reprinted or reproduced or utilised in any form or by any electronic, mechanical, or other means, now known or hereafter invented, including photocopying and recording, or in any information storage or retrieval system, without permission in writing from the publishers.

Trademark notice: Product or corporate names may be trademarks or registered trademarks, and are used only for identification and explanation without intent to infringe.

British Library Cataloguing in Publication Data
A catalogue record for this book is available from the British Library

ISBN: 978-1-138-56537-1 (Set)
ISBN: 978-0-203-70248-2 (Set) (ebk)
ISBN: 978-1-138-57104-4 (Volume 17) (hbk)
ISBN: 978-0-203-70275-8 (Volume 17) (ebk)

Publisher's Note
The publisher has gone to great lengths to ensure the quality of this reprint but points out that some imperfections in the original copies may be apparent.

Disclaimer
The publisher has made every effort to trace copyright holders and would welcome correspondence from those they have been unable to trace.

The Economic Organisation of a Financial System

Edwin H. Neave

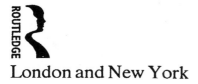
London and New York

First published 1991
by Routledge
11 New Fetter Lane, London EC4P 4EE

Simultaneously published in the USA and Canada
by Routledge
a division of Routledge, Chapman and Hall, Inc.
29 West 35th Street, New York, NY 10001

© 1991 Edwin H. Neave

Typeset by NWL Editorial Services, Langport, Somerset TA10 9DG
Printed and bound in Great Britain by
Biddles Ltd, Guildford and King's Lynn

All rights reserved. No part of this book may be reprinted or
reproduced or utilized in any form or by any electronic,
mechanical, or other means, now known or hereafter invented,
including photocopying and recording, or in any information
storage or retrieval system, without permission in writing from
the publishers.

British Library Cataloguing in Publication Data
Neave, Edwin, H.
   The Economic Organisation of a Financial System
   1. Financial management. Decision making. Theories
   I. Title
   658.151

ISBN 0–415–05353–6

Library of Congress Cataloging in Publication Data is available

For Liz

Contents

Figures	ix
Preface	xi
1 Introduction	1
Existing approaches	3
Present approach	5
Outline of remaining chapters	6
2 Financial system agents and environment	12
System characteristics	13
Transactor information	16
Transactor capabilities and criteria	21
Anatomy of transactions	25
Transactions and governance costs	27
Summary	30
3 Governance mechanisms: major types	32
Governance mechanism capabilities	32
Market governance	39
Intermediary governance	42
Other governance mechanisms	46
Summary	48
4 Specialised governance mechanisms	50
Specialised markets	52
Specialised intermediaries	60
Relations between mechanisms	67
Evolution of system organisation	72
Summary	73
5 Aligning mechanisms with transactions	76
Demands for funds	76

Contents

Financiers' supplies of funds	81
Markets for corporate control	85
Markets for financing intermediaries	88
Summary	91

6 Managing transaction terms — 94
- *Principles* — 94
- *Complete contracting* — 97
- *Incomplete contracting* — 101
- *Effects of informational differences* — 106
- *Summary* — 108

7 Managing portfolios — 110
- *Portfolios of marketable securities* — 111
- *Portfolios of non-marketable securities* — 115
- *Intermediary income management* — 119
- *Managing closely held investments* — 121
- *Summary* — 122

8 System organisation and performance — 125
- *Perfect markets and securities prices* — 126
- *Completeness and incompleteness* — 131
- *Securities markets and information* — 135
- *Intermediation and finance* — 141
- *Routine and innovative transacting* — 145
- *Summary* — 146

9 Financial system change and performance — 149
- *Forces of change* — 149
- *Performance problems* — 154
- *Remedial intervention* — 159
- *Actions and responses* — 161
- *Summary* — 164

10 Finance and economic development — 166
- *How domestic finance affects economic development* — 167
- *How external finance affects development* — 173
- *Effective development policies* — 173
- *How economic development encourages financial activity* — 177
- *Summary* — 180

11 Conclusions — 182

References — 186

Index — 194

Figures

3.1 Transaction information and governance mechanisms 33
4.1 Technologies and governance mechanisms 51
6.1 Transaction circumstances and governance structures 96
6.2 Information and contract terms: risk 98
6.3 Sources of uncertainty and governance structures 102

Preface

This book develops a descriptive theory of a financial system's organisation and functions. It attempts to reconcile neoclassical financial theory and managerial finance by synthesising the main findings of these studies within an institutional economics framework. There seems to be considerable need for such a work. Most financial theorists do not develop a financial system perspective, since they usually restrict themselves to studying those institutional details with which their theories are directly concerned. Partly as a result of this specialisation, financial executives and students of managerial finance do not have ready access to summaries of the principal theoretical results, and are consequently inhibited in commenting on current theoretical perspectives from an institutional point of view. Accordingly, this book is intended to help relate the complementary perspectives of current theory and current practice. Synthetic works like this book can, if they are successful, eventually strengthen the relations between current theory and current practice.

The contents of this book have been used in financial institutions courses offered to three very different audiences: undergraduate students in business, economics, and law, graduate students in business administration, and financial system professionals continuing their education. With each of these groups, the material has been used to outline the principal elements of modern financial systems, to examine the economic forces which shape the manner in which these elements interact within any given financial system, and to sketch how financial systems change.

Since this book applies the theory of organisational economics to the study of a financial system, its contents can also serve graduate students by presenting them with a detailed illustration of how organisational economics can be put to work. Indeed, this material has been used for several years to supplement the regular selection of journal articles typically covered in a doctoral seminar in organisa-

Preface

tional economics, and student experience indicates it helps to round out the lessons of the more traditional readings.

Through their insight, interest and persistent inquiries, many students have helped to shape the form in which the material is now presented. I hope the resulting book does justice to these students' very real contributions, and that the work will thus prove useful to others in structuring their studies of financial systems. The students' contributions are too numerous for them all to be detailed. Nevertheless, some readers of the manuscript's more recent versions should be recognised explicitly. I have particularly appreciated the comments of Byron Lew, Yue Li, Melissa Lu, Harold Ogden, Yang Hoon Pang, and Bo Pazderka, all of whom have read and commented on parts of the present work. Their interest has helped to improve the exposition; whatever errors and lack of clarity remain are my own doing.

It is also a pleasure to acknowledge the support of a sabbatical leave from Queen's University, Kingston, which greatly accelerated the preparation of the manuscript. I am grateful too to the University of St. Andrews, Fife, and particularly to Peter Grinyer, for hospitality and support during the early stages of the writing.

Finally, my sincere thanks to the people at Routledge who helped bring this work to fruition: Peter Sowden, Alan Jarvis, Jennifer Binnie and George Moore. Their enthusiasm, professionalism and support have been invaluable.

Edwin H. Neave
Kingston, Canada

Chapter one

Introduction

The questions of how a financial system is organised and of why financial systems assume certain configurations are important topics for economic analysis, but they are questions which have not yet been examined extensively. Rather, financial theorists have focused on explaining various specialised aspects of financial system functions, and empiricists have applied their skills to testing such specialised explanations. Thus modern financial theory and the empirical studies based on it consider some financial system components in great detail, but leave others almost wholly unexamined. For example, many relations between securities prices are explained by arbitrage pricing theory, and a considerable number of such explanations are supported by data. On the other hand, speculative bubbles in securities prices, or enthusiasms for expanding certain lines of business at certain times, are much more controversial phenomena, and are currently much less satisfactorily explained. Yet these phenomena are also prominent features of modern financial systems.

Similarly, modern financial theory addresses only some of the relations between a financial system's specialised components, while leaving others quite unexplained. As already mentioned, modern financial theory emphasises price relations based on arbitrage, and many tests of arbitrage-based theories have been carried out. But neither theorist nor empiricist has yet devoted a corresponding degree of attention to, say, the linking functions performed by financial intermediation.

The methodology employed by modern financial theory helps to explain why its results have developed in the current specialised fashion. Nearly all modern financial theory uses the methods of neoclassical microeconomics, the approach of which assumes that each economic agent has a well-defined goal, such as maximisation of current wealth. These single-minded agents are faced with highly structured decision problems, within the framework of which they can readily select actions (optimal actions) best suited to achieving their purposes. The body of financial theory based on these assumptions of highly rational, highly structured decision making is work referred to henceforth as *neoclassical financial theory*.[1]

The explanations of neoclassical financial theory are valuable in developing descriptive theory, not only because many theoretical propositions are highly satisfying from an intellectual point of view, but also because many of the theories' predictions are supported by careful examination of financial market data. Work on the functions of public securities markets is a case in point. For, this work explains how market prices of securities are determined at equilibrium, and data from highly active public securities markets supports many of its principal predictions. As an additional advantage, this theory both complements and is complemented by microeconomics: it helps to define the circumstances in which markets can best perform the task of allocating financial resources.

As a second example of how neoclassical finance can contribute to developing a descriptive theory, other works explain some of the functions of financial intermediaries, and empirical studies provide information about intermediaries' operating costs. When fitted into an appropriate synthetic framework, these results can be employed to help explain why a financial system is typically composed of both specialised financial markets and financial intermediaries, and to show how these different system components relate to each other.

On the other hand, the very strengths of neoclassical financial theory lie in assumptions which restrict the applicability of its explanations. In particular, decisions to enter new lines of business are not well explained by neoclassical financial theory, which offers little more than the view that innovation will be stimulated by perceptions of new profit opportunities. Neoclassical financial theory has little to say about how potential profit opportunities might be detected, nor about how strategies to exploit them might be formulated. Thus, other bodies of thought are needed to help organise and elaborate a more comprehensive view of financial system activity. For example, theories of decision making under uncertainty can be examined in a search for some explanations of how agents might take tentative, exploratory actions.

If agents' characteristics and capabilities are to be viewed more broadly than they are within the confines of neoclassical financial theory, an integrating framework is needed to relate the neoclassical findings to other theories and to current practice. Although it has not previously been applied in extensive detail to the study of entire financial systems, *institutional economics*, with its focus on descriptive economic theories of actual institutions, can provide such a framework.[2] In particular, Oliver Williamson (e.g., 1972, 1988) argues that

Introduction

different, specialised kinds of financing arrangements are deliberately aligned with the requirements of different kinds of financial transactions in ways which render financial transacting as cost-effective as possible. Since it uses a broader interpretation of cost-effectiveness than does neoclassical financial theory, Williamson's approach provides a framework capable of synthesising the findings of the present study.

Since it examines relations between financial systems and economic growth, development economics can further supplement institutional economics' explanations of financial system evolution. For, development economics addresses questions regarding the real and financial impacts of monetary, fiscal and regulatory policies, all of which can help supplement an understanding of financial system function and change. Incidentally, the converse may also be true: the analyses of this book may eventually contribute to the field of development economics. For, the latter has not yet extensively considered the importance of financial system composition: i.e., the influence of specific institutional arrangements on relations between economic and financial development.

The foregoing overview suggests that combining findings from the different fields just mentioned could be a worthwhile endeavour, and the rest of this Chapter outlines such an approach in greater detail. The next section provides a more detailed overview of neoclassical financial theory, and its successor indicates how these findings can be related within the institutional economics framework. The last section sketches the rest of this book's development.

Existing approaches

Considering a financial system in its entirety shows both where existing studies contribute to explaining system organisation and where additional work remains to be done. Neoclassical financial theory offers valuable explanations of how securities prices are determined, and empirical studies of highly active public securities markets confirm many of its propositions. Neoclassical theory has also made considerable progress in establishing the allocative and efficiency properties of financial markets. However, the results from neoclassical theory are derived under special assumptions which are simultaneously valuable and limiting. The value of the usual neoclassical assumptions lies in their potential for clarifying difficult analytical issues. As for limitations, the same assumptions rule out important practical considerations which also influence financial system form and functions.

Neoclassical financial theory largely depends on the assumptions of no (or inconsequential) transactions costs and well specified informational conditions. Theoretical investigations almost always assume either that agents use the same probability distributions or, if their views differ, that the differences can still be described as differences between well-defined probability distributions. Theoretical investigations rarely examine how such probability distributions are determined, nor do they consider what might occur if agents were not able to formulate the distributions at reasonable costs. In essence, neoclassical financial theory assumes that agents can formulate complex decision problems precisely and costlessly, and that they can determine the problems' solutions accurately and costlessly. In the rest of this book, such agents will sometimes be referred to as hyperrational.

When agents are hyperrational, they understand clearly the relations between alternative decisions and the decisions' impact on their respective wealth positions.[3] Thus, the assumption of hyperrationality makes it easier to predict how agents will behave, and in some instances the predictions will be descriptively accurate. On the other hand, the assumption of hyperrationality excludes many interesting situations pertinent to a complete explanation of how financial systems are organised in practice, and how the agents in them actually operate. For these reasons, it is important to assess the scope of neoclassical financial theory's descriptive validity, and to consider what alternative, complementary explanations might be applicable when the neoclassical approach has a lesser degree of descriptive validity.

In practice, agents do not always have the computational capabilities possessed by their hyperrational counterparts. Moreover, the information on which real life agents base their actions is not always as well structured as neoclassical theory assumes. Rather, formulating decision problems and finding their solutions can prove to be costly tasks which agents are less than wholly competent to carry out. That is, nearly all neoclassical theory studies financial decisions in the highly structured settings which Knight (1933) referred to as risk, but many practical problems arise under conditions better characterised as Knightian uncertainty. These possibilities are only infrequently recognised: few recent financial theorists other than Williamson (e.g., 1988) examine circumstances which effectively retain Knight's (1933) classic distinction.

The importance of Knight's distinction rests on its ability to explain what would otherwise be puzzling phenomena. In the arguments to follow, many features of financial transactions will be explained in terms of their usefulness in dealing with uncertainty. Indeed, many existing financial practices cannot fully be explained

Introduction

unless the effects of uncertainty are recognised explicitly. To give a straightforward example, neoclassical financial theory cannot explain why practitioners use such rules of thumb as payback criteria, since examples can be constructed in which payback rules clearly conflict with the prescriptions of present value maximisation. Yet the problem with such demonstrations may be the manner in which the decision problem is posed: payback rules can also be interpreted as attempts to recognise and to deal with the effects of uncertainty.[4]

Neoclassical financial theory is similarly limited in its ability to explain financial system change. Indeed, it may fairly be said that the theory is better at explaining well established practices rather than it is at illuminating the creative or exploratory aspects of finance, the dynamics of technological change, or the evolution of sophisticated financial systems from primitive ones. For, financial system change largely occurs under uncertainty rather than under objectively specified risk, and many of the interesting features of uncertainty are assumed away when decision problems are formulated in a manner conducive to neoclassical investigation.[5]

Present approach

In its attempt to provide a descriptive theory capable of bridging some of the gaps between existing normative concepts and current practice, this book uses institutional economics to explain financial system organisation and change. Following Williamson (1988) the book first defines three basic *governance mechanisms* which can be used to effect and administer financial transactions – markets, financial intermediaries, and internal allocation procedures. Next, this book analyses the relative advantages of using each mechanism. These advantages differ according to the capabilities of the mechanisms, and according to how the capabilities relate to transaction requirements.

Each mechanism can be used to administer particular and distinct classes of transactions cost-effectively, but no one mechanism has an absolute advantage in administering all types of financial transactions. Differences between capabilities, along with differences in transaction requirements, mean that each governance mechanism has a cost advantage for administering at least some types of transactions. If this were not the case, the different types of mechanisms could not all continue to survive in a competitive financial system.[6]

This book also contends that the contractual terms of a financial transaction are chosen to meet transaction requirements cost-effectively. Accordingly, each transaction's *governance structure* – the combination of governance mechanism and contractual terms used to administer it – is chosen for its capabilities in dealing with the transaction's particular requirements.

The most effective way of carrying out a transaction depends on both the transacting agents and the transaction itself, particularly its informational environment. Thus the subsequent analysis specifies agents' purposes, their capabilities, and the risks or uncertainties they perceive. In addition, some aspects of choosing a governance structure depend on interactions between the kinds of agents and the kinds of transactions with which they are concerned. For example, agents' levels of competence, and changes in those levels, can determine whether transactions are better regarded as uncertain or merely risky. Thus agents with greater competence sometimes perceive transactions as merely risk, while their less competent fellows will behave as if facing uncertainty.

Agents' attempts to transact cost-effectively explain financial system change as well as its static structure. Thus when transaction economics are changing, studying the changes' effects can show how financial systems will typically evolve. Such explanations have more than descriptive usefulness: they can also be used to help choose appropriate policies, either for financial regulation or for enhancing financial and economic development.

To summarise, this book develops a positive theory of the economic determinants of financial system organisation and change. Its theme is to show how transactions' requirements are aligned with governance capabilities to determine financial system form. Its development is based on a combination of neoclassical financial theory, institutional economics (largely as elaborated by Oliver Williamson), and observations of current practice. Principal findings of development economics are used to help round out the picture.

Outline of remaining chapters

The book is organised as follows. Chapter 2 defines the dimensions along which financial system activities are analysed. These dimensions include the nature of agents, their goals and the conditions under which they transact. While agents' goals determine the system's basic driving forces, the nature of any informational differences between them, and the costs of dealing with these differences, profoundly affect the ways agents transact.

For example, transactions are much more simply effected when financier and client both view a transaction as merely risky, and particularly if they both assess the risks similarly. If one or both parties views a transaction as involving uncertainty (in which case their respective assessments are also likely to differ importantly) it may not

Introduction

even be possible for them to transact. However if they are still able to come to a mutually agreeable arrangement, the governance structure financiers employ will typically be more elaborate and more costly than in the case of agreed risks, and will very likely incorporate attempts to deal with differences in the agents' information.

Chapter 3, following Williamson, distinguishes three mechanisms for governing financial transactions – markets, intermediaries, and internal allocations. Each mechanism has specialised capabilities, giving it an advantage in administering some, but not all, kinds of transactions. The advantages are best explained by elaborating the main costs of using each mechanism and comparing them to the benefits it can realise. Both governance costs and governance capabilities differ according to mechanism type, and transactions differ in their governance requirements. Choices between capabilities and transaction requirements are made on the basis of perceived cost-effectiveness: the financial system is organised to align these capabilities and the requirements of different transaction types (cf. Williamson, 1988).

Chapter 4 explains that most governance mechanisms are specialised in attempts to enhance their particular capabilities. Specialisation is intended to increase revenues, decrease operating costs, or both. In any of these cases, specialisation restricts the classes of transactions for which a governance mechanism can be used cost-effectively. As a result, specialised mechanisms play complementary roles within a financial system.

Chapter 5 elaborates how agents' purposes influence the alignment of transaction requirements and governance mechanism capabilities. With regard to financing demands, system clients choose between alternative sources on the basis of perceived costs and benefits. Firms, for example, consider using such alternative sources of funds as debt, equity, and retained earnings. Further specialisation is also possible: a firm faces, at least potentially, the alternatives of obtaining debt financing either through public markets or from intermediaries. In addition, the terms of a debt financing can be varied in many different ways. Clients' preferences are reconciled with available financing alternatives using a combination of all these devices.

Similar considerations explain the supply choices of financiers, who must price various kinds of risks or uncertainties and choose among alternative mechanisms, and alternative sets of terms, to govern the transactions they effect. Nearly all financiers operate specialised[7] mechanisms suitable for governing only specific types of transactions.

Transaction requirements differ importantly according to the parties' views of the informational conditions under which they

7

negotiate. The parties' perceptions can differ in both kind and degree. Moreover, perceptions can change over the course of a transaction, either because of new environmental information, learning, or both. Chapter 5 illustrates these issues in the context of two prototypical situations.

The first examines how informational asymmetries can be anticipated and dealt with when a transaction is first set up. Mergers and acquisitions are used as examples to focus the discussion. To function effectively in such circumstances, a governance structure must provide recontracting flexibility as negotiations proceed. Since not all of the necessary adjustments can be specified at the outset, the governance mechanism must recognise the original contract incompleteness and provide for flexible adjustments to the incomplete contract as and when the circumstances arise.

The second prototypical situation illustrates how agents deal with emerging asymmetries which they did not originally anticipate. An instance of this problem arises from time to time in the markets for intermediary securities and liabilities. When an intermediary is threatened with insolvency, the governance mechanism which worked well for investors or depositors during normal conditions can prove inadequate to handle the impending crisis. Consequently, the original mechanism is likely to be replaced by a costlier, more flexible arrangement. While the change toward a mechanism with greater flexibility can be effected quite quickly, reversion to the original, and typically less costly, mechanism (as and when the intermediary's problems are resolved) can be a much more protracted process, if it takes place at all. The manner in which expectations are revised creates an essential asymmetry in changing from one governance mechanism to another, as the chapter shows.

Chapter 6 observes that even after selecting a governance mechanism, agents must still choose among contractual terms to complete the governance structure for any particular transaction. In particular, there may be informational differences to be dealt with through choices of contract terms. Financiers screen, and clients signal, in attempts to manage whatever informational differences are recognised when negotiations begin. Financiers also choose contract terms and *ex post* adjustment mechanisms in further attempts to control evolving differences in the risks or uncertainties they perceive. These choices reflect attempts to manage informational differences either through using incentive schemes to encourage truthful revelation or through providing for different modes of adaptation as information is gradually revealed.

Appropriate choice of contract terms and *ex post* adjustment mechanisms can mitigate the impact of any unfavourable outcomes

Introduction

which may eventuate. However, such sophisticated choices of contract terms can also increase transaction costs, sometimes to the point where the costs exceed the benefits of transacting.[8] The chapter discusses these costs of managing informational differences, costs which stem from attempting to assess signal reliability, from managing the impacts of moral hazard and adverse selection, and from setting up mechanisms to make any necessary *ex post* contract adjustments.

Chapter 7 recognises that while financiers originate transactions on an individual basis, they must also manage the resulting portfolios. Several of these portfolio management tasks differ from the origination problems discussed so far, and thus merit additional, separate discussion. The principal task of portfolio management is to assemble and administer assets which generate a return appropriate to the investment risk or uncertainty assumed.

All portfolio managers are concerned with generating a target level of income while keeping the income risk as low as possible.[9] Financiers managing marketable securities portfolios try to manage return versus risk mainly by trading assets, while financiers managing portfolios composed mainly of illiquid assets (e.g., intermediaries' portfolios) must manage risk–return tradeoffs without relying heavily, or perhaps even at all, on active trading. In either case, management competence affects portfolio operating costs, and ultimately the transaction costs which must be levied by financiers against their clients.

The ways individual agents' actions combine to determine financial system organisation and performance, are next examined. Chapter 8 first considers how securities prices are determined, and how these pricing processes affect the financial system's operating characteristics. The chapter then examines how the system's intermediaries affect financing availability. In both cases, the theory of institutional economics is compared with neoclassical financial theory and empirical findings in attempts to note which system properties can presently be well explained, as well as some which currently appear anomalous.

Chapter 9 considers additional system effects: namely, characteristics of system change and the performance problems typically associated with highly evolved financial systems. The effects of regulation on system change, and the likely prospects of ameliorating performance difficulties through using regulation are both examined.

Chapter 10 considers performance problems in less developed financial systems. It recognises that finance and economic development are interrelated: financial systems both shape economies and are

9

shaped by them. For, the availability of financing can either encourage or constrain economic growth, while economic growth usually leads to further development of a financial system. Development economics primarily discusses the importance of monetary, fiscal, and regulatory policies. However, this book argues that the institutional details of a financial system exert an important, but less often recognised, influence on economic development. Accordingly, the potential contributions of institutional economics to further advances in development economics are sketched.

The eleventh, concluding chapter reiterates the book's purposes and summarises its findings. It compares and contrasts an institutional economics theory of a financial system with the much better known neoclassical financial theory, using elements of both to explain the economic organisation of a financial system. The book argues that while neoclassical theory has helped to define important properties of financial transactions and their aggregate effects, it leaves many features of financial activity unexplained. In particular, the neoclassical approaches have little power to explain the details of financing transactions and resulting system features. Institutional economics provides complementary explanations of both financial system organisation and change, and some of the findings of development economics further round out the picture. The combination of approaches thus illuminates a greater number of system features than it is possible to do using current neoclassical theory alone.

Further progress toward understanding financial system activity will, it is hoped, benefit from the first steps taken here. For, the comparison and contrast of different theoretical approaches inevitably sets up tensions which require resolution, and it is from the syntheses resolving those tensions that greater understanding eventually emerges.

Notes

1 Further characterisations of neoclassical theory and its methods are discussed extensively in the succeeding chapters.
2 For a recent survey of the scope and nature of institutional economics, see Barney and Ouchi (1986).
3 Usually, these agents are viewed as striving to maximise some function of their wealth.
4 Some observers will immediately object that such attempts, being crude and ill founded, are necessarily suboptimal. But to object that the attempts are suboptimal is to assume a precisely formulated problem in which an optimal act can be determined. The objection thus ignores the possibility that precisely formulating the investment decision problem in order to determine an optimum may be a very costly exercise. Clearly,

Introduction

what is needed before the charge of suboptimality can be defended is a theory of the costs of and benefits to problem formulation, as well as a theory of how to decide within the confines of that formulation.

5   Arrow (1972) observes that once a problem is placed on an organisational agenda some means of solving it is likely to be determined. In the present context, we are contending first, that neoclassical financial theory places only certain classes of problems on its research agenda – the problems which are tractable given the tools presently available. Attacking only tractable problems is, of course, a sensible and highly productive research strategy. But it is not always likely to stimulate the development of new tools for attacking new classes of problems; research within an existing paradigm is usually conservative. Thus, our second contention is that expanding the research agenda can lead to new ways of defining tractable problems, to new ways of analysing these problems, and eventually to new understanding.

6   It might be countered that different mechanisms could all survive if they were capable of carrying out the same kinds of transactions at the same costs. But this observation would then pose the problem of deciding whether the mechanisms are somehow fundamentally different, and still exhibit the same operating costs, or whether the differences are apparent rather than real. The present discussion assumes that as a general matter fundamental differences in design will lead to differences in operating costs.

7   In the sense of this paragraph, even a financial supermarket combining commercial and investment banking activities is a specialised governance mechanism: it makes greater use of discretionary supervision than do such transactions as public market sales of new securities issues. Later chapters deal with finer details of the functions such financiers might perform, thus further delimiting the kinds of governance structures (mechanisms plus detailed transaction terms) they employ in different circumstances.

8   In such cases informational differences can be termed the cause of the resulting failure to transact; cf. Akerlof (1970).

9   Agents are assumed to be risk-averse.

Chapter two

Financial system agents and environment

This chapter defines the dimensions along which financial system function and organisation will be analysed. It begins by noting how the combined actions of agents determine the form of a financial system. It then discusses agents' goals, their capabilities, and the informational conditions under which they strive to attain their goals. Finally, the chapter considers how the costs of information processing and of administering transactions affect agents' choices.

Agents employ specific governance structures to administer individual transactions. Since agents strive to maximise the benefits they derive from transacting, the choices are driven by efficiency considerations, but this book interprets efficiency rather more broadly than do other contemporary studies. For, it recognises that agents can have limited information and limited insight into how best to attain their desired ends, and that such limitations can affect agents' interpretations of efficiency. That is, agents attempt to choose efficient forms of governance structures, but their choices are limited by available information and available knowledge.

Hence, the form of a financial system is determined as an aggregate effect of choices which are intendedly efficient, but may not always be so in an objective sense. Nevertheless, if the financial environment did not change too rapidly, and if financial markets were sufficiently competitive, the continuing pursuit of improvements to existing practices could result in a system which was both intendedly and objectively efficient. In practice, the situation is rather more complex. A financial system is continuously adapting, and at any point in time some parts may operate efficiently in an objective sense while others are only intendedly efficient. Those parts which do operate efficiently in an objective sense can be analysed using neoclassical financial theory, but those parts which are only intendedly efficient can be better understood using institutional analyses which postulate environmental uncertainty.

Financial system agents

System characteristics

This book attempts to explain financial system organisation, using a combination of neoclassical financial theory and institutional economics to do so. It begins with the view that a financial system's main function is to act as a transmission mechanism linking up funds provided by original suppliers with the funds used by final demanders. Financiers extend funds and administer the liquidation of financings using combinations of institutions and contract terms called governance structures. Different forms of governance structures are chosen to achieve different purposes: agents effect discriminating alignments between transaction requirements and the structures used to govern them (Williamson 1988).

Financings and governance

A financial system usually performs its transmission role indirectly: original suppliers of funds generally differ from proximate suppliers. Exchanges of funds between original suppliers and ultimate users can be channelled through market transactions in securities, through intermediary borrowing and lending arrangements, or internally between corporate divisions. These three channels are henceforth referred to as a financial system's three main types of governance mechanisms. The combination of governance mechanism and contract terms used to administer a given transaction is called a governance structure.[1]

This book's principal task is to explain why different governance structures are aligned with different transaction requirements, and to show why many different kinds of alignments will coexist in any financial system. It will be argued that the different mechanisms derive their importance from their respective abilities to carry out particular kinds of financings cost effectively. Different forms of governance structures are selected according to agents' goals, the ways they attempt to achieve these goals, the informational conditions under which they act, and the costs and technologies of transacting. Governance structures play complementary roles in that each offers certain advantages not possessed by the others. There are many different kinds of financing requirements, and the specialised advantages of different governance structures means each offers advantages for effecting a particular class of transactions.

Self-interest

Financiers pursue their own interests, and their clients do the same.

13

The Economic Organisation of a Financial System

Unless otherwise stated explicitly, this book interprets self-interest as meaning that agents attempt to increase their wealth and thus, ultimately, their consumption choices. Since financing arrangements create both possibilities for mutual benefit through exchange and for losses through opportunistic behaviour, each transaction offers a mix of cooperative and conflicting features. A client wishes to obtain funds, a financier to supply them, and both expect to benefit from the exchange. However, each desires to capture as large a share of the mutual gains as he can.

There is a possibility that an agent will use deception (i.e., act opportunistically) to gain an advantage over others who are less well informed. Agents do not always act opportunistically, but the possibility of their doing so means that other agents must take precautions against opportunism, incurring additional costs as they do so.

Contract terms

Agents try to manage transactions through negotiations which usually revolve around a set of standard terms defined by current practice and current financial system conditions. These prototypical arrangements are usually modified to reflect a given transaction's particular requirements. Some of the factors thus taken into account are the kinds of transaction information available, whether or not each agent's information differs, the expected reactions of each agent to the other, the anticipated effects of environmental change and the costs of administering transactions.

Contract terms can be chosen from a variety of possible arrangements, but their choice is constrained by the particular governance mechanism agents utilise. For example, a bank may be legally restricted from purchasing a client's equity, but a stock market investor is not usually limited in this way. Within the constraints of using a particular governance mechanism, contract terms are selected with a view to satisfying agents' conflicting concerns to the maximum possible extent. As an illustration, the less a financier knows at the outset about a particular financing's likely profitability, the more likely he is to require, as a condition of providing financing, interim reports about the project's progress. So long as the client understands the financier's purposes in making such requests, and regards the implied compliance costs as reasonable, the reporting requirement is likely to be incorporated in the financing contract. As many such issues can arise in a given transaction, reaching agreement can be a relatively complex process.

Financiers try to select cost effective governance structures, which implies that they operate governance mechanisms as efficiently as

Financial system agents

they can, subject to managing the risks or uncertainties they face. Striving for cost-effectiveness also means that financiers assess the limitations of whatever kind of mechanism they operate. For example, a banker will define a class of transactions he can profitably conduct. This class will generally include a variety of loan transactions, but will likely exclude others, such as the investment transactions typically entered by merchant bankers. The banker will specialise, not in transactions which he knows to be profitable to some financier, but in those which he himself can profitably conduct.

In some cases a client may be able to secure several offers of financing, in others none at all. The number of potential offers he can generate depends on the nature of the transaction's requirements, as will be discussed subsequently. For example, a client seeking external financing will choose, frequently in consultation with one or more financiers, whether to offer securities in a public market place or through private negotiations. The client's eventual choice among the offers he can secure will depend on their comparative costs, the amount of information requiring to be released, the parties who will become privy to the information, and the effects of such information release on the client's competitive position.

Aggregate effects

Financial system organisation is an aggregate effect, resulting from the ways individual transactions are originated and administered. At any given time, financial system organisation reflects a consensus regarding which transactions can be effected profitably, and in what ways. Further, it reflects a consensus regarding cost effective ways of carrying them out, a consensus based on current knowledge. While the principal features of system organisation are likely to persist through time, a financial system is not a static entity, since both transactions economics and financiers' technical knowledge can change with time.

It is possible to explain both the static determinants of financial system organisation and the forces which lead to changes in the system's form on the basis of transaction economics. Financiers attempt to balance conflicting forces which are subject to changing economics: they attempt to minimise costs through using routine ways of transacting on the one hand, and to enjoy the prospects of earning extraordinary profits through addressing client needs in novel ways on the other.

Technological change influences costs, as does learning. Learning itself has both an experiential component – with practice routine transactions can be carried out more efficiently – and an innovative component – new ways of transacting are discovered from time to time. At the same time, client needs change as their businesses evolve. Balancing the resulting tensions determines system form at any point in time, and drives the changes within the system.

The rest of this chapter describes and analyses the different environmental conditions under which agents can transact. These conditions are distinguished according to the kinds of information agents possess, the ways they attempt to realise their goals, the costs of and other dimensions to the transactions they enter. Succeeding chapters then examine how agents attempt to deal with different combinations of these conditions.

Transactor information

The most common paradigm in current (neoclassical) financial theory assumes that wealth maximising agents, with unlimited conceptual and computational powers, take decisions under conditions of risk. Initially, neoclassical financial theory assumed that agents view risks homogeneously, but more recently situations of heterogeneously distributed information have been analysed. Valuable insights have developed from these perspectives, but they are not sufficient to explain the nature of a financial system completely. For, not all agents possess the conceptual and computational capabilities that neoclassical theory assumes.

In addition, many financial transactions are not well enough specified (particularly if they are relatively novel) to be categorised usefully as risky decision problems. That is, for purposes of descriptive theory it is often helpful to recognise that agents' limited conceptual abilities mean in effect that they can usefully be viewed as acting under uncertainty rather than under risk. The reasons for this are straightforward: not all agents are able to define, with any precision, the environmental states with which many neoclassical financial analyses begin. Alternatively, limited computational abilities can prevent agents from calculating which action might best be taken. In both cases, agents' limitations create forms of environmental uncertainty. In addition, agents may face behavioural uncertainty: it is not always a straightforward matter to specify the alternatives their competitors might consider, let alone which of these is likely to be selected.

The distinction between risk and uncertainty was first posed by Knight (1933), but it has not frequently been used in recent financial theory, mainly because financial theory has recently been primarily normative in intent. If uncertainty looms sufficiently large in a given financial transaction, the paradigm of costlessly calculating actions to maximise some measure of well being may help to organise thoughts about the nature of the problem, but have little explanatory power. When this is so, neoclassical prescriptions become a poor guide to action. Decision making under uncertainty is much more tentative, and much more concerned with managing key environmental reactions, than neoclassical financial theory usually recognises.

To advocate the distinction between risk and uncertainty is not to overlook Savage's (1951) observation that, given a set of axioms, a decision maker's choices can be used to define an underlying subjective probability distribution. Savage's findings are useful both for defining some decision problems more precisely than would otherwise be possible and for analysing the nature of decision problems which have already been defined in a precise way.

But the Savage argument does not always help to formulate positive explanations. In effect, Savage studies decision problems whose elements, if not already structured, at least have the potential to be cast into convenient analytic forms which then further and significantly assist in selecting an appropriate decision. However, many important real life decisions involve defining a problem's structure rather than solving a problem that has already been structured. For studying these kinds of situations, the traditional distinction between risk and uncertainty remains valuable.

There is no definitive separation of risk from uncertainty: one merges into the other along a continuum of increasingly precise quantitative description. Nevertheless, it is possible conceptually to distinguish the categories, at least in a relative sense. Risk means the unknown future can be relatively well specified in quantitative terms. Uncertainty means the unknown future is less easy to specify, and therefore more difficult to quantify. In distinguishing risk from uncertainty for analytical purposes, the crucial issue is how an agent views a decision problem,[2] for his perceptions of whether or not precise analyses are possible influence his choices.

Risk

An agent is said to view a situation as risky if his decision making can be assisted by modelling the effects of actions using states of the world and a probability distribution of outcomes defined over them. As a practical example, putting a working prototype into production might be defined as a typically risky situation arising in manufacturing. In finance, a decision to grant a working capital loan secured by inventories is often well enough structured to be called risky.

Actions taken under risk can be described as tactical: while demanding care and anlysis, there is much of a routine nature about them. In theory, the problems of deciding how to face risks involve such matters as specifying probabilities and calculating which actions will maximise a criterion such as the expected utility of an agent's ending wealth position. Thus an agent will assume a risk if, for example, the expected utility of doing so is positive; he will try to choose among available alternatives to maximise expected utility.

In practice, an agent will assume a risk if the anticipated rewards seem large enough in relation to the risk. Judgements may be made according to rules of thumb which have been found to work well in the past. In sufficiently well-structured problems, it may be possible to check whether rules of thumb lead to decisions which also maximise expected utility; if they do not, agents may change their behaviour when any inconsistencies in their reasoning are pointed out. Thus, in sufficiently well-structured situations, the paradigms of decision making under risk can prove useful either as guides to action or as consistency checks on whether accepted rules of thumb might be effective guides to action.

Nevertheless, the prescriptions of decision making under risk still need to be employed with care. Neoclassical theory frequently advocates maximising the market value of a firm; it has defined conditions under which such a criterion is a guide to acting in the best interests of the firm's owners. But such guides may need to be modified to explain observed choices. For example, market value maximisation approaches do not always recognise that clients can obtain satisfaction in other ways, say through benefiting privately from controlling a corporation. The possibilities of private benefits can both affect the kinds of financing clients seek and create agency problems for financiers.

Uncertainty

Uncertainty means inability to formulate a decision problem precisely. Agents face uncertainties because of their limitations: an agent with limited conceptual or computational capabilities faces environmental uncertainty if he cannot adequately define states, outcomes, or outcome probabilities.[3] He faces behavioural uncertainty if he cannot predict the actions of others. While behavioural uncertainty is a particular form of environmental uncertainty, it is sometimes useful to distinguish it, since an agent may act differently in dealing with behavioural than with other kinds of environmental uncertainty.

Actions taken under uncertainty, particularly unstructured uncertainty, can be described as strategic actions. The "problem of meeting uncertainty ... passes inevitably into the general problem of management, of economic control" (Knight 1971, p. 259)). The management problem to which Knight refers is not the everyday stuff of financial operations; rather, it is the essence of long range financial planning. Analysing how agents deal with uncertainty is thus profoundly important to studying financial system evolution. For, financiers' strategic choices determine how financial firms, and consequently the financial system, will change through time. Equally, clients' strategic choices influence the kinds of demands that financiers will face.

Just as it is useful to distinguish between risk and uncertainty, it is also useful to distinguish qualitatively between kinds of uncertainties. Structured uncertainty refers to a situation which can be characterised in alternative ways. In such circumstances decision makers may devote much effort to refining these alternative possible representations. Research and development of a working prototype provides an example of a situation arising in manufacturing. Venture capital investing, particularly in firms using an already established technology, is a typical example in finance.

Unstructured uncertainty refers to a situation in which even an activity's parameters are not defined. Deciding which of several areas might profitably be explored through research and development constitutes an example in a manufacturing context. A decision to acquire a new company to change the thinking within the acquirer, such as General Motors' acquisition of EDS (a large information processing firm), offers an example which is at least partially concerned with finance.

Symmetric versus asymmetric views

Individual agents' views of transaction circumstances can differ. Thus financiers and clients may not view available transaction information in the same way, or even as belonging to the same structural category. Moreover, each agent makes assumptions as to how those with whom he negotiates regard the transaction, complicating the picture further. Thus a transaction's context may be classified in any of the following ways:

- agents perceive risks symmetrically
- agents perceive risks asymmetrically
- at least one agent perceives structured uncertainty
- at least one agent perceives unstructured uncertainty,

where the categories are ranged in order from most to least well structured. Except where otherwise indicated specifically, the rest of this book will consider transactions in which the client's information is at least as well structured as that of any financier. Also unless otherwise specified, the transacting parties both accept that the client's information is at least as well structured as the financier's.

Under symmetric risk, both parties are assumed to use the same probability distribution. Under asymmetric risk, this book assumes throughout (again, unless the contrary is stated explicitly) that the client views the payoff distribution as less risky[4] than does the financier. For example, a firm's manager can usually be presumed to know more about likely product sales figures than the financiers providing the capital for production and sales. If a financier perceives a situation as uncertain, the client does not perceive a greater uncertainty, and may indeed regard the situation as only risky.

Reasons for informational differences

In analysing the effects of informational differences, it is important to specify why they arise. For, depending on the source of information differences, financier and client may attempt to resolve them in different ways.

The actual points of disagreement can involve payoff distributions, the effects of actions, or both. A payoff is a value assumed by a payoff function; i.e., a mapping from the space of acts and states to the set of real numbers. Unless otherwise stated specifically, this book interprets payoffs in terms of monetary reward; before they are realised, agents model risky payoffs as random variables. Agents can differ in their choices of the random variables' distributions. They can define relevant states of the world differently, assign different probabilities to the states, or both. With respect to actions, transactors can disagree either on which actions are possible or on the payoffs to them. Again, transaction terms will vary according to whether these outcomes are costlessly known to both or whether it is more difficult for one party to ascertain an outcome.

Informational differences complicate negotiations, even under risk. If transactors disagree, either on the distributions to be valued or on the ways to value them, they may find it difficult to specify terms regarded as equally satisfactory to both parties. Indeed, their differences may even prevent a transaction from taking place, as theories of market failure argue (Akerlof, 1970).

In situations regarded by one or more agents as uncertain, the likelihood of their agreeing on the nature of a transaction's informational conditions is remote. Hence for discussion purposes little is

Financial system agents

lost by considering only situations in which the uncertainties are viewed differently. In these circumstances, both parties are still concerned to profit from any new information they might obtain. Equally, each party recognises the importance of self interest: each notes the possibility the other might use any privately obtained new information opportunistically.

A financier will try to guard against opportunistic exploitation by writing contract terms or using incentive payments to ensure he will become informed of any unfavourable developments of which the client may first become apprised. A client might do the same if he thinks the financier will be the first to obtain some kinds of important information. Before attempting to control client actions or to devise incentive schemes, financiers must try to decide whether the relevant contract terms will generate benefits at least equal to the cost of writing and enforcing them. If financiers cannot gain such net benefits, they may avoid the transaction altogether.

In some cases, financiers may be more competent than their clients in aspects of the business. When this is so, financiers are likely to require considerable control over any transactions they enter, and may also refuse some for reasons the client does not understand. A classic instance occurs when the technologically innovative entrepreneur approaches a lender who understands little about the business the entrepreneur is trying to finance. The difficulties can be compounded by the financier's scepticism regarding the entrepreneur's managerial (as opposed to his technological) capabilities. To the entrepreneur, the proposition may only be risky; to the financier it may be one of considerable uncertainty.

Transactor capabilities and criteria

Uncertainty is the counterpart of agents' limitations. Agents can have limited conceptual ability, limited computational ability, or both. In practice, they may well wish to act rationally (i.e., to further their own interests), but they may not know how best to do so. Such agents are said to have bounded rationality.

Agents whose rationality is bounded cannot always select acts from within the set of all available alternatives: rather, they may be faced with problems of defining what alternative choices they actually have. Many of the financial transactions to be discussed in this book involve such attempts. For example, financiers funding the production and marketing of a new product in a new market may need to learn a great deal about the business before they can assess its likely profit distribution with any degree of precision. While they are learning, the financiers are likely to proceed in a somewhat disorganised, hit or miss fashion as they try to determine the key features of their financing decisions.

While individual financiers usually remember the lessons they have learned, at any point in time a financial system has a certain proportion of inexperienced agents. This continuing fresh supply of inexperience means that some of the lessons of the past must be learned repeatedly. For example, Wall Street traders are famous for short memories; the lessons of the past are frequently being re-learned by new traders. Thus in the aggregate certain kinds of bounded rationality are as likely to persist as to be eliminated.

Three views

At present economic theory offers three major views of transactors and the criteria they use. Littlechild (1986) calls them the neoclassical (NC) view, the Austrian (A) view, and the radical subjectivist (RS) view. In the NC view, agents deal with risk and revision of probabilities, using the maximising criteria already described. In the A view, agents are initially ignorant, but are also alert to the possibility of discovering previously unperceived opportunities. At least initially, their main purpose is to learn more about the situations they face. The RS view is characterised by indeterminacy and imagination; agents are seen as attempting to create or at least influence future environments.

This book will frequently identify NC views with standard financial practice on the one hand, RS views with financial innovation on the other. Thus the NC view is most closely associated with analyses under risk, while the RS view is most closely associated with analyses under unstructured uncertainty. The A view, being an intermediate category, can fit either some forms of standard practice or some forms of financial innovation, depending on particular circumstances. It is most closely associated, however, with analyses under structured uncertainty.

Characteristics of the three views

The NC view of decision making under risk embraces search for a best decision within a structured framework. In contrast, the A view regards agents as trying to determine what is worth searching for. According to the A view, agents try to cope with a lack of knowledge using two devices. First, they assume the likelihood of an opportunity will depend inversely on its value; hence they often regard new alternatives sceptically. Second, these agents actively seek new opportunities: they try to place themselves in situations where the opportunities are more likely to present themselves. In particular, agents may emulate the actions of others in attempts to find advantageous new opportunities.

Under the A view, agents try to define and to rank alternatives according to their expected importance, using such indices as expected profitability. Thus some actions are aimed at discovering what is worth searching for, others at defining new alternatives. Trying to value a new security about which little is known, particularly if the issuer is employing a new technology, is an example of trying to discover what is significant.

With the unstructured uncertainty of the RS view, agents have still less understanding of the situations with which they are faced. Hence they are likely to focus on major sources of potential loss which might arise from the actions of others or through adverse environmental changes. To deal with the first of these possible losses, financiers can attempt to restrict clients' permitted actions. To deal with the second, either financier or client might attempt to create or control future environments. Trying to assess the returns to taking over a firm when the takeover might be opposed constitutes an example.

Usefulness of the different views

Each of the three views proves useful in this book, since each is related to a different informational perspective. Recognising the importance of differing informational conditions permits offering alternative explanations for the ways transactions are governed. With alternative explanations, it is sometimes possible to explain financing arrangements which are puzzling when regarded solely from the perspective of neoclassical financial theory. In some circumstances the three views offer equally plausible hypotheses regarding transaction governance, thus creating useful tensions between more than one possibly valid explanation. These tensions in turn stimulate empirical testing in attempts to resolve the differences, although assessing the validity of A and RS views is generally much more difficult than testing the implications of NC views.

To show how the different views generate different explanations, consider a firm acquiring an equity stake in a new company. According to the NC view, the firm bases the decision on an index such as expected profitability. The RS view does not deny the point, but continues by arguing that in some cases the investment might be premised on a desire to gain access to a technology with which the firm is currently unfamiliar. The firm might do so because the investment promises possible future profit opportunities which are difficult or costly to assess precisely. It is possible to define this problem formally by assuming some form of probability distribution for the benefits.[5] Such information might even sometimes be helpful to decision makers, but it obscures the point that some acquiring firms experiment, not because they have a good estimate of expected profitability, but because they are trying to gain an initial estimate of an opportunity's distribution.

Firms which act according to the RS view behave strategically. Their managers act as if the possible results of an experiment cannot usefully be quantified (at least at any reasonable cost). Thus if asked to explain their decisions such managers might cite such reasons as a need to match or anticipate competitor actions. The explanation may be sufficient for the managers, but to many neoclassical theorists it would be *prima facie* evidence of irrationality. The difference arises from differing assumptions regarding which problem aspects can usefully be quantified. The pragmatic manager facing such a situation recognises that the firm might have subsequently to withdraw from the activity, and in such cases protracted attempts at problem definition might not be cost effective. On the other hand, few neoclassical analysts are likely to acknowledge this possibility.

Thus there can be some circumstances in which a neoclassical approach is altogether inappropriate. For if the costs of formalising a problem are sufficiently great, and if the time needed to effect the formalisation is sufficiently long, it will not necessarily be cost effective to structure the analysis formally before carrying out the experiment.

It is worth reemphasising that agents' views of the world are partially determined by their competence; i.e., by the degree to which their rationality is bounded. To an agent with a low degree of competence (i.e. with tightly bounded rationality), a situation might appear as unstructured uncertainty, while to a more competent agent the same situation might appear to be one of structured uncertainty or even of risk. In a well structured, competitive, stable situation evolutionary adaptation should drive out incompetent behaviour over time, with the result that the surviving agents may sometimes usefully be modelled as if their rationality were unbounded. However, the assumption of unbounded rationality is much less useful in poorly structured, unfamiliar situations, where even the most able agents have a low degree of competence in relation to situational requirements.

Recognising degrees of boundednesss means that the manner in which a financial system effects transactions depends to some extent on the distribution of competencies within it. Moreover, the combined effects of competition and learning may eventually result both

Financial system agents

in more structured ways of doing business and the elimination of less competent agents. Both these effects should be distinguished in analyses, but it is not easy to do so, since currently available information about relative competence is mainly anecdotal. Thus, while this book recognises the existence and importance of bounded rationality, it cannot fully determine its sources, nor can it account fully for how competence might change with the passage of time. Instead, it is possible only to focus on some of the consequences of bounded rationality.

Anatomy of transactions

The environmental specifications given above still do not capture all relevant transaction dimensions. Transactions also differ with respect to how completely contracts can be drawn up, the specificity of the assets being financed, and the frequency with which the particular kind of transaction arises. Degrees of contract completeness also depend on how agents view transaction requirements, given their information and abilities.

Contract completeness

In analyses under risk, contracts are assumed to be complete. For, theoretical investigations under risk assume it possible to structure decision problems completely, including the specification of any contract terms. On the other hand incomplete contracting is to be expected under uncertainty. Either a highly rational agent who faces a highly unstructured decision problem, or an agent with bounded rationality faces the same difficulties: he cannot specify precisely what might happen, nor can he specify precisely how to deal with a realised event.

While agents cannot contract completely under uncertainty, this is not to say their decision problems cannot be analysed at all. For example, Heiner's (1983) concept of a gap between agent competence and problem difficulty suggests that stereotypical behaviour is more likely to be observed as problem difficulty increases relative to agent competence. On the other hand, transaction economics suggests that agents compensate for an initially imperfect understanding by creating governance structures which permit them to learn over the course of a transaction. That is, an initially prevailing competence–difficulty gap may be ameliorated, through time, by adaptive contracting.[6] However, the greater the degree of contract incompleteness, the costlier the learning, and the more elaborate the structure needed to effect any necessary ex post adjustments. In these circumstances, stereotypical behaviour may persist for some time.

The fundamental transformation

An initially incomplete contract can be transformed as the contracting parties interpret it opportunistically (Williamson, 1972, 1986, 1988). When negotiating, client and financier may be dealing in a competitive market. After obtaining the financing under an incomplete contract, client and financier are linked in a relationship of bilateral monopoly which continues until the financing is liquidated. The likelihood of this change in negotiating position, which Williamson calls the fundamental transformation, is one of the principal reasons incomplete contracts provide for discretionary adjustments. Since *ex post* adjustment needs cannot be specified in advance, agreeing to make adjustments as and when the need arises is really all the parties can do at the outset.

Asset specificity

It is particularly difficult to write complete contracts for financing assets with highly specific uses. Such kinds of financings are especially subject to the fundamental transformation, because the more specific the uses for assets acquired, the less developed is the secondary market for the assets, and the less valuable they are as collateral. Hence, keeping the assets operating satisfactorily is important to the security of the financing arrangement, and creates a greater need for discretionary rather than rule-based contracts. For example, many new ventures, and particularly the most innovative ones, will be financed with equity (a discretionary form of contracting) rather than with debt (a rule-based form of contracting; see Williamson (1988)).

Human capital often represents a highly specific asset the value of which financiers find difficult to establish. For this reason financing arrangements dependent on particular individuals' performance are likely to be incomplete contracts permitting considerable use of discretion. Discretion is needed because in many situations human performance is difficult to describe precisely.

Transaction frequency

If a given type of transaction recurs frequently, the skills needed to effect it are likely to be readily available. Thus, increasing transaction frequency should, other factors remaining the same, lower governance costs. When transactions recur only infrequently, financiers may not develop or retain the skills to carry them out cost effectively. The result is a greater discrepancy between financiers' competence and transactions' governance requirements, with the result that if

Financial system agents

they are entered at all, infrequent transactions are likely to be viewed as involving uncertainty.

The most frequently entered transactions are likely to be those offering relatively high profits in relation to the risks or uncertainties involved. Large profit potential can derive from small margin but high volume business, from high margin but low volume business, or combinations of the two. Financiers are likely to avoid marginally profitable, unfamiliar kinds of transactions because of the possibility of incurring greater costs than originally anticipated.

Transactions and governance costs

It is useful first to distinguish between transaction and governance costs. Then, the ways in which each type of cost differs under different informational conditions will be examined.

Transactions and governance costs distinguished

Transaction costs mean the costs incurred by a client, both costs paid directly to the financier and any indirect costs such as the search costs incurred in locating a financier. The governance cost of any transaction is its share of the total costs of using a governance structure; i.e. the total cost to the financier of handling the transaction.

The transactions costs incurred by a client will normally include the financier's incremental costs of operating the governance structure, a share of the governance mechanism's fixed costs, and any search costs incurred, even though they are not paid over to the financier. Thus transaction costs include both direct costs such as the brokerage or loan application fees paid to complete an arrangement, and any indirect costs of carrying out investigations of available financings. All need to be taken into account by the client. For example, a small business might look long and hard to find a financier willing to invest long-term capital in the business, but these costs will typically not form a part of the payment to the financier.

A governance structure's operating costs depend on its capabilities. These costs can be expressed as the sum of the resource costs of setting up and operating the governance structure, plus any losses which can be incurred if the structure fails to offset a particular transaction's possible unfavourable outcomes.

Costs and risk

Transaction requirements affect governance costs. Under risk, it may be possible to define all governance costs in monetary terms. It is useful to begin with this relatively straightforward setting, later extending the analysis to uncertainty. Even under risk, governance costs include more than just the value of physical resources utilised in managing transactions. Additional costs arise from the need to manage the effects of bounded rationality and opportunism, and from the need to absorb any losses resulting from failure of the governance structure to offset them. Still other costs arise from the contract terms used to deal with informational asymmetries.

Governance mechanisms' operating costs can exhibit scale or scope economies. Second, a mechanism's long run cost function can shift as a result of learning or technological change. For example, a new way of standardising transaction terms can lead to cost reductions represented by a downward shift of the curve. For any given mechanism, the operating costs' magnitude can further be influenced by transaction type and frequency. For example, exchange operations exhibit scale economies, so that unit governance costs decline, at least over some range, as more transactions are carried out. Thus trading a small number of shares can be more costly, on a unit basis, than trading a larger number.

Financiers can reduce costs through learning by doing: more efficient techniques are likely to evolve from experience in performing a certain type of transaction. These properties of governance mechanisms' cost functions bias a financial system toward performing regularly recurring, familiar transactions. Financiers are as likely to avoid using unfamiliar, specialised forms of governance mechanisms as they are to avoid unfamiliar forms of transactions, at least unless the new mechanisms offer a potential for greater than normal profit margins.

If risks are viewed asymmetrically, transaction costs include both the costs of efforts made by the client to affect the asymmetries and the governance costs the financier incurs in removing or otherwise dealing with informational asymmetries. These costs are associated with signalling, verification, and possibly monitoring of a transaction after it has been entered. Under risk it is usually possible to quantify all these costs, so that both parties can balance them against a quantifiable distribution of transaction benefits.

Clients will also try to minimise the transactions costs they pay, but as with financiers, their search may fail to locate the least costly method of transacting. Clients whose rationality is bounded, and particularly those who also face relatively high search costs, may not always avail themselves of a least cost financing, but may instead accept the first feasible arrangement they find. Moreover, search costs are likely to be lower on a per unit basis in highly organised markets like the stock exchanges than they are in less organised markets such as those for venture investments, because effective methods of undertaking the search can readily be ascertained. Hence, clients will be biased toward exploring familiar rather than unfamiliar sources of funding.

A financial system effects many kinds of transactions, and because either market exchange or intermediation can be carried out using a number of alternative specialised mechanism, there will usually be a least cost way of carrying out each type. (It is, of course, logically possible that two or more ways will be equally costly.) The most efficient method of transacting will depend on the type and frequency of the transaction as well as the nature of the environmental conditions under which it is typically carried out.

If the markets for providing funds and other financial services are competitive, financiers are highly motivated to minimise their operating costs. They may, as already mentioned, try to keep costs low by taking on only regularly recurring, familiar transactions. Thus in competitive markets there is at least one force working against innovation. Indeed, under competition financiers may be less likely to innovate than in monopolistic or oligopolistic markets where they can influence the prices they charge for performing services.

On the other hand, even in a competitive market, a financier with a new product or method can gain a form of monopoly or oligopoly power for the period of time it takes other competing institutions to emulate the new development. Since innovation is costly, even novel forms of transactions, or novel forms of governance structures, will usually evolve from well-established technologies. Radically new ways of obtaining operating efficiency cannot only take much longer to evolve, but may be avoided even when first recognised because they will likely exhibit higher operating costs until the new technology becomes familiar.

Costs and uncertainty

Under uncertainty, the foregoing anatomy of costs remains valid, and all the costs previously discussed will still be incurred. However, additional costs related specifically to managing uncertainties need also to be recognised. For example, clients may expend additional resources in searching for new alternatives. Because available alternatives are less well-defined, clients must expand their searches accordingly. On the other hand, in particular situations some clients might actually expend less on search costs under uncertainty, since any benefits to finding new alternatives are also less precisely defined. Nevertheless, on average it is probably correct to conclude that search costs increase.

The same is likely true for governance costs: there may be particular instances under uncertainty when they are less, but as a general matter they are likely to be greater than under risk. Finally, the likely costs of opportunism are higher than under risk, since uncertainty means greater difficulty in detecting opportunistic behaviour. Hence, financiers are likely to find that governance costs under uncertainty are greater than they are under risk.

Summary

To analyse the economic organisation of a financial system, this book follows Williamson in using the transaction as the basic unit of analysis. The transactions economics view holds that transaction requirements and governance structure capabilities are aligned, through the combined choices of clients and financiers, in ways that are intended cost-effectively to serve the parties' collective and individual purposes as well as possible. The form of a financial system results as the aggregate effect of choosing structures to govern individual transactions.

One of the most important transaction features affecting governance structure choice is the information available to transactors. It is useful to distinguish transactions' informational conditions on the basis of risk or uncertainty, because to study only risk is to presuppose an ability to structure financing decisions that is not always available in practice. Hence to construct a descriptively realistic picture of a financial system, the distinction between risk and uncertainty proves useful in explaining the nature of the governance structures chosen. In addition, distinguishing between symmetric and asymmetric information helps further to round out the picture.

Agents' abilities to structure decision information can be described either in environmental terms such as risk and uncertainty, or in terms of their conceptual and computational limitations. Thus, to observe that agents attempt to deal with uncertainty is to observe that they exhibit bounded rationality, at least with respect to a given situation's requirements. Viewing decision making under uncertainty in these complementary ways helps to define the sources of uncertainty and the kinds of criteria agents are likely to employ.

Different forms of governance structures are employed to deal with different sources of uncertainty. Informational differences constitute a highly important transaction circumstance, but not the only relevant one. Bounded rationality means that many contracts can only be drawn up incompletely. Transactions based on incomplete contracts pose different governance requirements than do those based on complete contracting: they are subject to Williamson's fundamental transformation and the consequent need to provide for

Financial system agents

making *ex post* adjustments. Asset specificity and the frequency with which particular transaction types occur are additional important dimensions. Only some forms of governance structures have the capabilities to govern infrequently recurring transactions, or those for financing assets with highly specific uses.

Transaction costs are the costs, both direct and indirect, paid by clients to carry out a transaction. On average, direct transaction costs must cover the costs of transaction governance. Governance costs are likely to increase as transaction requirements become more complex. In particular, transactions under uncertainty are likely to have higher governance costs than transactions under risk. A transaction whose informational conditions are viewed differently by financier and client is likely to be more costly than a transaction whose conditions appear the same to both parties.

Notes

1 The terminology is due to Oliver Williamson, and indicates this book's heavy indebtedness to his perspectives (1972, 1985, 1986, 1988). This book uses the term 'governance mechanism' to refer to the organisation effecting a transaction (market, intermediary, hierarchy, or any specialised form of these categories), and governance structure to mean the combination of mechanism and contractual terms used to effect any individual transaction.
2 The agent's view may be altered by advice, as in Savage's famous comment regarding his gratitude at having his attention drawn to what would otherwise have been an inconsistency in reasoning.
3 It is presumed here that the effects of facing the uncertainties are regarded as significant.
4 Formally, degrees of risk can be defined using standard measures such as a distribution's. Alternatively, stochastic dominance criteria can be used partially to rank distributions of differing risks (Hadar and Russell, 1969, Rothschild and Stiglitz, 1971).
5 Alternatively, the acquisition decision itself might be used to infer the probabilities with which benefits are assumed to be realised.
6 Thus, incomplete contracting with subsequent adjustment can be viewed as an evolutionary response to the competence–difficulty (CD) gap, offering an alternative to Heiner's stereotypical responses. This view raises the empirical question of whether as a CD gap increases behaviour becomes increasingly stereotyped throughout the negotiations or whether it is only in the use of an incomplete contract that stereotypical behaviour is manifest. If the latter, the rational adjustment processes are merely deferred, not forgone altogether. Finally, the two kinds of response need not be mutually exclusive. A refined empirical analysis might seek to establish a set of circumstances under which stereotypical behaviour resulted, another under which *ex post* adjustment was the more likely.

Chapter three

Governance mechanisms: major types

Chapter 3 examines the three basic types of mechanisms for governing financial transactions: markets, intermediaries, and internal financings. Each type's specialised capabilities gain it competitive advantage in administering some, but not all kinds of transactions. Since transactions present varying requirements, specialised mechanisms play complementary roles within a financial system.

A financial system uses three principal governance mechanisms to effect financings: markets, intermediaries and internal financings (Williamson, 1972). This chapter surveys the most important capabilities each mechanism offers, and the next chapter continues the examination in greater detail.

It is convenient to discuss the mechanisms' complementary roles by assuming a fixed point in time and a fixed amount of funds for allocation among competing users. This focus rules out such long run questions as how economic growth and the supply of finance are interrelated, as well as such short run questions as relations between economic activity, credit and monetary policy. The longer run questions involving relations between economic growth and finance will be explored in Chapter 10. The shorter run relations between financial systems, credit and monetary policy are fully discussed in many economics texts and will not be considered in this book.

Whenever a transaction is arranged, a governance mechanism (or sometimes a combination of them) is chosen to effect the transfer of funds to the client, and to administer the arrangement until its liquidation. Since the capabilities of different mechanisms are aligned with transaction requirements, the mix of transactions determines the proportion of total funding administered by each kind of mechanism.

Governance mechanism capabilities

Mechanisms' capabilities derive from the specialised technologies they employ, and the resulting capabilities limit the kinds of transac-

Governance mechanisms

tions which each mechanism can carry out. First, any financier will only enter transactions which are potentially profitable when administered with the mechanism he employs. Second, any mechanism's capabilities affect the financier's evaluations of risks or uncertainties, thus influencing his profitabililty estimates. Third, mechanisms with only minimal monitoring and supervisory capabilities are usually suitable for transactions under risk, while transactions under uncertainty require more highly developed monitoring and supervisory capabilities. Finally, governance capabilities determine a financier's ability to attract potential clients, who seek to have their particular requirements met as cost effectively as possible.

Governance and transaction information

Since different mechanisms offer different capabilities for initial screening and for subsequent supervision, informational conditions profoundly affect the alignment of mechanism capabilities and transaction requirements. Figure 3.1 shows how qualitatively different kinds of information and governance capabilities are usually related.

Figure 3.1 indicates that transacting under risk normally requires the least amount of screening. In addition, risky transactions pose no need to make *ex post* adjustments (i.e., to alter contract terms after a financing has initially been extended). For, the definition of risk means that contract terms, even if they involve contingent adjustments, can be determined completely in advance. Transacting under risk is generally cheaper than transacting under uncertainty because it usually requires less screening and monitoring.

Transacting under uncertainty requires additional governance

Figure 3.1 Transaction information and governance mechanisms

Type of transaction information	Type of governance mechanism; typical function performed
Risk	Market transactions. Assessment of outcomes, valuation of financial instruments, trade.
Structured uncertainty: recognition of what is not yet known but needs to be known	Financial intermediation. Reduction of ignorance; definition of new alternatives; structuring additional alternatives.
Unstructured uncertainty: determining areas of ignorance	Specialised intermediation or internal allocations. Discovery of new financing methods; facilitating joint ventures.

The Economic Organisation of a Financial System

capabilities. The less well-structured a transaction's environment, the greater the need for additional governance capabilities. In particular, the more difficult it is to contract completely in advance, the greater the importance of *ex post* adjustment capabilities. In comparison to markets, intermediaries and internal financings offer greater governance capabilities. Hence, as the following discussion shows, transactions requiring more supervision, especially on a continuing basis, will more likely take place through intermediaries or by way of internal allocations.

Governance mechanisms which have higher degrees of potential adaptability, and which offer control capabilities even in the event of unforeseen circumstances, are generally more costly to operate. Since financiers will only extend funds where they believe transaction benefits will outweigh governance costs, any transactions which are entered under uncertainty are likely to be regarded as more rewarding than transactions entered under risk.

Efficiency and effectiveness

Throughout, this book assumes that agents seek to transact efficiently. However, depending on the informational conditions they face, agents will not always know whether their actions are efficient. To reflect this difference, the term effective will be used to mean that agents search for efficiency to whatever extent they find possible, given their bounded rationality. The term efficiency will be reserved for situations which can be modelled with enough precision to provide an objective basis for assessing whether, given the model's assumptions, the actions it prescribes will maximise some criterion such as current wealth. In this usage, efficiency implies effectiveness, but effectiveness does not necessarily imply efficiency. The settings of neoclassical financial theory are settings in which efficient choices can be discussed. However, under uncertainty (that is to say, in many practical circumstances) it will be necessary to write less precisely of effective choice.[1]

The concept of efficient decision making provides useful but limited insights for descriptive theory. The useful insights derive from isolating and manipulating key decision variables within a formal model, and determining relationships between them. In a logical sense, the insights' validity is limited to the theoretical conditions assumed when constructing the model.

In addition, however, insights from studying efficient decision making can sometimes serve as an approximate guide for effective choice in less well-structured situations. For example, neoclassical financial theory predicts that any governance mechanism which remains viable in a competitive environment must be able to carry out some kinds of transactions at least as efficiently as any other mechanism. For purposes of descriptive theory, a governance mechanism which survives over long periods in apparently competitive conditions can be presumed to be at least as effective as any other known mechanism. Otherwise, it would not be used.

In normative theory, the mix of governance structures that result from a search for efficiency can be determined, at least in principle. Descriptive theory can use these findings as guidelines, but cannot reach conclusions which are as precise. One problem is that agents with bounded rationality may satisfice (Simon, 1961) i.e. choose any quickly found, satisfactory alternative without continuing to search for others which might offer greater payoffs. If agents satisfice, the forces driving a system toward equilibrium can either be muted or work in an uncertain fashion. For with satisficing, the most efficient alternatives will not always be chosen, as agents may cease searching once a satisficing (i.e., effective) alternative has been found.

The practical possibility that less than wholly efficient mechanisms can survive for extended periods of time means that financial systems will not always attain maximum possible efficiency. Nevertheless, even satisficing agents recognise that every mechanism is costly to operate, and given a transaction's expected revenue, seek to govern it using the lowest cost method they are able to determine. Morever, in a competitive environment satisficing decision makers can be forced, over time, toward increasing degrees of effectiveness. For, any decision maker who is less effective than his competitors will eventually lose business to the more effective firms.

Specialisation and costs

Greater mechanism capabilities are likely to be gained only at increased costs, because the extra capabilities require additional resources. For example, the ability to make *ex post* adjustments requires more than just contractual recognition that some adjustment might prove necessary. It also requires a means of determining what kinds of adjustments might be made, of discovering when the adjustments are needed, and providing a means of carrying them out.[2] Thus effective operation means that increasing a mechanism's capabilities can only be realised by incurring additional costs. These additional costs will be incurred even after allowing for cost savings resulting from economies of specialisation, as well as from learning and adaptation.

Most governance mechanisms can be operated more cheaply if they are specialised to some degree. In markets, economies of specialisation can be realised by trading large volumes of particular kinds of securities under conditions of homogeneous risk. For example, the market for government bonds efficiently organises and consummates trading in securities whose default and income risks are similarly assessed by most traders. As a second example, standardising terms in options trading greatly contributed to the trading increases which took place during the 1970s and 1980s. In addition, options exchanges' decisions to provide performance guarantees enhanced the ability of parties to deal without the need to screen each other's creditworthiness.

Intermediaries can also benefit from specialising. For example, screening costs can be lowered on a unit basis if an intermediary screens only one or a few transaction types. A firm specialising in venture capital investing offers an illustration. While the initial costs of assessing a venture investment might be relatively easy to calculate, the costs of its continuing administration might not be, nor might the ways in which it would best be carried out. Thus given the magnitude and uncertainty of both setup costs and the costs of continuing to administer transactions, only a few firms might perceive a profit opportunity in entering the venture capital business, and then only by keeping costs low through specialising.[3]

Learning and adaptation can lead to discovering new ways of specialising and of reducing operating costs over time. For example, as traders learned to make use of new technology, screen-based trading largely replaced open outcry trading on the floor of the (London) International Stock Exchange. As computing technology becomes ever cheaper and more powerful, even smaller stock exchanges may find it profitable to adopt the new technologies. If so, the smaller stock exchanges of the future may exhibit new operating cost characteristics. For, with traditional technology smaller exchanges exhibit higher operating costs than their larger counterparts, but with electronic technology capable of linking numbers of small exchanges into a larger network that may no longer be the case.

Effectiveness and informational conditions

Governance mechanisms are chosen according to effectiveness criteria. Under sufficiently well-specified theoretical conditions, mechanism choice can be examined more rigorously using efficiency criteria. For example, if agents exchange homogeneously assessed risks, if markets are perfectly competitive, and if investors maximise expected utility by maximising their current wealth, efficiency can be assessed in terms of how a given mechanism affects financiers' current wealth. If market prices of securities can be maximised by maximising profits, efficiency can be assessed using profit maximisation criteria.

On the basis of costs per transaction, markets are probably cheaper to operate than other kinds of governance mechanisms, both in theory and in practice. While administratively less complex than intermediaries or internal allocations, markets are nevertheless highly effective under risk. A considerable body of evidence also shows that at least the larger public securities markets are not just effective, but both allocatively and operationally efficient. In these cases the markets are so competitive that they drive satisficing decision makers beyond the maximal effectiveness discussed above, and actually lead agents to attain the efficient outcomes predicted by normative theory.

With competition under risk, attempts to maximise wealth in the face of changing environmental conditions drive the search for efficiency. The fact that nearly all market agents now make extensive use of computer technology is one result of searching for greater efficiency. As another example, consider the sale and resale of bonds. In most western countries, bond trading is carried out by market agents acting as dealers; i.e., taking inventories. While they may be handled by the same market agents, less frequently traded, less liquid bond issues are usually traded on a brokered basis. Broking replaces dealing when the costs of assuming an inventory position become large relative to the typical revenues earned from trading.

Markets' advantages are also their weaknesses, meaning they are not a suitable mechanism for governing every type of transaction. Transactions posing the more complex governance requirements associated with uncertainty will more likely be effected using intermediaries or, in the most complex cases of all, internally. Intermediaries and internal financings offer greater capabilities for *ex post* adjustments than do markets, and the kinds of incomplete contracting that result from uncertainty can be handled more cost effectively by mechanisms capable of effecting *ex post* adjustments.

Mechanisms governing transactions under uncertainty are also intended to operate efficiently, but the assessment criteria are less clearly defined, and choices are likely to be made less precisely than under risk. As a result, it may well be that many choices under uncertainty are perceived to be effective, but there is no objective basis for determining whether or not they are efficient. For the counterpart of uncertainty, bounded rationality, means that financiers cannot always determine exactly how to maximise profits. Indeed, they may not even be clear as to what kinds of actions are likely to increase profits. For example, under structured uncertainty a governance mechanism may be regarded as efficient if it is useful in finding new ways of extending finance and in administering the resulting transactions: capacity to innovate may take precedence over narrowly defined profit maximisation criteria.

Since uncertainty also implies a lack of competitiveness, there is no guarantee that satisficing decision makers will be driven toward efficient choices under uncertainty. For example, either when financing new technologies, or when strategically changing a business's organisation, choices can only be shown to be intendedly effective. If the uncertainties in a transaction cannot be structured, firms will likely regard a mechanism as effective if it allows for some control over the effects of client actions, forms of environmental change, competitors' reactions, or any combination of these factors.

The governance structure used with sovereign loans provides an example of both the usefulness of *ex post* adjustments and the workings of uncertainty. Consider each in turn. Granting the loans on a floating rate basis offers the advantage of insulating financiers from changes in market conditions, thus allowing them to make *ex post* adjustments which offset interest rate risk. For such loans are typically funded by liabilities whose costs can also fluctuate with market conditions, and in this case intermediaries can earn a stable profit margin even while market conditions are changing.

Bounded rationality explains why the disadvantages of granting sovereign loans on a floating rate basis were revealed only with experience. In at least some sovereign loans, it was gradually realised that financiers cannot pass on risks to their clients regardless of any consequences. Financiers are not insulated from all risks if the floating interest charges become high enough to affect importantly the borrower's ability to repay the loan principal. Indeed, in such cases the financiers may have created additional problems for themselves. Second, sovereign loans were sometimes granted on the fallacious assumption that a country's legal powers of taxation, and not its ultimate ability to generate export earnings, ensured the safety of the loan. In actuality, the *ex post* adjustment mechanism proved ineffective because it relied on taxing power which had not been related to the country's ultimate earning power.

As another example of how uncertainty increases the difficulty of writing complete contracts, consider venture investments in comparison to collateralised bank loans. The terms of a venture investment, but not those of a collateralised bank loan, usually provide for the financier to have a seat on the board of the company and may also provide for mutual buy out of company shares. The board position allows financiers to monitor company affairs on a continuing basis. The mutual repurchase conditions allow for further adjustment to changing conditions as the fortunes of the client un-

Governance mechanisms

fold. The arrangements are chosen precisely because the venture investor finds it difficult to assess the likely course of the client's affairs in advance, and wishes to provide a mechanism for effecting *ex post* adjustments as and when they are needed. Even though the financier believes the venture will prove profitable, it may not be possible for him to specify very clearly in advance just what adjustments to the original contract may be needed to realise these profits as the client's project evolves. In the case of the bank loan, much less supervision is needed because the collateral secures the arrangements.

Market governance

Financial markets allocate scarce funds amongst competing users by means of interest rates. Market transactions are carried out at arms' length between original borrowers and final lenders; i.e., a quantity of funds is exchanged at an interest rate intended to compensate for the use of funds and the risk of their not being recovered. Apart from contract terms specified at the outset, market transactions usually do not provide a means of adjusting a contract in the light of new circumstances.

Advantages to market transacting

One advantage of a market is that it provides a locale for exchange: buyers or sellers initially unknown to each other can either meet directly in a market place, or trade indirectly using the services of easily identifiable market agents. Second, markets efficiently coordinate the actions of buyers and sellers through publicising the interest rates at which different kinds of financings can be arranged. Third, market prices enhance the efficiency of the resource allocation process, ensuring that resources are allocated to the highest bidders for them.

Markets also play an information dissemination role: they can mitigate initially prevailing informational differences as trading occurs. For example, trading commodities futures may begin between participants with widely varying information about the futures' worth. After several rounds of trading, however, the information is likely to be more equally distributed, and a consensus estimate of the commodity's market price can be established.

Financings regarding which there is considerable agreement, and which pose few requirements for *ex post* adjustments, can likely be effected at lowest cost if they are arranged as market transactions. For example, publicly selling a new issue of securities can very often prove the lowest cost way of raising funds for a well-known firm, at least when the firm does not believe that complying with statutory disclosure requirements will give its competitors an advantage. Secondary market trading of well-known securities illustrates another valuable property of financial markets: they can make it easy to reallocate invested funds as and when necessary.

Informational conditions

In exchanging funds as in exchanging other commodities the advantages of markets are realised most fully when risks can be assessed readily and reflected completely in transactions' market interest rates. The advantages can be seen most clearly when agents agree on the risks involved, have few concerns about the stability of these risks through time, and little scope to exploit each other opportunistically, either at the time a transaction is first arranged or subsequently. Secondary market trading shares of well-known companies is a classic example of a transaction well suited to market activity.

While market transactions can also occur under asymmetric risk, the scope for market transacting becomes more restricted as informational conditions differ more importantly, become less well specified, or both. Markets can remain an efficient governance mechanism for some transactions under asymmetric risk because the competitive advantages of governance mechanisms change gradually as transaction circumstances change. Parties who disagree greatly may not be able to negotiate, but parties who differ only in some details of their expectations regarding a transaction may be able to use the market place.

In particular, markets can effect exchanges of funds in the presence of informational asymmetries if parties can agree on the value of the securities being exchanged. The simplest example is if both parties agree that an instrument is (nearly) risk free. More complex examples using combinations of options have been studied by Neave (1989). If the informational asymmetries cannot be resolved through finding a combination of securities on whose value the transactors can agree, and if the parties deal anyway, at least one of them will be less than completely satisfied with the terms of the exchange. In such cases the dissatisfied party will likely contend that the implied interest rate on the transaction is not a competitive rate for that kind of risk.

On the other hand, markets can fail when interest rates do not reflect possible quality differences (Akerlof, 1970). These situations are much more likely to arise under conditions of asymmetric risk or uncertainty. Even if markets do not fail, such phenomena as equilibrium credit rationing can result from informational asymmetries (Stiglitz and Weiss, 1981). The crucial factor determining markets' advantages is whether

Governance mechanisms

agents believe they are likely to be harmed by any information differentials that may emerge subsequent to arranging the funding. If neither client nor financier believes he can be exploited by the other to any considerable degree, each is more willing to trade. These considerations offer, for example, a rationale for prohibiting insider trading. However if one party regards the other as having insider information which can be used opportunistically against him, trading can be inhibited or prevented completely. For example, there may be no willing buyers of shares offered for sale by insiders if the potential purchasers believe the insider might have adverse knowledge regarding the securities' future value (cf. Milgrom and Stokey, 1982).

Markets can sometimes effect financings under uncertainty, although the circumstances in which this occurs are even more restricted than under asymmetric risks. For, uncertainty implies contracts will be incomplete, and thus pose *ex post* adjustment needs. Very few market transactions can be structured to facilitate *ex post* adjustments. Certainly shares are traded in markets, and shares provide a vehicle for discretionary governance of firms (cf. Williamson, 1988). But apart from those shareholders whose control positions enable them to exercise an effective influence over a firm's affairs, most shareholders only exercise an influence by selling their investments. These minority shareholders have few if any prospects of effectively managing *ex post* adjustment processes.

A few market exchanges may take place even under unstructured uncertainty, as when highly speculative shares are traded on the basis of the opportunities they might eventually create. For example, in the early days of biotechnology firms their shares were traded actively, but seemed to be valued more nearly like options than on the basis of expected future earnings. Such transactions are not well explained using neoclassical theories, but may be explicable as the actions of boundedly rational individuals seeking to define new alternatives.

Some market transactions that appear to take place under uncertainty actually bypass its effects, as when guarantees or collateral are used. For example, purchasers of options contracts do not face the problems of assessing issuer creditworthiness if the options are guaranteed by an instrumentality of the exchange[4] on which they are sold. Similarly, financial intermediaries lending against collateral with a readily established market value need not usually concern themselves about the transaction's underlying uncertainties, since they can rely on the collateral for repayment of the loan.

Trading in certain kinds of market instruments can also sometimes offset the effects of uncertainty. For instance, options can be purchased or sold in attempts to mitigate the effects of alternatives whose possibility is recognised but deemed not very likely to occur.

41

Thus a currency speculator might acquire an option to purchase a foreign currency at some future date, fixing a purchase price at which a profit could be made if the currency were to increase in value unexpectedly. Such a transaction might be entered even though the speculator has only a vague suspicion that such a movement might occur.[5]

Intermediary governance

Like markets, intermediaries transfer funds from original suppliers to clients. Intermediaries maintain many borrowing and lending transactions on their own books for the duration of the financing arrangements, but this interposition between transactors is not sufficient to distinguish intermediated from market transactions. For, market agents acting as dealers also enter both sides of a transaction on their books, although normally only for a short time. Intermediaries are distinguished from markets in that they issue liabilities against a portfolio of acquired assets, meaning they actually transform the risks or uncertainties they originally assume. On the other hand, market agents normally buy and resell the same instruments. Intermediaries are further distinguished from market agents in that they usually exercise a higher degree of governance over the assets they hold.

Advantages to intermediation

Intermediation, being generally more complex than market exchange, is also more costly. Thus to gain a net advantage over markets, intermediaries must offer products or services whose value is commensurately higher. Both transaction economics and agency theory help to explain how intermediaries create such benefits.

Transaction economics holds that intermediaries can employ and enforce transaction terms different from those available to markets. The difference in governance capabilities allows intermediaries to make loans or investments that markets cannot effect profitably (Williamson, 1972, 1985). Agency theory argues that when either acts or states can be hidden from one of the transacting parties, controlling the potentially damaging effects of self-interested dealing requires a more complex system of incentives and enforcement than a market transaction can provide. Intermediaries are better able to put such incentive schemes in place and to administer them over longer periods, indeed over the life of a transaction if necessary.

Intermediaries also create net benefits through reducing governance costs over time. Both intermediaries and markets can learn to adopt new technologies, thus shifting their cost curves downwards. In addition, intermediaries can develop and retain experience histories which are usually lost in a series of individual market transactions. This capability is attributable to intermediaries' continuing relationships with both their depositors and their borrowing clients, but especially the latter.

Screening and diversification

Intermediaries can and usually do perform more intensive screenings than market agents. Through screening, intermediaries produce information about individual transactions that is normally used privately, allowing the intermediary to retain any benefits for itself. In contrast, market trading based on private information can serve quickly to disseminate the information, thus attenuating the benefits of its use. In some cases, public dissemination of costly information can occur so quickly that most of the potential rewards from gathering it privately can be lost.

Some recent theoretical studies help to explain screening and information production processes further. Chan (1983), using the venture capital market as an example, argues that intermediaries can realise scale economies from gathering information. Boyd and Prescott (1986) emphasise that with the more intensive screening intermediaries can bring to bear, they can deal with some adverse selection problems more effectively than can securities markets.

Intermediaries frequently specialise their screening functions and, as a result, the kinds of assets they acquire. In some cases intermediaries use an evaluation technology which can reveal more information than is available to the client. However, it is more likely that an intermediary's screening processes will work better than those of markets and yet reveal less information than clients possess. When screening does not generate all the information an intermediary requires, additional contractual arrangements may be employed to compensate for the effects of not having all necessary information. For example, intermediaries may require continuing reporting from clients in a form unavailable to market transactors.

One important kind of intermediated transaction is small in size and exhibits risks with well-known parameters. Screening assesses these limited variations in risks by routine methods, sometimes employing rules of thumb which attempt to reflect the risks' underlying nature. Automobile loans in consumer finance provide an example. These loans are made against consumer earning power. They are generally secured by a charge against the auto and possibly also by life and disability insurance to guarantee continuation of the consumer's income from which the loan is to be repaid. Another typical

43

intermediary transaction involves providing working capital loans to small businesses. Apart from their larger average size and some differences in security, working capital loans are similar to consumer credit in that they involve screening and accepting risks within relatively well-defined parameters.

Diversification within an intermediary is of no value in a perfect capital market, because individuals can diversify costlessly on their own account by using market-traded instruments. However, the diversification is a valuable service if intermediaries can carry it out more cheaply than their clients, as is quite frequently the case in practice. Also in practice, when intermediaries screen numerous small loans they are taking on assets which cannot, because of transactions costs, be traded readily in the market place. The liabilities intermediaries sell against portfolios of such loans have different risk characteristics, generally being less risky than the originally acquired indvidual assets. Intermediaries both effect non-market forms of diversification and reduce the impact of informational asymmetries by aggregating individual risks at lower unit costs than their clients would incur.

Monitoring and ex post adjustments

Expanding on concepts in Leland and Pyle (1972), Diamond (1986) and Bhattacharya and Pfleiderer (1985) recognise the importance of screening and monitoring in creating a diversified portfolio. Diamond argues that the monitoring possibilities open to intermediaries permit them to assume risks which could not profitably be traded in markets. The benefits to monitoring can be enhanced by judicious choice of financial instruments: for example, under some conditions debt instruments provide incentives for truthful revelation of insider information. Monitoring by intermediaries can increase potential net benefits by saving on the setup costs that would be incurred if individuals monitored transactions separately, as would be necessary in market transactions.

Markets do not normally provide for continuing supervision of a financing arrangement: once the terms of exchange have been agreed the buyer is entitled to whatever claim the purchased securities convey, but does not usually have the privilege of later changing the nature of the arrangement. In contrast, intermediated transactions often incorporate possibilities for continuing negotiations between financier and client as well as for communicating new information as it becomes available. Such continuing arrangements are clearly more valuable in situations where transaction information may become better structured with the passage of time.[6]

Informational conditions

Intermediaries, like market agents, transact under a variety of informational conditions, choosing contract terms as dictated by transaction circumstances. Under symmetric risk, lending normally uses routine screening and only minimal amounts of continuing supervision. The consumer loans discussed earlier offer one example; they may be granted according to preset scoring criteria and repayment supervision may be largely automated. When intermediary and client differ in their assessments of a transaction's initial risk, monitoring through time can sometimes attenuate the initial asymmetry. Making recurring loans to the same client over time provides an example.

Intermediated financings extended under structured uncertainty, such as venture investments, often employ both monitoring and learning mechanisms as already indicated. Another way of dealing with unstructured uncertainty, used for example in forms of real estate financing where possible uses for the land are still being determined, is for investors to take an equity stake in the venture. The equity stake allows them both to share in any profits which may result from the venture and to exercise voting privileges, the latter enabling them to influence the project's evolution.

While intermediaries normally produce information mainly for their own private use, they do also sometimes sell it. For example, banks may sell the results of their industry studies to interested clients. There are, however, some problems in producing information for sale. First, intermediaries wishing to sell privately produced information can face credibility problems, particularly if they use the information themselves. Second, they must also be able to insure that the information does not become a public good, for that might prevent either the intermediary or its clients from getting full value for the information. Millon and Thakor (1985) provide a theoretical setting in which an information gathering agency can both diversify its risky investments and profitably share information.

Choice of organisational form

Ramakrishnan and Thakor (1984) ask when it will be beneficial for information producers to form coalitions; i.e. to search for organisational forms which will reduce information production costs. The resulting organisations can improve welfare if informational asymmetries are initially present and if individuals cannot generate similarly reliable information as cheaply by acting on their own. As practical examples, firms like diversified information brokers or investment bankers may be able to produce reliable information at lower costs than can private individuals, because they can resell it a number of times. The incentive costs arising from individual information processors' propensities to produce unreliable information can decline with group size, if, as the authors suppose, the members of the firm can costlessly monitor each other's activities.

The Ramakrishnan–Thakor framework helps to explain the existence of several kinds of information producing firms: individual agents who produce financial information for sale, research firms which produce information for sale, and firms which produce information for their own use. In each case, the technology of information production and the likelihood of revenues being attenuated as any information sold becomes a public good are likely to differ, and the chosen organisational structure reflects an attempt to deal with these cost and revenue differences as effectively as possible.

Financial intermediaries can also vary their organisational structures to take advantage of information production and exchange. The organisational economics debates regarding the comparative merits of centralisation and decentralisation consider tradeoffs between information sharing and coordination on the one hand, incentives and efficiency of decision making on the other. In Williamson's terminology, organisational economics debates the relative merits of hierarchies and markets, but the debate also specialises to financial intermediation. In the latter context, relevant questions include whether an intermediary is better broken up into specialised divisions (e.g. consumer or commercial lending divisions) or into units delivering a range of products to given target groups. Since both offer advantages as well as disadvantages, oscillation between the two organisational forms is commonplace in practice, as agents with bounded rationality focus on first one type of advantage and then on the other.

Other governance mechanisms

Combining the activities of financiers and clients within a single organisation is a third kind of governance response to the contracting problems that develop between autonomous agents either when asset specificity is great or informational differences (especially if they involve uncertainties) are particularly important.

Internal governance can prove cost-effective in some situations where neither markets nor intermediaries can transact profitably. For example, a financial conglomerate's[7] investing in one of its subsidiary companies offers important possibilities for dealing with informational asymmetries, both at the outset and over the life of the investment. Thus internal financing is used when screening, continuing supervision and *ex post* adjustment are regarded as posing greater difficulties than can be met using the capabilities of intermediaries.

Internal financings offer both the greatest amount of information about transactions and the greatest ability to exercise *ex post* control over risks. The perceived risk of a transaction is likely to increase as informational asymmetries increase. However the difficulties associated with increasingly asymmetric informational conditions can sometimes be offset by continuing supervision of a client's affairs as they unfold – a consideration that is particularly important if the transaction involves investing over a relatively long period. Different types and degrees of informational asymmetries call for different types of internal governance mechanisms, as do different types and degrees of asset specificity.

Competitive advantages of internal governance

Internal governance allows for highly sophisticated screening and subsequent control over the managers whose activities are being financed. Internal governance also provides: ready possibilities for recontracting if conditions change, the ability to audit project performance, and the legal authority to change project management in case of need. Agency problems of an intrafirm nature may still exist, but their impacts are likely to be less costly than are similar agency problems arising in either market or intermediated transactions. Transfer or other forms of notional market prices are sometimes used with internal financing, but as the parties are part of the same organisational unit they usually exhibit greater goal congruence than they would if dealing at arm's length in a marketplace. In such circumstances, transfer pricing can perform effectively even when a market price would not. For, in markets the agents might treat each other more opportunistically.

Since intensive internal screening and supervision are likely to be more costly than other forms of governance, internal financing is likely to be used mainly for viable investments which pose particularly difficult governance requirements. The costs are not just the direct costs of governance: internal governance can also attenuate performance incentives to a greater degree than do market transactions. Nevertheless, firms do use internal finance, particularly at those times when they cannot readily raise funds externally. For example, some projects may not be viewed favourably by external financiers and firms wishing to undertake them must provide their own funds to do so.

The Economic Organisation of a Financial System

To see the differences in governance with internal financing, contrast it with a public share issue. In the second case information is widely shared by many parties, in the first it is not. Moreover, in the first case there are much greater opportunities for continuing supervision of the business subsequent to the financing being provided. Internal financings may also be useful in keeping information about development plans from being revealed to competitors as would be the case if a public securities issue were made by a prospectus offering. Thus combinations of financial and non-financial industries are frequently organised as financial conglomerates.

Combinations of mechanisms

Sometimes transactions use more than one governance mechanism. The recently evolved practice of securitisation is a hybrid of intermediary and market governance. Intermediaries screen transactions at the time of origination and place them on their own books while assembling a portfolio. Later, securities are issued and sold in the public markets against the value of the portfolio. In some cases third party guarantees or insurance of the securities' value is offered. Whether or not additional guarantees or insurance are used, the intermediary effectively acts as a market agent to sell the securities it issues. The activity thus combines original screening, subsequent transformation of risk and a market transaction subsequent to that. It represents a refinement of understanding in which intermediaries become more nearly precise about which of their activities represent added value and which do not.

Summary

The three basic governance mechanisms – markets, intermediaries, and internal financings – each have specialised capabilities for meeting transaction requirements. These specialised capabilities mean that each can offer cost effective governance of some transaction types, but not others. Recognising the advantages of each means in essence that the discriminating alignment of mechanism capabilities and transaction requirements is based on effectiveness criteria. Under sufficiently well-specified conditions, effectiveness can lead to efficiency.

Markets are an effective governance mechanism when transaction information is relatively well structured and when the assets involved are liquid (i.e. can readily be resold). In such cases, any necessary *ex post* adjustments are effected by subsequent market transactions without the need for specialised forms of governance structures.

Governance mechanisms

Markets are also used for managing portfolio risk, again because the instruments used for these purposes are relatively liquid and regarded in much the same way by numerous transactors.

Intermediaries have greater capabilities for initial screening and for subsequent administration, particularly forms of *ex post* adjustment, than do markets. These capabilities mean that intermediaries are better equipped to deal with uncertainties than are markets. They are also better equipped to deal with novel forms of transactions, because their *ex post* adjustment capabilities make certain kinds of learning less costly for them than it is for market agents. The economics of information processing explains both different types of information producers and differences in internal organisation.

Internal governance offers the greatest potential for intensive screening, as well as for supervision and adaptation through time. Internal governance structures are likely to be even more costly than those of intermediaries, but on the other hand they can handle more complex financing arrangements as a result.

Notes

1. There may be some circumstances in which, if they could be objectively defined, an effective choice could also be shown to constitute an efficient choice.
2. Cf. Arrow (1964) on the problem of selecting organisational control mechanisms.
3. Even these firms would not do so unless they perceived a demand large enough at least to cover their initial setup costs.
4. In many cases the guarantees are provided by a clearing corporation associated with the exchange.
5. It is not always easy to decide what beliefs underlie a transaction. If a speculator has performed what he regards as a thorough analysis of the transaction's expected profitability, the transaction is more properly regarded as taking place under risk. Even if he has not, and the counterparty has performed such an analysis, the transaction does not appear risky to the latter.
6. Huang and Litzenberger (1988) develop the economic foundations of how information about risks can gradually be refined as time passes.
7. Not all holding companies operate as financial conglomerates with highly developed governance structures; cf. Barney and Ouchi's (1986) discussion of Williamson and others. In this book the term conglomerate refers only to those organisations which do have highly developed structures for governing subsidiaries' transactions.

Chapter four

Specialised governance mechanisms

This chapter shows how and why the competitive advantages of governance mechanisms are enhanced through specialisation. Specialisation increases profitability, mainly through realising a combination of scale and scope economies. The economics of specialisation explains why different governance mechanisms play complementary roles within a financial system, and also helps to explain how a financial system adapts to clients' changing demands.

This chapter expands the Chapter 3 discussion of governance mechanisms and their capabilities by examining specialised forms of markets and intermediaries. Financiers strive to maximise transaction profitability, which under competition means they will choose the lowest cost mechanism[1] available, providing it handles transaction information effectively. A specialised mechanism can generally operate more cheaply than a general purpose one, since its capabilities can be focused on a relatively narrow set of transaction requirements. Thus, specialisation can bring competitive advantage in handling a restricted class of transactions.

Specialised mechanisms use different technologies, including exchange, screening, monitoring, bonding, and risk management technologies. Each governance mechanism employs the given technologies in particular ways, as Figure 4.1 shows.

As Figure 4.1 indicates, each governance mechanism makes its own particular use of a given technology. As a general matter, financial intermediaries have greater governance capabilities than markets, internal financings still greater capabilities. More complex governance mechanisms are needed to deal with more complex transaction requirements, particularly any initial informational differences, and any contract incompleteness which may later call for *ex post* adjustments to be undertaken.

Usually, a mechanism's costs increase along with its capabilities. The search for cost-effective combinations of governance mechanisms and transactions requirements means that simpler, cheaper

Specialised governance mechanisms

Figure 4.1 Technologies and governance mechanisms

Type of technology	Governance mechanisms		
	Markets	Financial intermediaries	Internal financing
Exchange technology	Anonymous transactions, usually with different agents even if repeated.	Continuing negotiation with the same parties.	Detailed, continuing negotiations with close supervision and control.
Risk management technology	Price mediated exchange	Price mediated exchange, swaps or internal management	Primarily internal management
Screening and monitoring technology	Initial evaluation	Continuing monitoring	Intensive, continuing monitoring
Bonding technology	Least capable of imposing penalties	Moderately capable of imposing penalties	Most capable of imposing penalties
Ex Post adjustment capabilities	Not used	Used in a limited fashion	Used extensively

market mechanisms are supplanted by more complex and costly intermediation or even still more costly internal financings as informational differences between transacting parties increase under conditions of risk. Transactions conducted under uncertainty pose still additional governance requirements, to compensate for which governance capabilities must be increased further still. As they do, governance costs also increase.

Transactions posing costlier governance requirements will only be entered by profit oriented financiers if the extra governance costs can be recovered through higher earnings from the financing transaction. Financial theorists generally believe that financiers require higher net returns as earnings risks increase. If a transaction's earnings risks increase even after using a costlier governance structure, the required market rate of return will be subject to a twofold increase: the financier must be compensated both for using the costlier governance structure and for taking on a higher risk. If this twofold increase cannot be obtained, the transaction will not be carried out.

51

The Economic Organisation of a Financial System

In the rest of this chapter, the combinations indicated in Figure 4.1 are used to discuss the capabilities and competitive advantages of specialised markets and intermediaries. It is beyond the scope of this book to consider specialised forms of internal governance in the same detail, as to do so would require a fully fledged discussion of the internal economics of the firm. For a summary of the present state of this field, the reader is referred to such works as Barney and Ouchi (1986).

Specialised markets

By creating a central trading place, a market minimises search costs: potential buyers and sellers can readily find each other. Without a market, search can be more costly, take longer, or both. Hence trading tends to concentrate in well-known markets (either physical or electronic) because search costs are usually lower there than anywhere else. This effect is enhanced by the operating economies of scale exhibited in many markets. For example, empirical studies of stock exchanges show that the largest exchanges can consummate trades at lowest unit cost, and are thus capable of attracting business away from smaller, less active markets.

Several types of specialised markets can be defined, each offering unique governance capabilities. The important characteristics of different markets are not the familiar categories used in everyday descriptions, but rather the markets' different economic functions. Extending the principles illustrated in Figure 4.1, different markets can perform their functions most effectively by using specialised forms of exchange technologies.

Primary and secondary markets: public and private markets

A primary market transaction is one in which new securities are issued, while a secondary market transaction is one in which outstanding securities are traded. Primary and secondary market functions are not unrelated. Primary market conditions are most immediately relevant to raising funds for new projects, but the terms according to which primary issues can be sold are influenced by the secondary market. Primary market terms are generally improved by an active secondary market in which the issuer's existing securities are traded.

Primary market agents depend mainly on an effective distribution network for their success, whereas secondary market agents depend largely on their ability to complete trades quickly and relatively cheaply. Thus firms which specialise in primary market transactions are those which can effectively manage the costs of searching for original purchasers, while the firms which specialise in secondary market transactions are those which can effectively manage trading costs. The two functions are often found within the same firm, because when combined they yield economies of scope which result largely from the fact that the two functions can use common inputs such as a research department and a securities sales staff. Nevertheless, the two functions are usually organised as separate divisions, because each also requires its own expertise.

Markets are often classified as either public or private, a classification which has economic meaning in that it refers mainly to the number of potential securities buyers and whether they are individuals or financial institutions. The public markets can be thought of as essentially retail markets, while the private markets can be thought of as closer to wholesale in function. For example, a new issue sold in a public market will usually be purchased by many buyers, a new issue sold in a private market may be entirely purchased by one or a few institutional investors.

When they are able to do so, clients choose between transacting in public or in private markets largely on the basis of the cost and informational characteristics represented by these two variants of exchange technologies. Costs include such considerations as the underwriting commissions paid for a given issue, and are relatively straightforward to assess. A decision based on cost alone will thus consider the different placement costs involved. As a general principle, very large issues are likely to be most cheaply placed in public markets, because of their usually wider distribution capabilities.

The informational considerations in choosing between the two types of markets are a little more complex. In the interests of distributing information to potential participants, regulation usually requires that primary public market issues satisfy disclosure requirements. The information disclosed must usually indicate key information about the client, the amounts of funds to be raised and the purposes for which they will be used. Disclosure requirements are normally satisfied by issuing a detailed prospectus stipulating the securities' terms and how the funds raised by the issue will be used. Since meeting disclosure requirements usually involves a relatively large fixed cost, only relative large new issues can economically be floated in a public market. However, without disclosure requirements, information might be less well distributed, leaving some potential buyers at a disadvantage. Disclosure can also bring advantages to the seller: a prospectus can sometimes provide information which helps the issuing firm to sell its securities successfully.

The Economic Organisation of a Financial System

A firm planning a public share issue will usually prefer to list its securities on the largest exchange for which it can qualify. The largest exchange will likely have the greatest amount of secondary market activity, which can improve the shares' liquidity and thus make their original placement easier. However, firms' choices are constrained by listing requirements, which are most rigorous on large exchanges. Listing requirements represent an attempt by the exchange to define minimum quality standards for the securities the exchange will trade. For, stipulating minimum trading quality can reduce investigation costs, and increase trading activity thereby.

Unlike a public issue, a private market transaction will usually be aimed at one or a few buyers. Since private market transactions are not usually subject to disclosure requirements, fixed issue costs are typically lower. Some clients also prefer private issues as a way of simultaneously revealing more information to financiers, less to competitors. First, financiers can utilise more intensive forms of screening than is possible with public issues, because in private issues financiers can enter individual, detailed negotiations with the client. Second, the disclosure requirements attendant upon public issues are sometimes strategically disadvantageous to clients because they force public announcements of plans which competitors may use to advantage.

As a final point, a public issue serves as a device for raising capital without surrendering a controlling interest to an outside group, at least so long as share ownership remains widespread. Private placements, on the other hand, can more easily result in some group's obtaining a controlling interest in the issuing firm.

Dealer and broker markets

A dealer provides transaction immediacy by assuming an inventory position in the instruments being traded, assuming risk on behalf of clients. A broker does not assume an inventory position, but simply matches up parties to a transaction. In effect, brokers provide an information service which helps sellers and buyers find each other. Whether a transaction is handled by a dealer or a broker depends on the relations between expected transaction costs and revenues, in this case the costs of managing risks and market agents' perceptions of normal commission charges.

Market agents act as dealers when they expect to recover their inventory costs from trading revenues. A dealer's competitive advantage rests on his ability to provide quick, relatively cheap trading services. Accordingly, dealer markets usually exhibit active trading in a relatively homogeneous class of instruments. In addition, dealer markets usually exhibit active arbitraging. For example, block traders (dealers who take what are effectively wholesale positions in large blocks of shares) can smooth out price fluctuations that might not be smoothed out by stock exchange specialists, who have more limited capital and customarily handle orders of smaller size.

Brokers replace dealers when the risks of taking inventory positions are relatively large in relation to typical transaction revenues. A broker acts like an information producer who earns rewards from fees charged for finding buyers for a seller, or sellers for a buyer. Broker markets are generally less active in individual securities than dealer markets, and also tend to be more fragmented than dealer markets because there is usually less arbitraging when market agents do not trade on their own account.

One of the clearest examples of the differences between brokers and dealers is found in the foreign exchange markets. In forward foreign exchange contracts dealer risks can change rather rapidly with changing market conditions, and over a relatively wide range. On the other hand, client commissions cannot readily be changed over a similar range. In these cases, the change from dealing to broking means one type of risk management technology is substituted for another as the importance of market risk or uncertainty grows in relation to customary commission charges.

Under normal conditions, foreign exchange traders act as dealers in forward contracts. Under unusual conditions, say when they believe a country's currency may come under considerable pressure, traders initially respond to the increased uncertainty by widening their bid–ask spreads on the forward contracts. If the uncertainty continues to increase, traders become unwilling to take positions in forward (and sometimes even in spot) contracts. In extreme circumstances, they may be willing to trade only on a brokered basis. If the uncertainty is later reduced to a level the traders regard as satisfactory, they will resume normal trading.[2]

Markets for trading risks

A good deal of financial activity involves trading risks.[3] While risks are exchanged in all financial transactions the distinguishing feature of the arrangements now being discussed is that risks are traded in their own right rather than incidentally as a result of raising funds. Options, futures, and foreign exchange markets are the most important markets for actively trading risks, but interest rate and currency swap arrangements are becoming increasingly important. These markets are not used for raising new funds, but they make it more attractive to undertake risky projects in the first place because they facilitate risk trading. That is, secondary markets for trading risks enhance the primary financing of risky ventures just as an active secondary market for a company's shares enhances the primary market for a new issue. The detailed features of markets for trading risks will be discussed below, but it is useful to provide an overall perspective first.

Risk trading is motivated by differing expectations regarding future events, by differing attitudes toward bearing risks, and by the differing portfolio positions of transactors. Different expectations or attitudes stimulate risk trading, but even if agents have the same expectations and attitudes they may wish to trade as a means of managing portfolio risk. For example, a bank with floating rate liabilities and fixed rate assets might try to exchange the interest costs of the floating rate liabilities for a set of fixed rate interest payments. If it were able to do so, the bank could reduce temporal fluctuations in its net interest margins thereby. It would do so if the cost of this form of risk reduction were sufficiently low.

Although most discussions classify risk trading according to transaction type, the most important differences between transactions involve their underlying economics. Thus both selling insurance and speculating involve purchasing (assuming) risks. The distinction between them is essentially one of motive, since both kinds of transactions mean that more risks or uncertainties are taken on.

Insurance companies strive to profit from the premiums they charge for creating liabilities (underwriting risks). In effect, an insurance company writes put options on assets possessed by the insured parties, and tries to profit from the charges collected for writing the puts. Fire insurance, life insurance, and mortgage principal insurance all provide ready examples of the activity.

Speculators usually assume risks in attempts to profit from short-term price fluctuations. Thus speculation means taking on a relatively high degree of risk or uncertainty, but with a view to selling off the risk at a profit within a relatively short time. For example, a speculative option purchase might involve buying options (most of which expire within several months of their issue date) rather than stocks. Fluctuations on an options portfolio's rate of return are generally much larger than on a portfolio of the stocks themselves, both because the options are higher risk securities than stocks and because their purchase price is lower, permitting greater gearing of the invested capital. Sometimes speculative activities are referred to using other terminology: speculating by buying large quantities of shares of a firm likely to be the target of a future takeover is usually called risk arbitrage.

Selling off a risk to an underwriter is usually called buying insurance, while selling off a risk in the markets is usually called hedging. Thus these similar economic functions are both based on similar motives, but are effected using different governance structures. The choice between market and intermediary forms of governance structure is subject to much the same economics as are different types of lending or investment transactions.

Insurance purchases are most often privately negotiated between client and insurance company because of the intensive nature of the screening involved, and because of the value of continually monitoring the contract. Hedging is usually negotiated in markets with many traders because the risks are characterised by readily ascertained parameters and the contracts require little continuing supervision. For example, a hedging transaction might involve forward sale of a foreign currency asset to remove an exchange risk from the books of a firm by fixing the price at which the foreign currency can be exchanged for domestic funds.

Options, futures, and foreign exchange markets

An option is an instrument which gives its holder the right, but not the obligation, to buy (call) some asset at a specified price for a specified period of time, or to sell (put) some asset at a specified price for a specified period of time. European options can be exercised only at the end of the specified time period, American options at any point in time during the life of the instrument. Options contracts are used both to speculate on and to hedge against price changes in an underlying instrument. Trading risks in the form of an options contract rather than in the form of the underlying security is usually a cheaper way of effecting the exchange, mainly because less capital is required to trade the options contracts. For the options represent only a portion of the security risk, and for a given period of time. In essence, they separate a security's capital value from the risk of fluctuations in that value.[4]

Traded options are written against shares, share indexes, bonds, and foreign currencies, to name a few kinds. One example of such a transaction is buying a put when one expects to sell a security at some future time, but wishes to fix the profit on it before the sale actually occurs. Traded options are presently used in such a large variety of risk management transactions that they cannot all be detailed here; for further discussion the reader is referred to such works as Cox and Rubinstein (1986).

If there is active arbitraging between an option and its underlying security, close price links will be maintained between the assets. The theory of option pricing depends heavily on an assumption of active arbitrage, most often modelled as occurring continuously. As a result, price changes in an option can be modelled as functions of price changes in the underlying asset. The development of options pricing theory has led to recognising that many different kinds of risk trading can be interpreted as trades in combinations of options. Partly as a result of these theoretical developments, the options markets have come increasingly to be used for risk management. At the present time, the options markets account for an important proportion of traded risks. Since all forms of risk trading seem likely to continue growing, activity in the options markets also seems likely to continue increasing.

While options contracts confer privileges, futures contracts create obligations. That is, a futures contract requires the parties to it to buy or sell a commodity, physical or financial, on a specified date for a specified price. Like options, futures contracts are often used to speculate on, or to hedge against, price changes in an underlying instrument.

Futures contracts are distinguished from forward contracts in that the former are usually traded on organised exchanges, where their values are adjusted as the value of the underlying asset changes. Forward contracts do not normally trade, and are therefore not normally "marked to market" (revalued frequently) in the same way as futures contracts.[5] One of the principal differences between financial forwards and financial futures is very much like the difference between going long in the bond markets and rolling over a series of short maturity bonds. Financial futures typically need smaller performance guarantees than do forwards, because changes in value are settled daily rather than being left outstanding until the end of the contract (Cox, Ingersoll and Ross, 1981b, pp. 324 and 335). Thus, again each specialised instrument also plays its own special economic role.

While risk trading began mainly in options markets, the futures markets are becoming increasingly important in performing the same functions. As suggested in the last paragraph, the financial futures market is of greatest concern in the present discussion: instruments traded include interest rate futures, currency futures, and stock index futures, all of which can be used for specialised forms of risk management.[6] For example, a bank wishing to offer fixed rate loans can convert its earnings to floating rate by taking an appropriately calculated short position in interest rate futures. This short position rises in value as interest rates rise, and falls as they fall. It thus increases earnings on the fixed rate loan as the costs of funding the loan increase, and vice versa.

Risks are also traded on the foreign exchange markets. Much of the world's foreign exchange trading resembles transactions in

Specialised governance mechanisms

wholesale markets because the amounts of individual transactions are so large. In contrast, options and futures market trading has some characteristics of retail trading, because the amounts involved are typically smaller, and because the contracts are often shorter-term. Each of the world's foreign exchange markets has a similar structure, being dominated by large dealing banks. In addition, foreign exchange brokers supplement these activities of the dealing banks. About two-thirds of all foreign currency transactions are spot, the rest forward. Forward transactions are the main vehicle used in risk trading. For example, foreign trade creates foreign currency accounts receivable whose risk can be offset through a forward sale.

Evolution of risk trading

Each kind of risk trading plays an economic function which is at least partially distinct, and specialisation helps the particular kind of trading to play this role efficiently. However, despite the present differences between the different markets for trading risks, the boundaries between them are not fixed permanently. As one example, the currency options and futures markets are becoming increasingly important in foreign exchange trading, particularly for transactions in smaller amounts. More changes of the boundaries between the different markets for trading risks are likely to be observed in the future, as the rest of this section indicates.

First, the present economies of specialisation are likely to change. For example, the various foreign exchange markets are becoming increasingly automated and ever more closely linked through international communications and international trading. Second, the economics of market operations is affected by standardisation and by other institutional changes. For example, options have only traded on organised exchanges since 1972. At that time trading was standardised and the option contracts guaranteed[7] by financially responsible agents of various options exchanges. These innovations stimulated an explosive increase in options trading activity both by making it easier for agents to find each other and by removing most of the risks in trading with agents whose credit ratings would not be known to each other.

Another feature of market evolution is displayed by considering how the different markets originated. For example, the options and futures markets were originated by securities firms familiar with the functions of market agents. Hence options and futures traders aimed at reducing trading costs through standardising the instruments traded, and at enhancing trading between anonymous parties by guaranteeing contract performance.[8] On the other hand, foreign exchange trading was mainly originated by banks and is not yet as standardised as options and futures trading. In part, the lack of standardisation is due to the larger size of individual transactions in foreign exchange.

But other factors are also at work. In particular, foreign exchange contracts' terms tend toward a standard as trading activity in a particular currency increases beyond a certain level. Foreign exchange contracts are not usually performance guaranteed: most traders are well enough known to each other that any concern over default risks is managed mainly by restricting the quantity of orders placed with any single counterparty in a given day. However, as the foreign exchange markets continue to expand and the number of traders increases further the need for guarantees is likely to increase.

The same developments seem likely to occur in the interest rate and currency swap markets. Although these markets are mainly broker markets operated by bank traders at the present time, securities firms have begun actively to trade both kinds of swaps. While the banks have been willing to arrange transactions on an individual basis, securities dealers are more closely attuned to the virtues of standardisation, and have begun to emphasise the importance of setting the same terms on swap transactions.

In all the cases discussed above, the relative emphases on brokered individual transactions as opposed to standardised, guaranteed dealer transactions reflect the experience of bankers on the one hand, securities dealers on the other. The two kinds of specialists have developed different kinds of expertise from their primary business, and in the markets for trading risks, each group has to learn which kinds of organisation are most economic, and under which circumstances. The evolution of the markets for trading risks toward greater standardisation thus provides a case study in the increasingly discriminating alignment of transaction requirements with governance capabilities. The increasing discrimination itself occurs gradually because agents with bounded rationality learn only gradually.

Specialised intermediaries

Intermediary functions are sometimes categorised straightforwardly as asset services, liability services, and accounting services. Asset services include financing client activities and managing the resulting asset portfolios. Liability services mainly take the form of issuing specialised claims: for example, banks sell deposits, insurance companies sell a variety of life insurance contracts. Finally, intermediaries perform accounting services for clients, services which in the case of banks and near banks include providing chequeing facilities.

While all intermediaries perform these same basic functions, they do so in specialised ways. In particular, different transaction requirements affect the way an intermediary is organised. For example, the managers of unit trusts (mutual funds in North America) spend relatively large sums on research as well as on marketing and sales activity. These expenditures suggest that fund managers are active in generating new information for the benefit of their clients, presumably realising scale economies in doing so. Lending intermediaries also produce information, but usually on a transaction by transaction basis to be used privately in negotiations with the client: credit assessment processes offer a prominent example. Hence, a discussion of specialised intermediaries should address the economic questions of why such differences occur.

Managing intermediary organisation

Even though intermediaries are specialised according to an emphasis on investment (such as unit trusts) or on lending (such as banks or near banks), most still remain multiproduct firms dealing in several financial markets. Typical practices suggest that intermediaries realise scope economies from providing related services. For example, many bank and near bank intermediaries now offer most consumer oriented financial services. Indeed, some observers suggest that retail banking is now more like retailing than traditional banking, in that it is currently organised to deliver whatever range of services seems most attractive to retail clients.

On the other hand, even the multipurpose commercial and retail firms known as financial supermarkets are limited in the activities they can profitably conduct. For example, clients representing large corporations wishing to purchase the services of financial specialists would not be likely to find retail banks well suited to their needs. Even the specialised divisions of a large bank might not offer the requisite expertise: some corporate clients prefer to conduct some of their financial transactions only with fully fledged investment bankers or merchant bankers.[9]

It is important to recognise that currently the traditional distinctions between formerly different forms of financial intermediaries (such as banks and securities firms) are disappearing. Changing technology, increasing competition and the gradual removal of restrictive regulation provide incentives for financial firms of various types to enter each other's traditional businesses. In doing so, the firms entering the new lines usually supplement the products or services they have traditionally offered, apparently seeking to realise scope economies, to take advantage of greater than normal profit levels, or both.

The perceived presence or absence of scope economies and of market opportunities varies with industry beliefs and economic conditions. Thus, international banks have recently begun curtailing at least some of the investment activities which they have entered since the mid-1970s. This change of strategy suggests the banks may originally have overestimated their possibilities for realising scope economies, possibly because they underestimated the difficulty of acquiring the requisite skills for competing with international investment houses. Alternatively, they may have correctly anticipated the net benefits to expansion of their business on its own, but neglected to adjust their profit forecasts for similar expansion by their competitors. The fact that virtually all international banks took the same actions simultaneously may well have changed the economics on which the expansion plans were based, and eventually led to the current retrenchments.

Whatever the size and function of an intermediary, in a rapidly changing financial system it may be able to gain competitive advantage by using an organisational structure which facilitates rapid adaptation to environmental change. Especially, the current pace of technological change offers radically new possibilities for organising financial firms, and firms which fail to adopt the new technologies can quickly be placed at a cost disadvantage. These kinds of developments are likely to continue: the cost of human resources relative to technology will continue rising and financial institutions will go on substituting relatively cheap capital for relatively expensive labour.

Some small, special purpose intermediaries are able to continue operating profitably over the longer run, suggesting they somehow gain and retain competitive advantages over larger firms. These advantages may stem from the larger units' being inhibited by restrictive regulation, or from specialised investment skills being needed to serve a small market. In the second case, it may not be possible to blend the cultural attributes attendant on these skills with the atmosphere of the large organisation, even if an autonomous specialised division is set up. In addition, the inertia of large organisations may prevent them from adapting rapidly to a changing financial environment, while small institutions may exhibit greater flexibility: in rapidly changing markets larger institutions may be at a disadvantage in effectively serving some types of new clients.

A few financial intermediaries act primarily as information producers, selling information but not investing on their own account. For example, some firms insure municipal bonds against default, but do not buy the bonds themselves. In contrast, a bank which investigates applications for credit normally does buy the client firm's securities. As discussed in Chapter 3, there are two economic reasons for these differences in practice: the difficulty in appropriating the rewards to privately produced information, and the possibility that firms selling information to third parties could be regarded as offering unreliable advice if they were to invest on their own account.

Economics of intermediary operations

Intermediaries enjoy economies of specialisation from standardising practice and thereby creating competitive advantage in providing certain classes of service. They also realise scale economies in screening and administering asset portfolios, particularly by taking advantage of computing and communications technology. Transaction economies of scale can usually be realised by increasing the numbers of transactions, possibly over a relatively wide range. Economies of scale in administering portfolios can also be realised by increasing portfolio size. Thus many intermediaries gain cost advantages from handling large numbers of small transactions whose screening is subject to scale economies.

Economies of scope or cost complementarities seem to exist mainly where transaction types are not too different. Where they can be realised, scope economies are often gained by sharing computing and communications resources across functions. The main factor limiting economies of scope from extending to all possible financial transactions seem to arise from the nature of human capital. Not all kinds of skills can easily be combined, especially when financings are complex and the skills necessary to consummate them are costly to acquire. Thus, for example, there may be economies of scope in combining the sale of fire and property insurance or in joint ventures between banks and securities dealers. However, in the first case the economies would probably not extend to combinations of insurance activity and venture investments; in the second case neither banks nor securities dealers might prove particularly skilled at making long-term development loans.

Large intermediaries have another cost advantage – they can usually effect geographical diversification more cheaply than their smaller regional counterparts, which may explain why securities analysts seem widely to believe that smaller financial intermediaries are riskier. However, to an increasing extent the advantages of diversifying geographically through a branch network are being attenuated by securitisation, a topic introduced in Chapter 3. Larger intermediaries may also benefit from lower overall costs of funding than can be enjoyed by their smaller counterparts. It seems at present to be an open question whether smaller intermediaries might be able to enjoy a similarly low cost of capital by purchasing funds *en bloc* in several different, geographically dispersed markets.

Intermediary average cost curves slope downward, at least over an initial range, because of a combination of scale and scope economies. There is considerable empirical evidence to show that small intermediaries can realise economies through growth. There is little or no evidence showing that financial intermediaries of large size exhibit scale diseconomies. The absence of evidence does not necessarily confirm an absence of scale diseconomies. Rather, it may simply mean that management is aware of when scale diseconomies start to manifest themselves and do not allow the intermediary to reach such a size.

Intermediaries sometimes set up specialised divisions to perform particular functions such as term lending to business. Specialised divisions permit concentrating the activities of highly skilled, costly personnel. They may also generate economies by utilising performance oriented reward structures for specialist personnel. Some intermediaries have segregated their activities into semi-autonomous groups, possibly as an alternative to being faced with scale diseconomies. Examples are the large pools of funds managed by life insurance and by trust companies. Some of the fund managers may administer several different specialised funds, such as fixed-income, share, or mortgage funds.

Sometimes intermediaries create affiliated organisations to realise scope economies from activities which regulation prevents the parent firm from carrying out. For example, specialised mortgage lenders are set up in countries where mortgage lending is subject to regulatory restriction. These tendencies are strengthened if there are tax advantages to be gained by conforming to the restrictive regulation. On the other hand, combinations of affiliated organisations seem to face rising costs because of the nature of human capital. Investment bankers and commercial bankers, for example, are often said to be members of different cultures, who do not easily work together, even within affiliates of the same organisation.

Traditionally, large securities firms have acted primarily as dealers and brokers, thus emphasising trading and agency activities rather than intermediary functions. However, large securities firms have now begun also to act as financial intermediaries, apparently realising scope economies in data processing and accounting. For example, securities firms might be able to offer cash management accounts or term deposits at relatively small marginal costs using existing accounting facilities. They might also be able to utilise existing staff to market the new products, effecting another form of savings.

Like banks and near banks, large securities firms can realise scale economies in research and can also diversify the profit risks of operating specialised divisions such as retail securities sales or corporate finance. Many of the recent securities industry mergers can partially be explained on the bases of these kinds of scale and scope economies. In addition, the larger capital bases of larger firms make it easier for them to compete for the position of lead underwriter or to arrange bought deals. For, these transactions involve outright purchases of large amounts of securities, which may be held in inventory for some period of time.

Cost-effectiveness of intermediation

The kinds of transactions which intermediaries can handle more cost effectively than markets change with time and technology. Moreover, industry understanding of what is currently cost-effective can change as intermediaries experiment with new forms of organising their activities. However, unless at least one intermediary's management perceives the possibilities of using a new technology, there is no guarantee that useful technological innovations will be quickly adopted. Thus, there is also no guarantee that at any point in time the industry will be as efficient as it might be.

The fact that technological innovation does not always spread rapidly is more a question of perception (i.e. of the degree to which rationality is bounded) than of motive. It means that possible new ways of doing business are not always discovered, or seen to be profitable, rather than that intermediaries are unwilling to experiment. Indeed, intermediaries frequently experiment with new lines of business which are later dropped if they prove unprofitable. Thus in the mid-1980s banks tried to offer investment services as one means of offsetting revenue losses stemming from corporations' return to market borrowing. However, in the late 1980s the same banks began to de-emphasise this kind of business, a trend which looks as if it will continue into the early 1990s.

If they are perceived as cost-effective, technological innovations can spread rapidly. For example, the use of computers now permits banks and other intermediaries to offer such products as daily interest savings accounts, which would have been prohibitively costly when interest calculations were done manually. It also came to be realised that consumer loans can be administered more cheaply by using modern computing equipment. Once these notions were accepted by intermediary executives, computerisation spread rapidly.

The Economic Organisation of a Financial System

Economics of information processing and screening

The economics of intermediary information processing informs the evolution of specialised intermediaries. Certain intermediaries have evolved different screening capabilities as a result of their history. This experience affects both the ways they are likely to evolve in the near future, and their current screening costs. When changing the nature of their activities, financial firms are more likely to enter lines of business related to their current expertise rather than to enter businesses with which they have no experience. While exceptions to this adaptive change can be observed from time to time, for the most part history constrains financial firms' current forms of experimentation.

Thus, some intermediaries specialise in particular kinds of screening functions for relatively long periods. For example, US banks operating in Canada have made proportionately more cash flow loans than their Canadian counterparts, probably because of the economics of screening just discussed. In particular, since the US market developed first, the US banks may have gained cost advantages from early learning. They could then extend these cost advantages by entering the smaller Canadian market, where local financial firms had not developed the same experiential knowledge.

Current screening costs depend on history because they can be affected through learning by doing. Thus, incumbent firms are more likely to have low costs than are new entrants. This experiential barrier to entry provides a second force constraining the nature of financial firms' change.

Intermediation and risk trading

The discussion of brokers and dealers on pp. 54–5 pointed out that risks are traded most actively when they are judged as somehow reasonable in relation to the returns from trading them. While much risk trading is effected in markets, other governance mechanisms are used as risks rise relative to expected returns, as screening costs per transaction rise, or both. Risk intermediation sometimes involves exchanging larger risks with unique characteristics, such as in an interest rate swap between two large financial intermediaries. Currency swaps also sometimes involve large amounts and unique terms. These kinds of transactions were the first kinds of swaps to be effected, explaining why these markets were first entered by banks and only later by securities firms.

Despite the foregoing, lack of familiarity with a transaction can inhibit even intermediary risk trading. It may be that some risks are viewed differently by sellers and potential buyers, or they are regarded as atypically large in relation to normal trading revenues. For example, a few years ago it was not possible to hedge long-term foreign currency loans, and for this reason, firms had until recently to offset this risk internally. However, as financial intermediaries have learned to take on long-term foreign exchange positions, the possibility of trading them has emerged.

Relations between mechanisms

The terms of transactions effected in a given market or through a given intermediary are related to those arranged in other parts of a financial system. In other words, a financial system's specialised mechanisms are not able to set financing terms in isolation. Rather, the terms they can set are constrained by and related to the terms in other markets. The forces constraining and relating terms are those created by flows between different markets, flows resulting from both arbitraging and intermediated transactions.

System components and links between them

Interest rates on securities which are close substitutes are kept at the same or similar levels by combinations of arbitraging and intermediary transactions among the instruments concerned. Both arbitraging and intermediation direct financial flows between markets in response to emerging interest rate differentials (appropriately adjusted for differences in risk, of course). For example, suppose a given instrument or market begins to post a larger than normal interest differential from closely related markets. Then arbitrageurs, intermediaries, or both will begin to direct a larger proportion of funds to it, tending to remove the emerging differential. If the differential is smaller than normal, the reverse will occur. The size of the flows linking various sub-markets, and their interest elasticities, will depend on whether arbitraging, intermediation or both are viewed as sufficiently profitable.

Neoclassical financial theory is largely built on the assumption that linkages are created by costless arbitraging, which is therefore profitable whenever an atypical interest rate differential emerges. Indeed, a perfect financial system is usually described as a single capital market because the theory holds that flows between different parts of the market would respond strongly and quickly to any deviation from equilibrium interest rate patterns. The risk–return relationship in the theory of securities market pricing, and the yield curve explained by theories of the term structure of interest rates, are examples of theories premised on active arbitraging. On the other hand, neo-

The Economic Organisation of a Financial System

classical financial theory does not recognise or address the effect of intermediated flows of funds between different parts of the system.

Without arbitraging or intermediation, linking flows may be relatively small and respond sluggishly to atypical interest rate differentials. Where the flows are small, sluggish, or both, a system is usually described as (partially or wholly) fragmented. The variation in price–earnings ratios of shares with apparently equal risks offers an example. For example, price–earnings ratios in Japanese stock markets are currently much higher than in the New York or London markets, indicating a lack of international arbitraging between these markets.[10] The two-tier structure of some domestic stock markets seems to offer another example of weak linkages.

When either financial economics or the perceptions of those economics change, say because of innovation or technological change, the size and interest elasticity of linking flows will also change. In a developing financial system, the linking flows usually become larger, and more interest elastic, as the system increases in sophistication. However the time scale of adjustment can differ importantly across different parts of a financial system. Merton (1987) observes that interest rate or securities price responses to announcements through standard channels are rapid, but funds flow responses to, say, scientific advance can be much slower. Thus interest rate anomalies which can only be eliminated by changing existing practices or by establishing new channels for intermediation can persist for relatively long periods of time.

Arbitraging between markets

Theories based on arbitraging are actually more extensive than the examples given in the previous section. In addition to the capital asset pricing theory and the term structure theory, they include the arbitrage pricing theory, theories of pricing of such derivative securities as options or futures, the interest and forward parity theorems, and the Fisher effect. These theories' predictions have all been tested empirically, albeit to varying degrees. They have been found to hold most closely in financial markets which most closely approximate the perfectly competitive ideal, such as highly active markets for publicly traded stocks. Less competitive financial markets only exhibit tendencies to develop the equilibrium patterns predicted by the relevant theory. In these markets, the patterns' realisation is inhibited by impediments to trading or differing expectations which remain unaligned through time.

Both the capital asset pricing theory and the arbitrage pricing theory hold that securities with the same risks will have the same interest rates, and that rates will increase with risk. The theories differ in their definitions of how securities risk should be assessed, but both have enjoyed considerable success in explaining relations between securities prices in the public markets. If an interest rate on some security is too high in relation to market perceptions of its risk, the security will attract buyers, its price will rise, and the effective interest rate on it will fall until a customary differential is restored. The customary differentials between, say, corporate bond rates and mortgage rates can be thus explained as attributable to the risk differences recognised in the capital asset pricing theory or in the arbitrage pricing theory.

Theories of pricing derivative securities hold that arbitrage relates the derivative security's price to the instrument against which it is written. As the price of the underlying instrument fluctuates, the price of, say, an option on it will also fluctuate, but usually over a wider proportional range. So long as cheap or costless arbitraging is possible, new information in either market is reflected virtually simultaneously in the other. Fragmentation of these markets can only occur if trading is somehow inhibited.

The Fisher relation holds that financiers seek to earn real rather than nominal rates of return, with the result that any nominal rate they specify equals the sum of a real interest rate plus an adjustment for expected inflation. Thus if expectations of future inflation suddenly rise, the prices of bonds expressed in nominal terms should fall; i.e. nominal interest rates should rise to maintain a constant real rate of interest. Although attempts to test the validity of the Fisher effect have been made, the tests are hampered by the difficulty of choosing an appropriate proxy for the expected rate of inflation. Nevertheless, the Fisherian view is probably valid in the sense that financiers are likely to take declines in purchasing power into account when making longer-term loans or investments – they may lend in Swiss francs at very low rates of interest, but will not extend the same interest rates on loans of the same risk denominated in, say, a South American currency.[11]

Interest parity theory holds that similar investments in different countries should, as a result of arbitraging, bear the same real rate of interest. Thus, if country A has a real interest rate of 4 per cent over one year, and country B has a nominal interest rate of 20 per cent, country B is, in theory, expected to have a 16 per cent rate of inflation. To equate real interest rates in the two countries, B's currency must fall, so the one year forward rate for which the currency of B can be exchanged for that of A is 16 per cent less than the prevailing spot rate.

Interest parity theory assumes perfect markets and certainty regarding future events, and therefore is not likely to hold exactly in practice. Nevertheless, it does provide a rough indication of both direction and likely magnitude of change in currency values in many practical situations. Where they are observed, deviations from the predictions of interest rate parity theory are generally attributed to market imperfections or central bank intervention designed to offset the workings of market forces. However, the market forces on which the relationships are predicated seem only to prevail after relatively long adjustment periods.

The forward parity theorem argues that spot rates and forward exchange rates should be closely related to each other whenever active arbitraging can occur. If there is no difference in two countries' expected inflation or interest rates, the forward rate and the spot rate should be equal. In essence, forward parity argues that forward and spot prices incorporate the same information about differential inflation rates between countries, adjusting the rate of change of currency values to compensate.

Such relations between spot and forward rates do often seem to be observable in highly developed foreign exchange markets. However as previously mentioned changes in confidence can inhibit forward trading to such an extent that there is a kind of temporal fragmentation to the foreign exchange markets. Whenever such temporal fragmentation occurs, forward parity relations will not hold, at least for a period of time until normal conditions are restored.

Interest arbitraging, particularly between government securities issued in various currencies, is a common short-term international investment transaction. It therefore serves as one vehicle which tends to bring about the relations predicted by the interest parity and forward parity theorems. It is also interesting to note that the foreign exchange risk on interest arbitraging transactions is often hedged in the forward markets. For, small changes in exchange rates can have relatively large impacts on short-term interest yields, meaning that the net earnings from interest arbitraging are only attractive when the foreign exchange risk is sold off at the time of the initial investment, thus fixing the net interest earnings. If the net earnings are not hedged against foreign exchange risk, many short-term investors find them unattractive, as the risk is too large in relation to the expected level of the earnings. On the other hand, since there are costs to hedging, interest arbitraging will tend to create the relationships predicted by interest and forward parity theorems only when the cost of hedging is more than covered by the emerging interest differential.

Intermediation between markets

Arbitraging is not well suited for transactions in which fund administration or information processing functions are subject to scale economies, but in these cases financial intermediaries can profitably perform a function analogous to arbitraging. For example, many intermediaries purchase securities whose prices they find attractive. In doing so, these intermediaries direct a pool of small savers' funds toward attractive investments by acquiring information about the investments that small savers could not gather on their own for the same unit costs.

As intermediaries reallocate funds among competing investments in response to differential profit opportunities, they help ensure that market equilibrium risk–return relationships are maintained. For instance, in most countries there is no direct arbitraging between government bonds and residential mortgages. Savers will allocate their funds between bonds and deposits on the basis of their relative interest rates. Hence if rates on bonds rise, so will rates on deposits. But a large proportion of deposits, particularly term deposits, is reinvested in mortgages, and in order to preserve their profit margins intermediaries will increase rates on mortgages to compensate for increases in their deposit costs. Thus the fact that intermediary deposits compete with bonds is sufficient to link the markets, albeit indirectly.

Financial system fragmentation occurs if the same transactions are carried out at different interest rates in different markets (after duly adjusting for any differences in risk, and assuming the interest rates are adjusted for possibly different tax rates and other similar costs). Fragmentation results when neither arbitraging nor intermediation transactions are seen as profitable, when the opportunities have not been perceived, or when it is not known how to carry them out. Financiers' perceptions may either be correct or based on inadequate technical knowledge. To the extent fragmentation arises from not understanding how to use available technologies profitably, its effects are likely to be mitigated by learning, although the process may be lengthy.

Complementary use of mechanisms

A transaction is sometimes governed using a combination of mechanisms. For example, syndicated loans involve both private market sales of loan participations and private information production. A syndicated loan is usually screened by a bank acting as syndicate manager, but because of the loan's large size the funds are usually provided by a relatively large number of banks, essentially in the form of purchases of loan instruments from the syndicate manager. Typically, these other banks do not screen the loan as intensively as the

The Economic Organisation of a Financial System

lead manager; sometimes, they may not screen it at all.

The various forms of insurance brokerage and reinsurance activity which can be observed in practice also represent combinations of intermediated and market transactions. Thus in reinsurance transactions, intermediaries (insurance firms) originate insurance liabilities, which they then exchange (partially or wholly) through the reinsurance markets. The reinsurance markets themselves are a sort of wholesale market in which relatively large amounts of insurance liabilities are traded, much as banks and other lending intermediaries repackage individual loans in the activity known as securitisation.

Securitisation represents a relatively new transaction type stemming from lessons learned by combining governance mechanisms. Intermediaries screen transactions at time of origination and place them on their own books while assembling a portfolio, which may later be used to back a securities issue. When the securities issue is sold, the intermediary effectively acts as a market agent. The activity thus combines original screening, subsequent transformation of risk, and eventual brokerage activity; in this sense it is a combination of intermediary and market activity. It represents a refinement of understanding in which intermediaries become more nearly precise about which of their activities represent added value and which do not. Securitisation will remain popular so long as no large losses are incurred by buyers of the securities, but since the securities are not always rigorously screened by purchasers, eventual losses from and a resulting cutback of securitisation activity seem inevitable.

There can also be complementarities to combining internal and external financing. It has long been standard practice for financiers to invest funds in many kinds of projects only if the project's owners do so also: perhaps the best known instance is the financial market's willingness to buy corporate debt only if the issuer has a sufficiently large amount of equity investment. The equity investment is intended to share the risks, to manage adverse incentives, and to obtain additional information about how project owners view the risks.

Evolution of system organisation

Financial system organisation adapts to changes in economic conditions. Thus, new financial firms or markets can evolve in response to changes in supply or demand conditions. For example, an increase in the number of high technology firms seeking venture financing might encourage new venture capital firms to enter the business. Any such new entrants premise their entry decision on notions, albeit sometimes vague ones, of being able to earn profits.

Private sector firms seek transactions whose profitability is commensurate with their risk. If a certain transaction's risk is perceived as too high in relation to the rewards it offers, financiers will not entertain it, no matter how actively clients seek the financing. This inability to come to terms is called market failure. Technological change or other forms of learning which lead to lower transaction or monitoring costs can eventually mitigate those forms of market failure which were originally due to inability to screen or supervise cheaply enough.

Financiers differ in their abilities to estimate probabilities, to discern alternatives, to execute plans, and to adapt to change. Thus some financiers will experiment while others will not; both may be acting rationally according to their own assessments of uncertainty and their ability to cope with it. For example, merchant bankers are currently active in arranging leveraged buyouts and bridging finance related to mergers and acquisitions. They hope to be able to earn profits by doing the business, but acknowledge that they cannot always wholly anticipate the consequences of the transactions they undertake.

Trying to develop new methods of profitable transacting can mean experimenting in the face of uncertainties with little or no clear idea of the transactions' ultimate profitability. "The existence of a problem of knowledge depends on the future being different from the past, while the possibility of the solution of the problem depends on the future being like the past" (Knight, 1971, p. 313). When they experiment, financiers understand that they are taking unquantified risks, feel uncomfortable with taking them, but regard the game as worth the candle nevertheless. "The whole forced necessity of doing things frightens me. You cannot afford to do nothing. But when things go wrong they have a habit of going wrong everywhere." (Leon Levi: quoted in *The Economist*, Survey 34, 11 July 1987.)

Thus financial system change, while intendedly rational and based on anticipated net benefits of some kind, cannot always be described using models of decision making under risk. For, actions leading to change may be premised on attempts to define new alternatives, or even to begin structuring the nature of the uncertainty. "Whatever we find it pleasant to assume for philosophic purposes, the logic of our CONDUCT assumes real indeterminateness, real change, discontinuity" (Knight, 1971).

Summary

This chapter examined specialisation by market agents and by intermediaries. With respect to markets, the discussion distinguished the economic functions of primary markets from those of secondary mar-

The Economic Organisation of a Financial System

kets, and of public from private markets. The differing economic roles of dealers and brokers were explained. Reasons for the emergence of markets for trading risks were given, and the economics of market operations discussed.

Various types of specialised intermediaries and their economic functions were also considered. The chapter examined questions of managing intermediary organisation, the economics of intermediation, and the economics of information processing and screening.

Finally, the chapter examined relations between governance mechanisms. In particular, arbitraging and intermediary links were discussed, along with the reasons that markets and intermediaries function in complementary ways. The economic forces determining financial system structure were then used to explain how the system evolves.

Notes

1. More precisely, they will choose the lowest cost governance structure, which might in unusual cases mean using a mechanism which does not operate at lowest cost. Except when these possibilities seem to be of practical importance, these qualifications are omitted.
2. The practice is so well known that traders have a name for the reversion to normal conditions. The time when uncertainty is resolved to the traders' satisfaction is referred to as the time "when the dust settles".
3. The single apparent exception, the theoretically defined risk free security, really does not exist in practice. Even if a transaction's nominal interest rate is fixed, its real rate is usually affected by uncertain inflation against which agents can hedge only imperfectly.
4. To see how an option separates risk and capital value, define single period European options with exercise time 1 and exercise price s by

$$P(X, s) = \begin{cases} s - X; X \leq s \\ 0; s < X \end{cases} \quad \text{and} \quad C(X, s) = \begin{cases} X - s; X \geq s \\ 0; X < s \end{cases}$$

where P and C indicate put and call options respectively. Then, any random variable X can be written as

$$X = s + X - s$$
$$X = s + \max[X - s, 0] - \max[s - X, 0], \text{ so that}$$
$$X = s + C(X, s) - P(X, s),$$

for any certainty outcome and exercise price s. The negative sign means that P is written rather than purchased. If the options in the foregoing identity are guaranteed they will be valued in perfect markets at equilibrium according to the put–call parity condition

$$v(X) = v(s) + c(X, s) - p(X, s),$$

Specialised governance mechanisms

where $p(.)$ and $c(.)$ refer to the time 0 market values of guaranteed options $P(.)$ and $C(.)$ respectively, and s is both a certainty outcome and exercise price as before.

5 A futures contract written in discrete time with one period to delivery is formally equivalent to a forward contract. Then, using the put–call parity relation of the previous note, either of these contracts is equivalent to

$$F(X, s) = v(X) - v(s) = c(X, s) - p(X, s).$$

The relation in earlier periods is more complex because futures contracts involve a series of cash payments as they are market to market at the end of each trading period.

6 A forward contract can theoretically be represented as a combination of a European call and a short European put position. The theoretical relations between futures and options contracts are more complex, but their close relations are recognised in reality. Both empirical study and casual observation confirm that arbitraging transactions relate, at least to a considerable degree, options and futures prices along the lines predicted by their theoretical relationships.

7 The practice of guaranteeing performance, although critically important to maintaining market confidence, is not universal. Following the stock market crash of 19 October 1987, performance under option contracts traded on the Hong Kong Options Exchange was suspended. Defaults were eventually avoided as market participants assembled an emergency fund to meet the obligations of failed or failing firms. Defaults also occurred on the London Metals Exchange about two years earlier, where contracts were not guaranteed by the Exchange.

8 The guarantor is usually an instrumentality of the exchange such as its clearing house corporation.

9 The interpretation is consistent with theories of organisational economics which recognise limits to the net value arising from expanding organisational boundaries. These limits are postulated to arise mainly from the increasing difficulty of coordinating larger numbers of activities.

10 The phenomenon seems to remain even after attempts have been made to allow for inter-country differences in valuation methods.

11 The index linked bonds issued in the United Kingdom and in Argentina seem to support this view. The interest yield on an index linked bond will be a good approximation of the real rate of interest if the index used to increase the bond's interest and principal payments is regarded as a good proxy for the effects of inflation.

Chapter five

Aligning mechanisms with transactions

This chapter also explains how transaction requirements and governance mechanism capabilities are aligned. It first examines why firms use different types of financing – debt, equity or retained earnings – in different circumstances. The chapter then discusses financiers' decisions, explaining how they price risks, and how they employ different governance mechanisms to deal with screening and information production problems, agency problems, and problems posed by incomplete contracting.

Since differences between transactions are largely differences in informational conditions, governance mechanism choice turns importantly on a transaction's informational setting. To examine these effects, the chapter considers two situations: one in which differing views are present before the transaction is arranged, the second in which they arise subsequently. The first is illustrated by mergers and acquisitions, the second by transactions in intermediary securities and liabilities when the solvency of the issuer is called into question.

This chapter also discusses how client and financier choices jointly determine a governance mechanism which furthers both parties' purposes. Since the alignment of transaction requirements and governance mechanism capabilities depends largely on informational conditions, the chapter examines the impact of information in two special contexts. These situations show how needs for *ex post* adjustments are sometimes recognised when a transaction is initiated, and how an incomplete contract is reworked when the need for adjustments is not recognised until after financings have been arranged. The first situation is illustrated by mergers and acquisitions, the second by transactions in intermediary liabilities.

Demands for funds

Clients propose financing terms which they regard as advantageous, subject to the constraint that financiers also find the terms acceptable. The main class of clients considered in this chapter is business firms, since as already mentioned most transactions in personal finance are relatively straightforward. When a personal transaction is more complex, the principles discussed below still inform the choice of governance mechanism. Hence the discussion applies to personal transactions as well, but it is more convenient to elaborate the principles by referring only to business clients. In seeking funds, these clients choose a firm's organisational structure and various forms of signalling and bonding mechanisms. The discussion considers each of these issues in turn.[1]

Organisational structure and financings

In seeking funds, management's first step is to choose an appropriate organisational structure. This choice depends both on management's own needs and on environmental constraints, economic and legal. For example, a firm is usually organised as a corporation if management intend to issue limited liability shares.

Fama and Jensen (1985) argue that management choose an organisational structure which best combines administrative and control mechanisms suited to their needs. Fama and Jensen contend that the balance between the administrative and control features of a governance mechanism differs according to whether or not management wishes to protect a non-tradable investment in human capital. Firms are usually organised as proprietorships, partnerships, or as closely held corporations when the investments they undertake are intended directly to serve owners' purposes. These structures provide tighter control of skilled personnel, and reward schemes which motivate them to continued effort. Both are necessary to protect firms' asset specific investments, especially in human capital.

Management may wish to sell shares only to themselves and their associates, thus retaining control over the firm. But selling some equity to outsiders, with a resulting attenuation of control, may be necessary if management is to raise the quantity of financing it needs. In either case, the equity investors can exercise greater control than is available to bondholders. Normally, a board of directors performs the economic function of protecting the equity owners' interests (Williamson, 1988).

Mayers and Smith (1986) note additional aspects of relations between interest groups and capital structure choice, observing that some North American life insurance companies have switched from joint stock (i.e. share ownership) to mutual form. The recapitalisation implies a possible change in the costs (or the perceived costs) of controlling conflicts between residual claimants and managers.

While conflict between policyholders and shareholders is reduced or eliminated by mutualisation, conflict between owners and managers is likely to be exacerbated. Hence mutualisation suggests that there are net benefits in choosing a capital structure with greater capability for managing the first kind of conflict.

A decision to use project financing can also be regarded as an organisational choice. A firm may propose setting up an investment project as a separate division for at least two reasons. It may be able to capture benefits from the resulting specialised administrative structure, it may be able to raise financing more cheaply for a specific project, or both. Project financing is favoured by financiers in circumstances where they wish to exercise closer supervision and control over cash flows from the assets. Project financing can also make it easier for financiers to regard specific project assets as collateral, again reducing financing costs.

Capital market sources

Given an organisational structure, management must also consider specific details of financings in which combinations of debt, equity, and other securities are selected. The combinations proposed by clients, and those sought by financiers, will depend on the kind of capital investment being undertaken and on the informational conditions under which financing is sought. To illustrate, consider the choice between debt and equity financing.

Traditionally, analysis of the debt–equity choice recognises that debt is less risky than equity for financiers, that it creates tax savings for the firm. As debt is substituted for equity, the argument recognises that at some point incremental tax advantages will be more than offset by incremental expected bankruptcy costs. For, the larger the debt issue, the greater the probability that the firm will be unable to redeem its promises. If a firm defaults, bondholders may force it to declare bankruptcy. To avoid the possibility of default, firms may either avoid debt altogether, or may use income bonds which do not have the same inflexible interest obligations as do standard debt issues.

In the traditional view, the choice between debt and equity is determined by balancing the different costs just outlined.[2] Williamson (1988) argues there are other, complementary reasons for choosing between debt and equity. To Williamson, the choice is between governance mechanisms with different capabilities. Firms may have a natural preference for debt, but the more specific the assets in which they invest, the more likely financiers are to require equity financing. Williamson observes that assets with specific uses are more difficult to exchange at prices close to their economic value. Hence, these assets need to be closely controlled in order to exploit their economic value fully, and unless financiers can exercise this control their expected returns may suffer. Thus, the debt–equity choice is determined by balancing the different costs involved – avoidance of losses by using more flexible governance mechanisms on the one hand, the increased cost of equity financing as opposed to debt on the other.[3]

Intermediary financing

Clients seek financing from intermediaries as well as through the securities markets. Intermediary financing can be more cost-effective than either public or private securities issues when transactions have specialised screening or monitoring requirements. For, intermediaries have better screening capabilities than market agents, and greater *ex post* adjustment capabilities than do debtholders. Moreover, they do not always require the transfer of ownership interest associated with equity financing.

Signals and bonding

If management believe themselves to be better informed than financiers, neoclassical financial theory suggests they attempt to convey their information by signalling. That is, management choose actions which credibly reveal the nature of their insider information to financiers. Management can also offer to bond themselves in ways that identify their own and financiers' interests more closely. Bonding restricts management actions, provides management incentives, or both. Bonding can enhance signals' credibility: management can commit themselves to pay penalties if their signals subsequently prove misleading.

Many different capital structure choices have been examined as signals. In a now classic treatment, Ross (1977) considers the signalling possibilities of debt–equity choice. In Ross' model, more debt is chosen by more optimistic managements and, given the incentive scheme he uses, can be used to establish an equilibrium in which firm quality is signalled by its debt–equity ratio. Ross' model imposes costly penalties on management to establish the signalling equilibrium.

More recent studies incorporate misrepresentation penalties into the instruments actually traded. For example, an incentive to give false signals and thus raise share prices unduly would be offset if management were required to buy back some of the shares at the inflated prices. Some of the different signalling possibilities explored use securities issues and repurchases (Constantinides and Grundy, 1986), delayed conversions (Harris and Raviv, 1985), or dividends (John and Williams, 1985).

Most of the signalling literature is, being in the mainstream of neoclassical financial theory, concerned with *ex ante* informational differences. Similarly, the bonding literature is concerned with creating appropriate incentives at the time a transaction is first set up. Both approaches assume any needs for adjustment can be specified in advance; even if they are specified as contingency plans, these specifications are presumed to be complete.

Williamson's (1988) emphasis on incomplete contracting urges a broader interpretation of signalling and bonding. For example, any contract which is initially recognised to be incomplete will specify a mechanism to ensure that financiers will be informed of any important changes in a firm's affairs, thus permitting them to consider making contract adjustments as and when necessary. If adjustments actually are necessary, bonding can help ensure that management will effect them. While *ex post* adjustment needs may be difficult to specify precisely at the time a transaction is first initiated, their importance for financings seems clear, particularly under conditions of uncertainty.

Other features

Although agency theory and transactions cost economics explain important aspects of financing choices, further explanations are still needed. For example, Smith (1986) raises some currently unresolved questions regarding public issues: Why are rights used more extensively in the United Kingdom than in the United States? Why are rights offerings and standby agreements both used together? Note that the very mention of rights issues indicates that even for the publicly financed firm wealth maximisation is not the only criterion in seeking financing: issues of shareholder group continuity and control are often of crucial importance.

Grossman and Hart (1987) consider a related question: how many voting rights should attach to a common share? Tying votes to shares on a one to one basis, they find, is a good device for realising the incentives in the market for corporate control: one share, one vote can be used effectively by an outsider to wrest control from existing shareholders if the outsider expects to be able to raise the market value of the firm. Voting control and management incentives are not completely separable, although they are conceptually distinct. It is possible a given management would want different ratios of votes to shares, say to maintain family control over an enterprise. Presumably in such situations the family would obtain private benefits from control, benefits not reflected in the prices other shareholders might be willing to pay.

Financiers' supplies of funds

The terms, if any, on which financiers will supply funds depend largely on how they view potential rewards in relation to the risks or uncertainties involved. If financiers believe a transaction is only risky, they will set a required return which depends quite precisely on the degree of the risk, at least in competitive markets. Under uncertainty, the required return will be higher, but will also be set less precisely. Most financiers are prepared to assume only limited kinds of uncertainties: they are sometimes unwilling to entertain relatively uncertain, unstructured proposals even if the expected returns are considerably higher than on other forms of business they conduct.

Financiers who specialise in less well-structured financings generally have more highly developed screening and monitoring capabilities. As a result, they also have relatively costly operations. To compensate for their higher governance costs, they usually demand a greater proportion of any profits generated from a project receiving financing. To offset uncertainties, they usually require a relatively high degree of control over the client's activities.

Screening and other forms of information production

A financier's initial assessment usually determines whether a project is likely to offer acceptable rewards in relation to its risk or uncertainty, and hence determines whether or not additional investigation is warranted. If financiers regard the results of the initial screening favourably, they usually outline terms for providing funds. If at this point client and financier are closely agreed as to the risks or uncertainties involved, they can likely agree on any remaining details fairly easily. Moreover, the terms will likely be close to those currently prevailing on other similar transactions.

If an initial screening does not produce a sufficient degree of agreement but agents still wish to transact, they must attempt somehow to deal with whatever informational differences remain. It has already been noted that under risk signals and bonding can either remove the differences *ex ante* or provide mechanisms for their satisfactory *ex post* resolution. In any case, financiers will still wish to verify information provided by the client as a way of guarding against possibly opportunistic presentation of data. Thus financiers normally incur verification costs even in simple transactions.

Screening capabilities affect financiers' risk assessments, and hence the kinds of transactions they can profitably consider. For example, banks make operating loans but do not usually extend venture financing because they have not developed the capabilities to screen new ventures. When banks do enter the venture financing business, they normally use specialised personnel or affiliated organisations to carry out the transactions. In this way the banks attempt both to realise economies of specialisation and to use the higher-powered incentives that smaller firms' managements usually face. The principal costs of setting up affiliated organisations relate to the conflicts they can pose – the culture of an affiliate is not always compatible with that of the parent firm.

Intermediaries enjoy screening advantages not possessed by market agents. First, intermediary personnel usually develop a greater capability to assess default risks than do market agents, because they often deal with the same clients continuously over time. Intermediaries also gain greater screening capability through using specialist personnel. For instance, some loan officers may acquire a relative advantage in assessing business loan applications where human judgement plays a relatively important role. In addition, intermediaries use more capital intensive operations which apply routine screening methods to relatively homogeneous transactions, realising scale economies not always available to market agents. For example, computers are used for such purposes as credit scoring and processing credit card and consumer loan applications, as well as for administering established accounts.

As an alternative to screening and verification, agents can try to bypass informational differences, say by using third party guarantees or collateral. If collateral is available, it may be cheaper and more convenient to use it than to rely on a more elaborate governance structure. This possibility seems to explain why many retail banking transactions stress the availability of collateral as a condition for many small business and personal loans.

Agency effects

Agency effects mean that a given group may be able to further its own interests, at the expense of others, without being detected. For example, managers might find it advantageous to further their ends at the expense of the firm's owners or financiers, and it is not always easy to determine whether they are doing so. Thus agency effects can increase payoff uncertainties, governance costs to offset the effects, or both.

There are many kinds of agency effects, arising from conflicts or potential conflicts between a variety of different interest groups, as the following examples show. First, there can be conflicts of interest between shareholders and debtholders: the latter are generally much less willing for the firm to take on risks than are shareholders. For, shareholders generally reap any benefits to increased risks, while debtholders incur any costs. To control these conflicting preferences, debtholders need to employ more costly governance mechanisms than would be necessary if the two parties' preferences were wholly compatible.

Second, management–shareholder conflicts can arise if a firm has professional managers with either no or proportionally small shareholdings of their own. In this case managers, cautiously attempting to preserve their reputations for successful operations, may be motivated to avoid bankruptcy to such an extent that investments are too conservative from the shareholders' point of view (cf. Grossman and Hart, 1987). Again, the effects of conflicting preferences can be mitigated, but only at the expense of using more costly governance mechanisms.

Third, even if firms' investment decisions are advertised as market value maximising decisions, financiers may constrain firm actions to ensure that value maximising criteria are indeed pursued. For example, if financiers acquire an equity position, they may use incentive schemes to align management rewards with firm value maximisation. Otherwise some of the firm's earnings could be diverted to management perquisites instead of being reported as earnings to which the shareholders have claim.

In neoclassical financial theory, financiers try to offset agency effects by devising incentive and monitoring schemes on an ex ante basis. For example, Grossman and Hart (1981) formulate the principal–agent problem as one in which the principal chooses a risk sharing contract (incentive scheme) to influence an agent's behaviour. The principal wishes to maximise his expected utility subject to keeping agent's utility above a reservation level. In an attempt to define optimality conditions, the principal's utility function is also required to attain a stationary point. However, without further specification the conditions just mentioned may not even satisfy necessary optimality conditions. Thus devising incentive schemes to resolve a principal–agent problem is not always an easy theoretical matter.

Bhattacharya and Pfleiderer (1985) consider how to elicit truthful information from agents without knowing their preferences. They formulate a single period model for employing portfolio managers whose efforts are not directly observable and whose results are also affected by randomness. The problem has earlier been considered in a single period planning context by Weitzman (1977), and in a multi-period context by Atkinson and Neave (1981), although only Bhattacharya and Pfleiderer specifically relate the design problem to financial transactions.

Any attempt to manage agency effects affects governance costs, which in turn have impacts on financing choices. For example, Kim and Sorenson (1986) argue that high growth firms are likely to use less debt; high operating risk firms more. The authors attribute these effects to managing the agency costs of debt versus equity. However, Williamson's (1988) argument offers a complementary explanation: greater flexibility of governance can offer net advantages in these higher risk, less well-structured situations. More detailed analysis of individual firms' decisions is needed before a clearer picture of two explanations' relative importance can emerge.

Incomplete contracting

The precise design of mechanisms intended to deal with agency problems can only be studied under risk. Under uncertainty, transaction circumstances are not well enough specified to permit equallly precise analyses. In practice, uncertainty poses the necessity for *ex post* adjustment mechanisms which permit changes to the original contract as and when circumstances dictate.

In practice bounded rationality (or its environmental counterpart uncertainty) prevents writing complete contracts. Contracts are incomplete whenever possible future changes in circumstances, even if anticipated, cannot be specified precisely. Whenever financiers recognise their inability to write complete contracts and believe that *ex post* adjustments may be needed, they will try to set up mechanisms to permit any necessary adjustments. These adjustment mechanisms can take many forms, but the most prominent are monitoring to detect the need for adjustment, and provisions for rewriting the contract to effect any necessary changes. The latter include various forms of bonding to give clients incentives to implement the adjustments.

Monitoring means policing client activities after initial financing has been supplied. To be effective monitoring must be accompanied by enforceable penalties should deviations from the initial agreement be detected. Bonding means using covenants or restrictions additional to those in the simplest forms of loan or investment agreements; to be effective bonding must also use enforceable penalties. Monitoring and bonding are both costly; in deciding whether or not to use them financiers must attempt to assess their expected benefits in relation to costs.

If monitoring indicates a need for adjustment, it is still necessary to make the requisite changes in contract terms. Thus if unexpected developments might affect asset values, it becomes important to consider how best to respond to such unexpected change. Flexible governance mechanisms are intended to "fill gaps, correct errors, and adapt more effectively to unanticipated disturbances" (Williamson, 1988). Most *ex post* adjustment mechanisms provide for some form of controlling firm decisions. For example, control can be implemented through acquiring a seat on a board of directors, or through acquiring a substantial proportion of the firm's outstanding shares.

Many financial transactions offer examples of *ex post* adjustment mechanisms. For example, in leveraged buyouts investment bankers will often provide bridging financing only on condition they can purchase equity in the resulting merged firm. A firm's owners may be reluctant to incur the loss of control attendant on selling shares, but in many instances financiers may require them to do so. While media accounts suggest that financiers are merely seeking a share of the profits by requiring a part of the equity, and while this reason is undoubtedly a factor in setting contract terms, financiers are not normally willing to invest in what they regard as an unusually risky project unless they can also play a discretionary role in its governance. A sufficiently large proportion of shares will give them the desired ability to influence client affairs.

Markets for corporate control

Transactions in the market for corporate control illustrate some important effects of informational conditions on governance mechanism choice. In most takeover situations outsiders (hereafter called the raiders) expect to profit through acquiring a target company. In effect, takeovers serve the economic function of linking markets that were not previously linked by using a new form of arbitrage.[4] But, unlike the more ususal forms of arbitrage, the negotiations to effect a takeover cannot usually be specified fully in advance. Hence the mechanism governing takeover financing must be a flexible one, capable of adjustment to changing circumstances.

Conflicting purposes

In an attempted takeover, the raiders hope to profit in one or more of several possible ways. They might believe that acquiring the target would allow them to realise scope economies in the combined enterprise. Or, the raiders might believe that the target is at present badly managed, and that they could improve both operations and profits through better administration. In other cases there can be tax or strategic advantages to a merger; in still others a raider may be interested in profiting through misrepresentation of the acquisition's potential. The rest of this discussion considers only the first two motives.

If the raiders believe a target to be badly administered but the incumbent management disagrees, any takeover attempt is likely to be contested.[5] If a struggle for control ensues, it can involve both attempts to convince particular interest groups their ends will be furthered by taking one side or the other (signalling) and attempts to muster enough shares, or at least shareholder votes, to attain the desired ends by force. From the incumbent management's point of view, the main issues are how to prevent the raiders from succeeding. From the raiders' point of view, the main issues are how to convince others of the validity of the raiders' views, to obtain financing for their acquisition, and to retain some of the created wealth for themselves.

Governance mechanisms permitting the use of discretion, and which maintain confidentiality of the raiders' intentions for as long as possible, are essential for takeover transactions. For, information about a possible takeover rapidly takes on the status of a public good, attracting other share purchasers (especially those known as risk arbitrageurs), possibly even before the raider has an opportunity to buy the shares at the initially prevailing prices.[6]

Financing a takeover

Both parties to a contested takeover attempt to muster resources to defend their respective positions. Incumbent management requires funds to purchase any needed additional voting shares. In the event the strategy of acquiring voting shares should fail, management may employ various forms of poison pills or poison puts to deter potential raiders. In essence, these strategies provide for *ex post* restructuring of the firm's financing. For example, outstanding bonds might be redeemed in the event of an attempted takeover, reducing the target's resources and making the financing of the acquisition more difficult. Management may also employ self-interested (but not necessarily untruthful) signalling to shareholders. In sum, management attempts to utilise, or to create in advance of an imminent takeover threat, a governance mechanism whose features will at least partially frustrate takeover attempts.

A raider requires both interim or bridging finance and longer-term financing to effect a takeover successfully. The funds are used both to purchase shares and to campaign in attempts to influence shareholder votes. The major traditional source of bridging finance has been bank loans. Bankers have usually lent funds to raiders so the latter can buy shares; the loans are usually intended to be repaid after the takeover has successfully been completed. Normally, repayment is accomplished by floating a debt issue subsequent to completion of the takeover.

Recently, investment bankers have begun offering bridging financing, again by extending loans or buying shares of the parent firm, either obligation to remain outstanding until longer term financing can be arranged subsequent to the takeover. The credit risks to providing bridging finance are quite different from the trading risks that investment banks take in their normal securities dealing business. The change in practice seems to result from declines in investment bankers' trading income, and the high profits which they can earn on successfully completed takeovers. However, the risks are also high: if the buyout is not successfully financed through eventual sale of bonds, a portion (perhaps a large one) of the investment banker's capital may be lost in the eventual forced liquidation of his lending position.

With regard to longer-term financing, raiders first attempt to use established financing routes. However these efforts may be unsuccessful, particularly if the proposed transactions are regarded by financiers as novel or as posing unusually large risks. The most popular recent form of financing involves using junk bonds; that is, to raise funds through issuing high risk bonds whose proceeds are used to buy out dissident and uninterested shareholders. In order for the manoeuvre to succeed, both the bond issue and the terms of share purchase must be attractive to the particular target groups of investors at which they are aimed. Moreover, the raiders must be able to avail themselves of the necessary financing at short notice, and in amounts which vary according to the way the negotiations have evolved. That is, the raiders must be able to set up, in advance, an incompletely contracted financing which keeps their intentions confidential for as long as possible and which permits making *ex post* adjustments as and when needed.

Economic effects

Takeover struggles turn on differences in preferences or differences regarding which actions are most likely to achieve some particular purpose. Grossman and Stiglitz (1977) offer a formal framework for reconciling managerial theories of the firm with neoclassical theories of value maximisation. Among other questions, they ask why are

The Economic Organisation of a Financial System

there both takeovers and disputed takeovers? Essentially, they argue the situations arise from differences between shareholder groups. Their formal analysis is aimed mainly at defining conditions under which shareholders will be unanimous in their choices of actions, thus helping to clarify the kinds of conditions under which disputes can arise.

In a sense, a raider both produces information and links transactions in quite different markets to finance an acquisition. Such manouevres can be successful if the secondary share markets are not closely linked with the primary markets for the junk bond issues. If these markets were closely linked at the outset, it would not be possible to raise enough funds from a junk bond issue for the manoeuvre to succeed. For, in relatively perfect markets the bond and share prices should be equalised by arbitrage, but a premium over existing share price is usually needed to complete the share purchases successfully.

Thus in effect, mergers and acquisitions create new forms of arbitrage between bond and share markets. Some of the rewards to successful takeovers are the profits to be earned in creating such linkages, particularly if they are based on the production of new information. The new information might well be based on the ability of the raiders to operate the firm more efficiently than the incumbent management. In sum, the market for corporate control can act as a stimulus to efficiency and to the dissemination of new technology.

Markets for financing intermediaries

The relations between informational conditions and governance mechanisms can be illuminated further by considering situations where a previously unanticipated need to make adjustments actually arises. The case of financing intermediaries during a time of crisis offers an instructive example.

Valuing intermediary liabilities during normal operations

Essentially, intermediaries raise funds through issuing deposits and by selling their own securities, both stocks and bonds. Deposits are normally valued at their nominal amounts, either because they are insured or because uninsured depositors have faith in the intermediary's solvency. On the other hand, securities values are related to the market's estimates of the value of intermediary net assets. Consider first the situation in which solvency is not in question; the complications presented by possible insolvency can then be discussed more easily.

The value of a firm's securities has been related to the value of its underlying assets using options pricing theory (Merton, 1974; Ingersoll, 1976). The principal theoretical work on valuing either intermediary deposits or the insurance which guarantees their redemption at par also uses option pricing theory (Merton, 1977). It attempts to determine the difference between the deposits' economic value, which derives from the worth of the intermediary's assets, and the nominal value underwritten by the insuring agency in the event of difficulty. Options valuation methods are used to derive a value of the deposit insurance and comparing it with the insurance premiums the intermediary actually pays.[7] In essence, these theories relate the temporal evolution of asset value to the value of securities or deposits issued against that asset portfolio. The theories recognise that asset values may not be observable, but can still be used to derive relations between liability values and those of the underlying assets.

Whatever the values the market attaches to them, in practice intermediaries' ability to issue new securities is limited by regulation. To avoid expository complications, the rest of this discussion assumes any new issues assumed to be floated fall within regulatory constraints. The market then faces the problem of valuing the claims. The main problem, recognised in the theoretical work mentioned above, is that the value of the underlying assets is not observable.

Information regarding intermediary liabilities

It can be much more difficult to value the asset portfolio of a financial intermediary than to value the assets of a non-financial firm. In practice, intermediary assets consist of many different types and sizes of loans. Moreover, not even the portfolio composition, let alone market prices of the items in it, is usually known (or is even potentially knowable) to investors. Intermediary assets are usually not marketable, and intermediary representations regarding value are likely to be biased – the problem of moral hazard. This lack of externally verifiable information regarding the worth of intermediary assets creates important problems if an intermediary's solvency is called into question.

Intermediaries and crises of confidence

An intermediary's financing capabilities can be affected radically when the safety of its asset portfolio is called into question. In such cases declines in securities value can occur suddenly, but any subsequent recovery is likely to be much slower. Rapid losses of confidence will mainly affect outstanding securities, because unless

The Economic Organisation of a Financial System

forced to do so by regulatory authorities, few intermediaries are likely to propose new public issues when they are in financial distress. For at such times management will almost surely find the market value of the firm's securities to be, in their opinion, unrepresentatively low.

Insured deposits are not usually affected greatly by changes in confidence, as depositors rely on the insuring agency to guarantee the safety of their funds. Uninsured deposits will, however, be affected.[8] To abstract from such effects, the rest of this discussion refers only to deposits which have no insurance coverage, formal or informal. During a crisis of confidence, such deposits will likely be rapidly withdrawn, causing a run on the bank. They will be replaced, if ever, at a much slower rate. The value of the intermediary's securities will be affected similarly.

Crises of confidence may be a long time in building, developing from the way information becomes available to the public. During normal intermediary operations signals regarding portfolio quality are infrequent, difficult to interpret, and may be ambiguous as to content. Accordingly there may be little new information about intermediary assets available to the public. This infrequent and partial information revision results in equally infrequent changes in opinion, but once they do occur the opinion changes are likely to be quite drastic.

If an intermediary's safety is called into question the information will often have been available to the public for some time, but somehow attitudes toward it undergo a sudden change. Whereas before information was regarded as either irrelevant or unreliable, it quickly becomes relevant. In these circumstances, bad news is treated as reliable, but good news is often not. A sort of contagion of pessimism (or realism which has too long been postponed) seems to spread among investors, causing a crisis. Investors become, more or less all at once, convinced that the informational situation is more uncertain than was previously believed.

Once intermediary safety has been questioned, even if the questioning is later found to have had little basis, restoring depositor and investor confidence is a lengthy and sometimes impossible task. This is probably because after a crisis of confidence any signals issued by the intermediary are treated as biased. Moreover, favourable signals, even if regarded as truthful, seem to be given less weight than those indicating unfavourable developments, perhaps because they are less surprising. With a crisis, perceived risk is replaced by perceived uncertainty. Resolving the crisis means reducing the current uncertainties to mere risks once again, often a lengthy process.

Changes in governance mechanisms

To survive a crisis of confidence, particularly if it involves proportionally large deposit losses, an intermediary normally needs access to a lender of last resort. The emergency funds provided by a lender of last resort are used to provide liquidity until, if ever, confidence in the quality of the assets can be restored. In effect the lender of last resort, be it a central bank or consortium of competing banks, replaces existing governance mechanisms for financing intermediary activity. The lender of last resort in effect temporarily buys an interest in the assets whose quality has been questioned, and takes greater control over operations than either depositors or purchasers of securities can exert.

Competing intermediaries sometimes act collectively as a lender of last resort. One reason they do so is to offset a so-called contagion effect (really a form of externality) in which their own asset quality can be questioned simply because that has happened to a competitor. The still sound competitors take such a possibility seriously because as the preceding discussion has argued, intermediaries are vulnerable to charges that asset quality has been impaired even if the charges are later shown to be groundless. When they provide emergency funds, the competitors will usually impose governance requirements of their own as part of the contract terms.

If no private sector lender of last resort emerges, the intermediary will likely fail unless the regulatory authorities step in. If the regulators do intervene, they will provide financing and a governance mechanism intended either to help the intermediary survive the crisis or to wind up its affairs, the choice depending on the authorities' resources and their view of the circumstances. Thus, with a change in information and a resultant unwillingness of agents in securities and deposit markets to continue providing finance, a spectrum of more complex, more costly governance mechanisms comes into play.

Summary

This chapter considered agents' choices of governance mechanisms. It began by examining firms' demands for funds. The nature of these demands is related to the firm's choice of organisational structure and to the financings it employs. The transaction requirements of firms influence their choices between market and intermediary forms of financing; they use signals and propose bonding mechanisms in attempts to influence the terms of the financing they can obtain.

The nature of funds supplies depends on the governance mechanisms firms employ and the economics of their operations. Different funds suppliers specialise in using different kinds of screening, which affect the kinds of transactions they will regard as profitable, and therefore be willing to consider. Financiers vary the forms of the governance mechanisms they employ in attempts to manage informational and agency effects and to deal with the problems posed by incomplete contracting.

The most important transaction requirements are informational, as illustrated by studies of the markets for corporate control and of the markets for intermediaries' obligations. In the markets for corporate control, attempts to forestall takeovers lead incumbent management to prefer adaptable forms of governance mechanisms. Raiders also prefer adaptable governance mechanisms, even for interim financing, because they need considerable flexibility of action in pursuing a takeover bid. The principal economic effect of takeovers relevant to the present discussion is the nature of the arbitraging links between different markets created by the takeover financings.

Preferences for different forms of governance mechanisms also become evident in cases when intermediary solvency is called into question. In such instances, the normal forms of governance are generally replaced by emergency forms with much higher capabilities for control and the exercise of discretion. The move to a more capable governance mechanism can be rapid, reversion to more normal and less costly forms is usually slower and less definitive.

Notes

1. The discussion assumes a firm's purposes are those of its management, subject to constraints imposed by such other groups as financiers, its labour force, and the like. Although only the constraints imposed by choice of organisational structure are emphasised here, others can also be important, as is recognised in both theory and practice. In theory, the circumstances are recognised by regarding the firm as a nexus of contracting parties (e.g. the agency theory of Jensen and Meckling, 1976) or as a coalition of at least partially disparate interests (e.g. Cyert and March 1965). In practice, many firms are managed by a controlling group which pays heed to the concerns of various constituents.
2. The importance of both the potential tax savings and the size of bankruptcy costs have been debated extensively, but to consider these issues here would not contribute to the book's purposes. For a review of these and other factors see Myers (1984). In the same way, the discussion recognises but does not emphasise the possibility that management will not use equity indiscriminately. For example, management will not issue equity if they believe a share issue might not raise financing on sufficiently attractive terms.

Aligning mechanisms with transactions

3 As Williamson has pointed out, governance arguments are closely related to agency theory views, although the emphases differ. For example, to Williamson (1988) Grossman and Hart (1982), Fama and Jensen (1986) see debt as compelling "managers to behave in a fashion more consonant with the stockholders' interests," which latter may frequently be identified with those of financiers. Agency effects are discussed further on p. 82ff.
4 The markets involved are the market in which the raider buys the firm's shares and the market in which institutional investors provide either short- or long-term takeover financing.
5 If management and the raider agree, the takeover bid is called friendly. In this case, of course, the transaction is simply a matter of financing a purchase between a willing buyer and a willing seller.
6 Grossman and Hart (1981) argue theoretically that takeover bids act as signals: in some cases even firms subject to an unsuccessful takeover bid may be revalued upwards.
7 Related work examines the value of a guarantee on life insurance policies (Brennan and Schwartz, 1976), and of insurance on mutual funds (Gatto, Geske, and Litzenberger, 1980).
8 Except in cases where the uninsured depositors believe the safety of their funds will be guaranteed by some government agency despite the absence of formal insurance.

Chapter six

Managing transaction terms

A governance structure consists of a governance mechanism and the contractual terms of a particular transaction. Choosing a governance mechanism constrains subsequent choices, but particular terms still need to be selected. This chapter discusses these choices and the reasons for making them. As with mechanism choice, choice of terms represents an attempt to deal with differing informational conditions. As informational differences increase, so do the difficulties and costs of managing them.

As discussed in Chapter 5, choosing to transact with a financier means working with the governance mechanism he typically employs. If a client's initial proposal is acceptable to a financier, the latter will outline terms for completing the transaction. If the terms outlined are acceptable to the client, the remaining contractual details can be negotiated. The principal economic function of these details is to manage each transaction's unique informational conditions.

Principles

Financiers treat familiar types of transactions routinely, particularly if they regard the transactions as taking place under risk and if they believe they have much the same information as their clients. In most such cases interest rates and other contractual terms are based on established practice and implemented using rules of thumb. When financiers have less information than clients, the differences require additional investigation and management, so that selecting terms to satisfy both parties becomes more complex. Satisfactory terms can be still more difficult to determine if the transactors face uncertainty rather than risk.

In any event, contract terms are chosen according to the same principles as governance mechanisms. Both the governance mechanism and the contract terms are intended to meet the purposes of financier and client as cost-effectively as possible. For example, earlier chapters have shown that an investment requiring continuing supervision would more likely be arranged with an intermediary rather than through a market. In keeping with the same principle, if financiers think that clients might substitute a riskier for a less risky project after obtaining financing, the contract terms will likely prohibit substitutions and stipulate penalties or other compensation (possibly including termination of the agreement) in the event the prohibitions are violated.

Informational conditions

Informational conditions are an important determinant of a governance structure's cost-effectiveness. Earlier chapters showed that progressing from least to most costly, the governance mechanisms are markets, intermediaries, and internal financings, and that this progression in costliness also reflects a progression in mechanism capabilities. The same is true for choices of contract terms: capabilities and costs increase commensurately with the complexity of transaction requirements, at least for those transactions which are actually carried out. The most complex and costly governance structures are generally employed to govern those transactions presenting the most difficult informational requirements.

Governance structures

Figure 6.1 provides a framework for analysing choices of contract terms, indicating that governance structure choices differ with transaction requirements, particularly noting that the structures chosen to administer complete contracts differ importantly from those chosen for incomplete contracts (Williamson, 1988).

Figure 6.1 displays a relation between risk and complete contracting on the one hand, uncertainty and incomplete contracting on the other. Even if contracting under risk involves contingency planning, it poses no *ex post* adjustment problems whose details cannot be specified in advance. On the other hand, since uncertainty implies contract incompleteness and the consequent possibility of needing to make *ex post* adjustments, greater discretion is needed to administer transactions. *Ex post* adjustment problems arise with incomplete contracting either because the parties do not know how to allow for all possible eventualities, or if they can conceive of doing so, they find it too costly to carry out their plans.

The Economic Organisation of a Financial System

Figure 6.1 Transaction circumstances and governance structures

(A) Alignments under risk (complete contracts)

Type of risk	Typical governance structure
Risk does not change. Agreement on payoff distribution.	Structure is rule-based; little or no provision for *ex post* adjustment.
Risk can change as time passes, but the process is specified in advance.	Structure is rule based but may use incentives and contingency plans. Any possible contract adjustments are specified in detail when financing is first arranged.

(B) Alignments under uncertainty (incomplete contracts)

Types of uncertainty	Typical governance structure
Structured uncertainty	Structure allows for discretionary governance as routinely speciſed in outline terms.
Unstructured uncertainty	Structure uses discretionary arrangements whose details may have to be individually negotiated.

Information and contract types

Transactions under risk can be analysed as differing with respect to states, acts, or payoffs. If the two parties do not use the same probability distribution, their informational differences must be dealt with. Moreover, differing information means each party may have opportunities to conceal information from the other. Nevertheless, the circumstances do not pose needs for *ex post* adjustment. Decision making under risk can employ contingency strategies which allow for different actions to be taken as information is gradually revealed. Since these contingent strategies are completely specified in advance, they are actually part of a complete contract.

In contrast, incomplete contracts can only stipulate the principles to be implemented in making *ex post* adjustments as and when the need for adjustment is recognised. Many current discussions of financial theory do not recognise this distinction, assuming implicitly that all transactions can be explained using only formal analyses under risk. Exceptionally, Williamson's work (e.g. 1972, 1985, 1988) argues the contrary.

Managing transaction terms

To employ a distinction between complete and incomplete contracting, between unbounded and bounded rationality, between risk and uncertainty, is not to argue that either the first or the second view is superior to the other. Rather, it is to argue for a discriminating use of different models according to the circumstances being analysed. Just as it is misleading to assume that all financial decisions can be analysed as if made under risk, it is equally misleading to argue that since formal studies are always idealisations and cannot completely reflect underlying realities, every practical situation must be analysed as one of uncertainty and incomplete contracting.

In some circumstances a formal analysis under risk can provide both useful normative results and a positive theory which fits the known data relatively well. For instance, Capital Asset Pricing Theory characterises relative prices for publicly traded stocks with considerable precision. In practice, CAPT can be used in a search for possible arbitrage profits, although these opportunities are relatively difficult to find in an efficient market such as the larger markets for publicly traded stocks.

In other circumstances, less formal analyses can provide more nearly accurate explanations of current practice. For example, venture capitalists often use rules of thumb for valuing the firms in which they invest. They use rules of thumb because they extend financing under uncertainty, and the information with which they deal is not sufficiently precise to permit more refined analyses. Whenever the venture capitalists' rules of thumb incorporate considerations not recognised in the CAPT, the pricing implications of the two approaches will differ. Moreover, in these circumstances the CAPT could be a poor predictor of a venture capitalist's willingness to finance a project.

The upshot of the foregoing is that normative theory based on risk, and descriptive theory based on uncertainty, play complementary roles in analysing governance structures. Where greater precision can be introduced, analyses under risk can usefully replace the less precise analyses under uncertainty. But a role for both is likely to remain, particularly since novel kinds of financial activity usually take place under uncertainty. The rest of this chapter considers examples of transaction terms used in the two contexts of complete and incomplete contracting. It also considers some effects of dealing with any informational differences which arise.

Complete contracting

Figure 6.2 presents dimensions of risk and governance structures for dealing with it. Since degree of risk is defined along a continuum

Figure 6.2 Information and contract terms: risk

Nature of information	Type and details of contract terms
Agreement on payoff distribution	Simple trade, as in market exchange.
Agreement on acts only	Resolution, signalling.
Agreement on states only	Restrictive covenants or arrangements conditional on certain states.
Clients can conceal information	Incentive schemes for truthful revelation; collateral to bypass the problem.
Financiers can conceal information	Guaranteed underwritings; private market or intermediated arrangements.

rather than as a set of distinct categories, the structures listed in Figure 6.2 are meant to indicate representative choices. In any particular transaction, certain details may require using a modified version of the contract types indicated below. Nevertheless, those indicated are typical of the terms used in many transactions.

Whatever type of contractual arrangement an agent enters, he seeks to obtain net benefits from it. For example, clients willingly incur signalling costs if they can reduce financing charges by more than the signalling cost. Similarly, the greater the degree of risk, the more anxious financiers are to gain greater discretion in dealing with it. For example, they may be more willing to incur costs to encourage truthful revelation of information. Up to the point where increased costs outweigh any increased benefits, financiers will attempt to increase their governance capabilities.

The next sections elaborate the choices of contract terms displayed in Figure 6.2. The sections respectively discuss resolution, signalling, and contingency planning. Restrictive covenants, guarantees, and incentive schemes are discussed in terms of how they contribute to signalling on the one hand, to contingency planning on the other. Only circumstances in which client and financier information differ are examined, since simple exchange under homogeneous information has been discussed sufficiently in earlier chapters.

Resolution and signalling

Limited forms of agreement can be reached even when the parties have different views of a transaction. For example, financier and client might disagree on the range of a payoff distribution, but they might be able to agree on a lowest possible outcome, and hence on the amount of financing that both could regard as riskless. It may also be possible to devise risky financial claims regarding whose value both client and financier agree, and if the incentives for misrepresentation inherent in such a transaction can be managed appropriately (see Neave (1989) for a method) there may be no need to deal further with any informational asymmetries. This kind of agreement, termed resolution, can be initiated by either party. A client might propose resolution in an attempt to reduce financing costs, a financier might employ it as a means of taking on new kinds of business. In either case, resolution carries a cost: the agreed amount of financing will usually be less than if transactors had the same information.

As an alternative to resolution, clients can attempt to ameliorate or even entirely eliminate the effects of informational asymmetries by signalling their private information, a topic introduced in Chapter 5. Financiers must assess the reliability of any signals they receive, since clients may have incentives to bias the signals in their own favour. Thus, some financiers will employ incentive schemes designed to counter the effects of biased signals.

The terms of a debt issue can be used to encourage truthful revelation of insider knowledge. Diamond (1985) shows that the optimal contract for maximising a risk neutral entrepreneur's expected return, given a minimum expected return to lenders, is a debt contract with a fixed face value and bankruptcy penalty, borne by management, equal to any decline in value from face. The arrangement ensures that management announce the true value of the firm when it becomes known to them. If management announce the firm to be worth the debt's face value or more, the debt must be repaid in full; if they announce the firm to be worth less than the debt's face value, they must pay the bankruptcy penalty. The scheme assumes management have resources to pay any bankruptcy penalties, a situation not enjoyed by entrepreneurs whose entire asset position consists of investments in their firm.

Heinkel (1982) argues that with insider information firms will use both debt and equity capital to raise funds, even in perfectly competitive financial markets. Insiders are assumed to know the distribution of firm cash flows, but capital suppliers do not. Taking into account management incentives to misrepresent firm type, financiers prefer a debt–equity mix that eliminates the adverse incentives of insiders and correctly prices securities. Heinkel finds necessary conditions for a costless, stable separating equilibrium in which the amount of debt issued by a firm increases with the firm's true value, which latter cannot be observed by outsiders.

Heinkel and Schwartz (1986) consider the choice between rights offerings and underwritten issues as a signal in a model embodying a range of possible firm qualities, unknown to investors. The situation provides incentives for firms to advertise their true quality. Even though advertising management's perception of firm quality may be costly, the expected benefits can outweigh the costs. Heinkel and Schwartz find that the highest quality firms will use standby rights offers, while intermediate quality firms choose a subscription price in an uninsured rights offer, and low quality firms use fully underwritten offerings rather than less costly rights offers.

John and Williams (1985) discuss how a firm might use dividends, even if subject to taxes, to signal quality. The dividend signal can be effective if increasing it means the share price will increase by more than the dividend tax. If the signal is to be credible, management interests must be served by the increase, as will be the case if management owns some of the shares.

Third-party signals

The basic aspects of signalling were discussed in Chapter 5, which pointed out that capital structure choices were the most common kind of signal treated in the theoretical literature. However, other kinds of signals should also be mentioned as part of selecting contract terms. For example, insurance purchases can serve as signals.

Thakor (1982) regards debt insurance as signalling the debt's value in an asymmetrically informed market. Each borrowing unit is assumed to possess perfect information about its own default probability, while the insurer can acquire the same information by investing in information production. A properly designed premium function will induce a borrower to obtain coverage that exactly signals the true probability of default. Municipal bond insurance coverage is used as a case in point. Benson (1979) discusses the information production role of agents underwriting municipal bonds, arguing that by finding a set of clients to whom such bonds can be sold, underwriters can reduce financing costs. The underwriters' costs of producing information will be less than the aggregate costs of transactors' producing the information individually.

Sometimes the signalling can be almost incidental to the nature of an arrangement. Fama (1985) argues that firms may use short-term bank borrowing as a signal: a bank's willingness to extend short-term financing may be regarded by other financiers as information about the firm's quality, and hence may reduce the firm's cost of information transmission.

Not all signals need be issued by management. When a third party can enjoy scale economies or other cost advantages in generating and providing specialised information, say by operating a rating service, financiers may find it more cost-effective to purchase the information than to produce it on their own. For, the third party may enjoy scale economies which an individual financier cannot realise.

Contingency planning

The solutions to decision problems under risk sometimes include contingency plans which recognise that gradual revelation of information can be used to advantage. For example, contingency planning can provide for certain acts to be taken only if certain events occur, and it can also provide for revising probabilities of future events as information is successively revealed.

Contingency planning is most often applied in situations of repeated negotiations. As an example, John and Nachman (1985) find that where a firm has to return repeatedly to the market for financing, the adverse incentive effects of risky debt on a levered firm can be ameliorated: there is less underinvestment with repeated transactions because in making each decision the firm considers its effects on securities prices in both the current and future periods. In another study, Flannery (1986) presents a sequential model in which firm's choice of risky debt maturity can signal insiders' information about firm quality. Riskier firms are found to issue shorter maturity debt; less risky firms prefer longer-term issues.

Harris and Raviv (1985) consider why the exercise of call options is sometimes delayed rather than being used to force conversion as soon as possible. They say that managers behave optimally given their private information, compensation schemes, and investors' reactions to their call decisions, but that optimal behaviour in a many period situation can differ from that in a single period situation. Thus, Harris and Raviv illustrate the principle that contingency planning permits linking the effects of actions taken in one period with those taken in another, in order to obtain greater long-run returns than would otherwise be possible.

Incomplete contracting

Agents do not always recognise that a contract is actually incomplete, and consequently do not always recognise a need to provide for *ex post* contract adjustments. However, when they do recognise the need, agents will attempt to devise cost-effective procedures to permit making adjustments as and when the need for them arises.

The Economic Organisation of a Financial System

Situations where the need for *ex post* adjustment is originally unrecognised may not be as common as situations where subsequent adjustment is contemplated, but it is useful to discuss both nevertheless. It is also worth noting that while the need to make *ex post* adjustments might be recognised, provisions to effect them could in some cases be more costly than the prospective benefits. Such situations arise, for example, in some speculative stock purchases, particularly if the purchaser does not acquire a control position. Rather than set up *ex post* adjustmemts processes explicitly, a dissatisfied investor will simply sell out his position.

Uncertainty and governance structures

Figure 6.3 classifies different possible sources of uncertainty and indicates the different kinds of governance structures typically chosen to deal with them.

Figure 6.3 recognises that under uncertainty, determining the precise nature of payoff probability distributions is either not possible or is regarded as overly costly. In such cases, financiers attempt to refine their understanding of the transaction's nature by attempting to discover important transaction features, or to obtain more nearly precise estimates of important problem parameters. For example, venture financing of a firm using a new technology can involve attempts to define the economics of the whole activity, since standards of comparison with other operations do not exist. The terms of such

Figure 6.3 Sources of uncertainty and governance structures

Source of uncertainty	Features of governance structure
Cannot estimate payoff distribution	Experimental attempts to assess nature of distribution; tentative forms of investment
Cannot specify acts of client	Request collateral to avoid the uncertainty; employ restrictive covenants
Cannot specify environmental reaction due to reactions of interested third parties	Attempts to control or accommodate third party interests; e.g., through forming conglomerates and resolving conflicting interests internally
Cannot specify environmental reaction due to economic change	Attempts to control environmental change or to offset its effects; e.g. floating rate loans

a financing are likely to be worked out jointly by client and financier.

Even when it is not possible to specify the kinds of environmental reactions that could affect a financing, it can be helpful to classify the source of uncertainty. For example, the uncertainty could result from the actions of clients, from the actions of interested third parties or from changes in the economic environment. In the case of uncertainty regarding the actions of clients or third parties, financiers can try to offset any effects through negotiation with the parties involved. For example, restrictive covenants can sometimes be employed to rule out or reduce the possible actions the client might take. Negotiations with third parties can sometimes achieve similar effects. For example, in the case of natural gas pipeline construction financiers sometimes can obtain the advance consent of regulatory authorities to pass on any construction cost increases by increasing the cost of the gas to consumers.

If it is not possible to deal with the likely reactions of interested third parties through negotiation, it may be possible to create an organisation of which they form a part. Some conglomerates are formed for these reasons. Financiers can also offer information they generate to clients, in attempts further to refine both parties' understanding. In this case, financiers might provide clients with estimates of a product's likely sales, and this research could in turn lead to the client offering different product specifications than were originally contemplated.

In the case of possible changes in the economic environment, the parties can attempt either to refine their information or to insulate themselves from the changes' effects. In seeking additional information, financiers might attempt to refine their estimates of project payoffs, or their probability estimates, by arranging some financings on an experimental basis. Alternatively, financiers can draw inferences from management actions. For example, management's willingness to join an endeavour likely evinces belief in the project's success, particularly if management invest funds of their own. On the other hand, resignation of key personnel from a firm could indicate their lack of faith in its future prospects.

Rating agencies are unlikely to play prominent information production roles under uncertainty, since their main function is to refine estimates of risks which have already been largely specified. However, under uncertainty consultants do perform a function analogous to that of rating agencies. For, experts with specialised knowledge can sometimes help to formulate or refine the structure of the uncertainties involved. In some cases, the advice provided by consultants can be helpful in learning how to control or offset the effects of environmental change.

Attempts to insulate the transaction from possible adverse effects can take many forms. One of the most obvious is to pass the risk on to another party, say the client. For example, interest rate risk is passed on to the client in floating rate lending. Japanese banks with large property loan portfolios, concerned about the possibility of eventual peaking in Japanese real estate prices, have been able to securitise some of their loans using equity instruments, which passes the risk of capital loss (as well as, of course, the possibility of any capital gains which might be captured by equity participation loans) on to the purchasers of the equities.

Uncertainty and ex post *adjustment*

The incomplete contracts written under uncertainty can lead, as a transaction evolves, to a degree of specialised interdependence between financier and client. This interdependence will be managed using *ex post* contract adjustments, at least whenever the adjustment processes can be devised cost-effectively.

The contract terms which permit *ex post* adjustments typically provide for greater discretion: equity in place of debt, a seat on a board of directors rather than a legal obligation to maintain, say, a given working capital ratio. Williamson (1988) points out that rules and discretion cannot usually be combined, because then discretion itself can be exercised opportunistically.

Providing for *ex post* adjustments can benefit both financier and client. An inflexible contract finely tuned to work perfectly under one set of circumstances can work badly if circumstances change only slightly. In contrast, discretionary arrangements can be robust in the sense that while they may not work perfectly under any set of circumstances, there can be many combinations of circumstances under which they are likely to work well. The differing costs and benefits to different forms of contracting mean that a given set of terms is likely to offer net benefits for some kinds of transaction, but not for others.

Ex post adjustments are also valuable because structuring incentives to ensure appropriate revelation of information is difficult to achieve under uncertainty. In fact, under unstructured uncertainty, incentive schemes may be replaced by detailed continuing negotiation, in part because neither party may know how to design incentives likely to achieve their desired ends. Sometimes, financiers may wish to monitor client affairs through board membership, direct ownership or control of the firm rather than attempt to utilise incentives.

Ex post adjustments thus allow financiers both to learn more about the risks to which an investment is exposed, and to deal with those risks more effectively. Possibly the most valuable use of *ex post* adjustments is their potential for structuring uncertainties. With adjustment processes in place, it may be possible to refine alternative possibilities, eventually to choose the most suitable kinds of transaction terms, and to determine how to control possibly adverse consequences of environmental change.

A current example illustrates some of these possibilities. Some third world countries have found[1] their financiers willing to accept equity investments in the countries concerned in exchange for their oustanding debt instruments. The country obtains the advantage of more flexible repayment terms, while the financier may find the value of the existing investment increased. With equity financing the technical possibility of default and any attendant renegotiation costs are both eliminated, an important consideration when the debt being exchanged carries fixed interest payments which from time to time become too great for the obligant to bear. When such payment difficulties are encountered, the obligant may be tempted to default unless the terms can be renegotiated without too much difficulty. Renegotiations of debt are frequently cumbersome, because they can involve obtaining agreement from a relatively large number of lenders with different purposes.

Bypassing the effects of uncertainty

Various forms of surety can be used to insure a financier against managerial fraud or incompetence, or against adverse environmental change. Guarantees or collateral can be taken to buttress a financing proposal which financiers do not think stands on its own merits. For example, insurance of mortgage loan principal makes mortgage financing more attractive to financiers. For with the insurance, mortgage lenders need only assess the borrower's ability to repay the mortgage from income while in good health.

A financing can offer highly uncertain payoffs, but the value of guarantees or collateral may be easily enough assessed to permit the financing to be arranged without structuring or resolving underlying uncertainties. For example, export credit insurance is often provided by exporters' governments. When goods shipped are insured against losses such as acts of war, acts which neither the financier nor the client can control, the financing transaction becomes similar to that of financing domestically marketed inventories, and involves only risks familiar to financiers.

Borrowers can be bonded so that financiers are insured against various developments or actions that might be inimical to financiers' interests. In some cases, financings are insured against such eventualities as death of key management personnel. Restrictive covenants and other forms of bonding are also used to manage agency costs (Smith and Warner, 1979).

Effects of informational differences

Contract terms are chosen with a view to balancing their costs against their likely benefits. This section provides further details of the cost effects of informational asymmetries. Under risk, these costs can be assessed quantitatively, but under uncertainty only a qualitative assessment is generally possible.

Assessing signal reliability

Clients may use biased signals in attempts to improve financing terms. Financiers try to counter this possibility by verifying client information and by designing reward schemes intended to offset any incentives for misrepresentation. Since there are costs to verifying information and to managing incentive schemes as well as to suffering any consequences of misrepresentation, an optimally designed reward scheme will attempt to equate the marginal costs of a scheme with the marginal benefits it is expected to bring. As well as trying to use a given reward scheme optimally, financiers must also try to choose among possible alternative schemes to find an overall best way of assessing client information. The choice of a particular alternative will depend on the mixture of costs and benefits it offers, and on how its net benefits compare to those of other schemes.

Moral hazard and adverse selection

Moral hazard and adverse selection are effects attendant on decisions to accept a pool of risks whose quality cannot individually be distinguished by financiers. Both can, unless offset, increase the realised losses from investing in the pool of risks. Either moral hazard or adverse selection can eliminate any net benefits to transacting if its effect is sufficiently great.

Moral hazard can best be understood in terms of relations between a financier and an individual client. It arises if a client's actions, taken subsequent to agreeing the terms of a financial transaction, alter the risks to which financiers are exposed. The example of setting fire to an almost bankrupt business to collect insurance on non-existent inventories provides an instance of moral hazard in the insurance business. It represents a situation in which a state (building burns down) has a higher probability subsequent to the act of insuring the building against fire damage. However, if the building does burn the insurer might not be able to determine whether the fire was accidental or deliberately set. Co-insurance provides one way of partially managing the problem, because it provides the insured with greater incentives to minimise the likelihood of fire damage.

Using the proceeds of a debt issue to finance a riskier investment than originally proposed offers a second instance of the workings of moral hazard. It arises when a project, inferior from financiers' point of view, is substituted clandestinely for the original. The shareholders receive any benefits from such a substitution, while financiers bear the increased risk. To offset these possibilities, financiers try to prevent project substitutions through continuing supervision of client affairs and use of contract terms which provide for sanctions if the terms are violated.

Adverse selection is best understood as resulting from the actions of many clients. Adverse selection works to increase expected losses if the terms announced by financiers for taking on a pool of risks are unattractive to lowest risk potential clients, who then turn to other financing sources. On the other hand, the riskiest clients in the pool are likely to find financiers' terms particularly attractive. Moreover, even high risk clients not originally in the pool may be attracted by the financier's terms. These combined actions, if not observable to financiers, can increase the originally estimated risks, sometimes substantially.

Clients are at least as likely to act opportunistically under uncertainty as they are under risk. For example, management may put less effort into making a project succeed than it appeared they would when seeking financing, creating a situation analogous to moral hazard. As an analogue to adverse selection, a financier who usually treats clients as if they are honest sometimes attracts a number of dishonest clients. A lender new to a geographical area frequently encounters this kind of difficulty.

Monitoring and learning

Monitoring is a policing activity intended to obtain compliance with existing contract terms. In itself, monitoring rarely enhances the safety of a financial arrangement, but the potential for discovery that it poses can discourage clients from taking actions which might otherwise impair the safety of a financial arrangement.

Since monitoring is costly, its use is only warranted if conditions materially affecting a contract can change and if through monitoring and taking corrective action the financier can offset the consequences of the change. Thus monitoring is mainly appropriate in structured situations where the possibilities of adverse effects can be assessed in advance: it is generally aimed at early detection of poor outcomes or violation of contract terms. The costs of monitoring are those of setting up and operating the monitoring mechanism, plus those of taking corrective action when it is needed. The benefits are gained through financiers' greater capability to offset possible losses.

Learning means discovering new information. Financiers will likely attempt to learn when they cannot easily ascertain the outcomes of a transaction in advance. Flexible or sequential contracting which provides for making *ex post* adjustments can help realise whatever benefits learning might bring. However, attempts to learn are also costly, and financiers will attempt to strike an appropriate balance between costs and benefits.

There may be net benefits to learning in many financial transactions, but they are likely to be greatest when financiers investigate the profitability of new lines of business or try to find new ways of conducting existing business. The costs of learning are the costs of using resources to experiment. They include mistakenly entering transactions which prove to be unprofitable because their true nature was not originally recognised. In practice, financial firms frequently do experiment with new lines of business, and regularly terminate attempts which do not work out as profitably as originally anticipated. Trying new lines of business suggests that financial managers regard experiments as useful learning devices; terminating unsuccessful lines suggests that financiers' experiments do not always confirm the obvious but rather represent genuine attempts to learn.

Summary

This chapter discussed choices of contract terms and reasons for using them. First, the chapter considered the importance of differing informational conditions, showing how transactions under risk are associated with complete contracting, while those under uncertainty are more closely related to incomplete contracting. Signals and contingency planning are used with complete contracting to deal with risks whose nature is gradually revealed through time.

Under uncertainty, contracts are usually incomplete. When the incompleteness is recognised, financiers attempt to set up mechanisms permitting *ex post* adjustments to be made. *Ex post* adjustments can deal either with changes in the economic environment outside the control of interested participants or with direct reactions of clients or interested third parties.

Contract terms are designed to deal with the workings of opportunism, whether manifest under risk or under uncertainty. The workings of opportunism are manifest through biased signals as well as through the effects of moral hazard and adverse selection. Monitoring and learning represent attempts to offset these effects. Sometimes the effects can be bypassed by using guarantees or collateral.

Note

1 In most cases these *ex post* adjustments were not anticipated when the contracts were originally drawn up.

Chapter seven

Managing portfolios

Portfolio management means screening and purchasing assets, funding their acquisition, and supervising the resulting holdings. The principal task in managing any portfolio is to generate a return commensurate with investment risk or uncertainty, but putting the principle to work in practice differs according to investor purpose and the nature of the assets held. The portfolio may be composed of assets which are mainly marketable or mainly non-marketable, and in addition some of the assets may have highly specific characteristics. Whatever the case, a governance structure which meets the portfolio's requirements will need to be selected.

Thus, portfolio management involves acquiring and financing an appropriate mix of assets, striving to generate as high a return as possible on them while simultaneously controlling the portfolio's aggregate risk. These tasks vary in kind according to a financier's purposes and the assets he acquires.

Managing portfolios of marketable securities principally involves selecting, purchasing and trading desirable investments to generate a target level of income while minimising risk. With marketable securities, asset specificity is not usually an important issue because in most cases an unsatisfactory investment is simply sold in the market place.[1] There are exceptional circumstances in which a block of market securities assumes a high degree of asset specificity: if the holding represents a large proportion of an issue, selling it off may not be a straightforward matter. Apart from these exceptions, which are discussed below, the main functions of a marketable securities portfolio's governance structure are monitoring financial data, identifying which securities should be bought or sold, and timing the transactions.

Managing a portfolio of non-marketable assets involves all of the above tasks except active trading. In addition, it poses the special governance needs of managing assets which cannot readily be liquidated. Moreover, management has a variety of ways to influence the income pattern of the aggregate portfolio by using a variety of derivative securities.[2]

The investment portfolios managed by some financial holding companies represent a third category – portfolios composed of a small number of large, closely held investments. These investments exhibit high degrees of asset specificity for at least two reasons. As already mentioned, any sufficiently large block of securities is not usually as easy to trade at market prices as is a smaller proportion of the same issue. Second, blocks of shares are often purchased so the owners can exercise a higher degree of control over the issuing firm than can an ordinary small shareholder. The nature of the investment is thus closely related to the individual characteristics of the firm issuing the securities. Hence, portfolios of large, closely held investments require the use of highly capable, but generally costly, governance structures.

Portfolios of marketable securities

Investors in marketable securities usually screen large numbers of securities with a view to buying the most desirable prospects, where desirability is assessed in terms of both income generating potential and contribution to portfolio risk. After their purchase, investors continue to assess the securities' earnings and risk contributions, thus deciding whether to continue holding them. Managing marketable securities portfolios requires understanding how diversification can be used to reduce overall portfolio risk, and management must also reinvest any funds deriving from sales or from maturing securities. Finally, managers need to understand the nature of derivative securities, since they can offer special opportunities for additional tailoring of portfolio risk and return.

The desirability of a given security can change with the fortunes of the firm issuing it. Errors in estimating a marketable security's contribution to a portfolio are normally rectified by selling it. Since the specificity of the investment does not normally change importantly subsequent to purchasing marketable securities, transactions are not usually subject to the fundamental transformation typical of incomplete contracts. Indeed, with such securities any problems of managing or selling them can usually be anticipated in advance, and the securities are thus not likely to pose important needs for *ex post* adjustment.[3]

Intermediaries such as unit trusts (mutual funds in North America) assemble portfolios of marketable securities to generate investment income. These intermediaries, members of a class known as portfolio investors, rarely attempt to control the firms in which they invest. Rather, they prefer to sell their holdings of securities issued by firms whose fortunes have taken an apparently undesirable turn.

Diversification

Portfolio theory studies managing asset portfolios under risk. To the portfolio theorist, the main management problems are estimating probability distributions of returns on individual securities and determining how different asset combinations will affect aggregate income risk.[4] Using variance of return as a definition of risk, and on the assumption that investors prefer to reduce variance for any given mean return, portfolio theory argues for selecting a diversified portfolio that offers a given expected rate of return while minimising its risk.

Portfolio theory shows that a diversified portfolio of assets whose returns are not perfectly correlated will have a lower variance of return than at least some of its individual components. That is, reducing risk through diversification is not just a matter of acquiring many assets. Rather it is a matter of judiciously combining assets with different statistical characteristics so as to achieve a given level of expected earnings at the lowest feasible risk.[5]

Practical considerations

In theory, the number of different assets used to achieve an optimal degree of risk reduction is determined by cost benefit analysis. Including more assets in a portfolio can, if their returns are not perfectly positively correlated, further reduce income risk. Sometimes it is possible to achieve this additional risk reduction without simultaneously reducing expected portfolio income. However, the effects of including more securities in a portfolio must be assessed net of transactions costs. For, these costs can limit the number of individual assets capable of maintaining or improving net earnings while reducing risk. On the other hand, since both the costs of and benefits to diversification are relatively easy to define, a theoretically optimal balancing of risk and return can be attained by equating marginal changes in portfolio risk to the marginal costs of the additional securities transactions.

In practice, determining an appropriate degree of diversification is less straightforward. First, the candidates for investment will be limited by the financier's knowledge: a financier cannot invest in securities of which he is unaware. Second, small portfolios are likely to

Managing portfolios

contain only a few securities, because transaction costs are usually large in proportion to the funds invested. Moreover, the marginal costs of additional transactions include not just transaction costs, but also the costs of assessing the securities' quality at regular intervals. Thus whether it pays to diversify further by purchasing additional different securities depends on initial screening costs, the costs of buying and selling securities, and the costs of monitoring them.

Large investors face the additional problem of finding a sufficient number of securities suitable for investment. Since the amounts involved in individual transactions are likely to be large, the large investor avoids small securities issues. For, a large investment in a small issue can create adverse price effects, both at time of purchase and at time of sale. On the other hand, managers of large portfolios can reap cost advantages not available to their smaller counterparts. Since the costs of securities analysis are largely independent of the amounts purchased, the unit costs of screening and monitoring are lower for larger portfolios, meaning their managers are more likely to conduct research. Moreover, managers of larger portfolios usually strive to increase portfolio size on the grounds of reaping economies of scale in screening and in administration.

Use of options and futures

Options, futures, and the markets in which they trade were discussed in Chapter 4. Portfolio managers buy and sell these instruments to help manage portfolio risks and returns. They trade in derivative securities rather than in the underlying instruments for two reasons: the derivative securities partition risks in different ways, and the costs of trading them can be lower than the costs of trading the underlying instruments.

Options and futures are normally used by portfolio managers to decrease portfolio risk.[6] For example, a call option can be used to ensure that, over its life, shares can be acquired at no more than the call's exercise price. As another instance, the holder of a put option can secure, over its life, the current value of an existing share holding. More sophisticated forms of insuring against declines in value are known as portfolio insurance, which is usually created using share index options and index futures. The next section discusses these possibilities further.

Dynamic portfolio management

Dynamic portfolio theories address the problems of managing portfolios through time, and some dynamic analyses complement the single period portfolio theory discussed above. In particular, Merton (1973) argues that investors can both diversify static risks, and structure their portfolios over time in ways designed to hedge against the risks of changing interest rates as well.

Portfolio insurance involves transactions in such instruments as index options and futures to affect the time pattern of a portfolio's capital value. These insurance schemes employ the same principles as hedging with put options, but rely on market trading of index instruments, at the values predicted by theoretical analyses, to create synthetic insured portfolios. Continuous trading can theoretically insure a synthetic portfolio against substantial declines in value.

In practice, synthetic portfolios do not achieve exactly the same income–risk tradeoffs as actual securities portfolios. However they do create approximately the same tradeoffs, and usually at lower transactions costs. The theoretical advantages of insured portfolios cannot always be realised in practice because instantaneous execution of trades at market prices is not always possible. At present the schemes work well under normal trading conditions, but not when markets are unusually turbulent. When securities markets exhibit rapid price change and atypically high trading volumes, actual options and futures prices can deviate substantially from their theoretically predicted values, and it can also be difficult to trade the instruments quickly.

Nevertheless, the more efficient markets become, the smaller the deviations between actual and theoretical prices are likely to be, since in an increasingly efficient market arbitrage works increasingly well. Arbitrage should also work more quickly, even with very active trading, as markets become increasingly efficient. Hence, the more impediments to efficient market trading can be removed or lessened, the better portfolio insurance schemes are likely to work.

In the future some of the institutional impediments are likely to be eliminated. The difficulties are due mainly to constraints on trading capacity and to slow and fragmented settlement procedures. Both these problems can be ameliorated, the first by changes in routines for handling high volumes of trading, the second by changes in procedures for settling transactions. As and when these institutional changes are made, portfolio insurance schemes' actual performance will approximate the theoretical predictions more closely than they now do.

Since portfolio theory deals with risk, it does not discuss how agents deal with any *ex post* adjustment problems resulting from incomplete contracting. Indeed, it does not even contemplate how to manage a portfolio if the distribution of the risks can change unpredictably subsequent to the assets' acquisition. For example, prior to

Managing portfolios

19 October 1987 most advocates of portfolio insurance did not contemplate situations in which turbulent market conditions would impede trading at or near theoretical values, and therefore had not worked out contingency plans to deal with such situations. The management problems which do arise in such situations are those discussed in the next section, which considers non-marketable securities.

Portfolios of non-marketable securities

The tasks of managing non-marketable securities include all those discussed above, except for active trading. That is, managers of non-marketable securities portfolios are also concerned with screening potential asset acquisitions and subsequently managing the orderly liquidation of the assets actually acquired. But managing non-marketable securities portfolios also involves additional tasks, as the assets can exhibit high degrees of specificity, and investments in them represent incomplete contracts which can require *ex post* adjustments.

While it was unnecessary to do so in discussing portfolios of marketable securities, it is now helpful, in discussing non-marketable securities, to distinguish between between income and default risks. Income risk refers to the possibility of unpredictable changes in an asset's earnings; default risk refers to the possibility of losing the entire capital. The difference is actually a matter of degree: the typical cost of default on a loan or investment held by an intermediary is large in relation to the income the transaction generates. Losses through default in portfolios of marketable securities are less common, and when they do occur are more likely to be partial rather than total losses.

The usefulness of the distinction parallels differences in how the risks are managed. In the case of marketable securities, both income and default risk are usually managed in the same way – by selling the securities if the investment is no longer regarded as desirable. However, different methods are used to manage income and default risks in portfolios of non-marketable securities. Income risks are managed using combinations of internal, intermediated, and market transactions in derivative securities, while default risks are managed using governance structures permitting the exercise of greater discretion than is usually possible in managing marketable securities.

As a practical matter the difference between income risk and default risk parallels what some financiers refer to as a difference between market risk and credit risk. Market risk means the risk of being able to trade at or near a given price, and is thus similar to income risk. On the other hand, credit risk refers to the risk of suffering loss from default. In practice, managing credit risk requires different skills than does managing market risk, and not all financiers possess both capabilities. For example, some investment bankers are skilled at assessing market risk, but not at assessing credit risk.

Accordingly, when these investment bankers use their own capital to take longer-term positions in the shares of firms, they assume credit risks with which they are unfamiliar, and are exposed to losses of a type new to them. Some such losses have recently been incurred by investment bankers taking positions in merger or acquisition transactions. In essence, the losses resulted because the investors did not realise that the governance structures appropriate for managing market risk (essentially, mechanisms for trading) are not appropriate for performing the monitoring and *ex post* adjustments which can be needed to manage credit risk.

In practice, the most important group of non-marketable securities portfolios is assembled by lending intermediaries such as banks and near banks, which mainly acquire debt instruments. Like portfolio investors, lending intermediaries acquire assets to generate income, but usually intend to hold the assets until liquidated.[7] The assets acquired are usually more specific than are typical holdings in marketable securities portfolios, and the contracts used by lending intermediaries are frequently incomplete.

Risk transformation

Lending intermediaries can transform the risks they assume, as Chapter 3 discussed. The capability to transform risks means that the aggregate risk of a lending intermediary's portfolio is influenced by its screening and management processes. Intermediaries mainly screen small heterogeneous risks or uncertainties. When arranging a financing, intermediaries assess income and default risk simultaneously. Subsequently, however, they deal with income risks in the aggregate by using special techniques, and deal with default risks mainly through individually tailored *ex post* adjustments.

To illustrate the differences between managing marketable and non-marketable securities, two residential mortgage loans can exhibit greater differences in risk than, say, two federal government bonds of different issue. Hence mortgage loans require a different kind of initial screening than do government bonds. Moreover, they subsequently require additional supervision, since after origination loans presenting difficulties cannot generally be sold off, while the bonds can. Supervising the liquidation of individual mortgage loans can involve the haggling associated with bilateral monopoly

(Williamson, 1972); each such situation becomes a special case in which the client gains a degree of power.

Diversification

Intermediaries offer their depositors a diversification service which the latter cannot obtain for themselves at the same cost. In addition, intermediaries diversify for internal management purposes. Consider each of these in turn.

As an alternative to diversifying on his own through market transactions, an investor can, through an intermediary, place funds in diversified portfolios of non-marketable assets that would not otherwise be available to him at the same cost. In essence, placing an uninsured deposit with a lending intermediary is such an act, because the worth of an uninsured deposit depends on the worth of the underlying assets. Other claims against diversified investment portfolios include shares in life insurance policies and the obligations of pension funds. In all these transactions the claims' values and risks depend on the underlying aggregate portfolio rather than on the individual assets composing it.

Intermediaries also diversify for internal management purposes, at least when regulation and the nature of the markets they serve permit them to do so. This kind of diversification can be highly important because it offers a way of managing default risk which differs from that used to manage a portfolio of marketable securities. In the absence of internal diversification, overly specialised portfolios can be created, and excessive specialisation can create default risks large enough to threaten an intermediary's survival. For example, some (particularly regional) intermediaries specialise in real estate lending within a given region, which can pose solvency problems for them if real estate values decline.

The main traditional defence against overspecialisation has been to syndicate large loans, selling portions of them to other banks. Syndication does not always meet the problem of overdependence on the economic fortunes of a given region however, because small individual loans cannot economically be divided and resold in the same way as large loans. In the 1980s intermediaries discovered a new means of selling off specialised risks using a technique known as securitisation.

Securitisation means selling claims against the original portfolios of specialised loans. When an intermediary issues such claims, the residual risk it continues to bear depends on the nature of the claims it sells. If the claims are equity and represent an actual transfer of income and default risk to the buyer, intermediaries can diversify against the risks of over-specialisation. For example, an intermediary with a large proportion of real estate loans in its portfolio might be able to package the loans and sell equity claims against them, transferring both default and income risks to purchasers of the equity. If the intermediary used a debt instrument for the same purpose, the default risk of the original loans would remain on its own books, and, depending on the terms of the debt issue, so might some of the income risk.

Incomplete contracting

Lending intermediaries' assets often represent incomplete contracts which can require *ex post* adjustments. The possibility arises because intermediaries are not capable of assessing all future eventualities which might affect each illiquid investment they make. To effect any necessary *ex post* adjustments, intermediaries utilise governance structures allowing them more discretionary control over their clients' affairs than is possessed by the managers of marketable securities portfolios.

Incomplete contracts are costlier to administer than their complete counterparts. On the other hand, the costlier structures have greater capabilities. Intermediaries' typically longer-term relations with clients give them greater potential for effecting *ex post* adjustments. If the net effect of costlier administration and greater capabilities is one of increased governance cost, transactions costs must be increased to compensate.

These effects of governance structure costs should be recognised in assessing financial system efficiency. For example, consider a financing using a cheap, low capability governance structure on the one hand; a second using an expensive, high capability governance structure on the other. Suppose that before the two governance structures are put in place, the risk of the first transaction is less than that of the second. But suppose further that the estimated risks and returns from the two transactions, given the difference in governance structures, are the same. The interest rates paid by the two clients would have to differ, since in each case the governance structure's costs must be covered, and in the second case risk management is more costly. It would be easy, in such a case, to compare the clients' interest rates with the risk–return earnings profiles of the two financiers and conclude that the system was either operationally or allocatively inefficient. But given the circumstances assumed, neither conclusion would be correct.

Intermediary income management

Managers of lending intermediaries strive to generate the most advantageous combination of high return and low risk attainable to them. This involves not just trading in assets, but also using special techniques to affect the aggregate incomes on those non-tradable assets. The several methods of intermediary income management include setting terms on loans and deposits, asset–liability matching, engaging in interest rate swaps, and using financial futures and options. The more effectively intermediaries can manage their incomes, the lower the operating costs to be borne by their clients.

To analyse the risk of a stream of net interest revenue from an intermediary's viewpoint, assume that default risk has already been evaluated in relation to the average return a loan or investment is expected to generate. It is then easier to consider managing the remaining income risks.[8]

Matching

Income risk can be reduced if a portfolio is financed with liabilities whose costs are positively correlated through time with the assets' revenue stream. Indeed, if the correlation is perfect the resulting income stream will be riskless, because a perfect positive correlation between earnings and costs means that net revenue, the difference between earnings and costs, has perfectly negatively correlated components, the fluctuations in which offset each other.

Matching means borrowing and lending on the same terms, at least with respect to the points in time at which interest rates can be adjusted. Matching means affecting interest rate risk without recourse to market trading of assets or liabilities. Intermediaries or other firms match transactions internally when, say, a floating rate loan is funded by floating rate deposits. Such practices are now commonplace in both domestic and international banking transactions.

Whether interest rates are fixed or floating, the amounts of assets must equal the amounts of liabilities on the same interest terms if risk is to be wholly eliminated. Of course, the markets faced by a particular intermediary may not permit this kind of balancing, in which case other means of offsetting income risks must be found, as with the swaps discussed in the next section. Alternatively, some intermediaries will prefer simply to assume the remaining risks, particularly if they believe a short-term trend in interest rates will work in their favour.

The Economic Organisation of a Financial System

Interest rate swaps

Lending intermediaries can hedge income risks externally using interest rate swaps. The swaps can be arranged either through private negotations or in an active market place.[9] If, for example, one intermediary has floating rate assets financed by fixed rate liabilities, while another has fixed rate assets financed by floating rate liabilities, an exchange of their interest costs can stabilise the interest incomes of both.

In practice, interest rate swaps were usually negotiated individually in the early 1970s when they first originated. However, as individual swaps have become more frequent, and agents have become more familiar with swap techniques, the cost and informational conditions under which they are effected have altered. As a result, at least some swaps can now be arranged in a relatively active market. The market developed because in order to hedge its portfolio fully, any given intermediary might have to engage in several transactions. In addition, transactions are now effected not just by intermediaries, but also by non-financial firms whose treasurers also wish to manage interest rate risk. With the increasing number of participants, search costs are reduced by the emergence of well-known market agents. Nevertheless, these agents still function primarily as brokers because few find it cost-effective to take inventory positions in the large, specialised risks involved.

Selling risks in markets

The interest rate swap market effects fewer but generally larger transactions than the interest rate futures market. Maturities are also shorter in the futures markets. Nevertheless, interest rate futures are also used by intermediaries to hedge interest rate risks, usually on individual transactions. The principle of such transactions is well illustrated by considering a specific market: that for government treasury bill futures.

Treasury bills have market values which are negatively correlated with changes in interest rates. Similarly, futures contracts written against treasury bills have payments streams that are negatively correlated with interest rates. However, a short position in treasury bill futures has earnings that rise as interest rates rise, and fall as rates fall. Hence the combination of a fixed rate loan and a short futures position (if the latter is of an appropriate size) behaves like a floating rate loan. If the arrangement is funded by floating rate deposits, the effect on the intermediary is that of matching a floating rate loan with a floating rate deposit, creating a position which is hedged against interest rate change.

For reasons discussed in Chapter 4, interest rate futures and similar contracts rarely have maturities in excess of one year, and accordingly they can only be used to hedge the risks of fairly short-term arrangements. Moreover, at the present time the amounts which can be hedged in the financial futures and options markets are relatively small in relation to the typical intermediary's total assets. Hence, intermediaries use the interest rate futures markets mainly for hedging risks on individual transactions rather than for purposes of affecting the interest rate risk of their entire portfolio.

Managing closely held investments

Managing the specialised portfolios of large, closely held investments mainly involves recognising the incomplete contracting problems which arise with asset specific investments, and devising governance structures capable of dealing with these problems. Some financial holding companies assemble such specialised portfolios of assets. The number of different investments they make is usually much smaller than those assembled by a lending intermediary, the individual investments are larger in size, and the transactions' governance structures usually permit exercising even greater discretion than do those used by lending intermediaries.

Even when they purchase publicly marketed securities, financial holding companies are likely to acquire control blocks, meaning their investments will have a high degree of asset specificity. Managing these assets mainly involves monitoring the evolution of the subject firms' businesses, learning when *ex post* adjustments are needed, and choosing ways to effect the adjustments. Such companies thus use governance structures which permit them to exercise active influence over the investments' operations.

Incomplete contracting

Financiers who specialise in administering large, closely held investments frequently invest under conditions of considerable uncertainty, with the result that contracting at time of acquisition is usually incomplete. This is one reason why conglomerate holdings usually take the form of control blocks: a highly discretionary form of governance structure is employed to deal with the asset specificity problems created by making large investments under uncertainty.

Some of the principal results of portfolio theory apply to closely held investments, and provide a point of departure for a fuller analysis. Under uncertainty as under risk, diversification offers potential for risk reduction. While it is less easy to quantify the benefits from diversification under uncertainty (it may not be quite as difficult to quantify costs) financiers can still attempt qualitative cost–benefit analyses.

Portfolios of large, closely held investments present the problems of using governance structures capable of dealing with unpredictable change, and of trading in what are essentially gaming situations. As an example of the first, management need to develop strategies for use in threatened takeover situations. As an example of the second, management must sometimes trade large blocks of securities in anticipation of what others will do. Both situations require governance structures which permit the use of considerable discretion, and which also allow for flexible responses to changing conditions.

Governance responses

The managers of large, closely held investments can experiment with unfamiliar forms of financing if their governance structures permit exercising discretion. For example, a conglomerate financier might invest in a new kind of asset because its returns seem unrelated to those on assets with which he is familiar. This is especially true when a firm considers taking on new lines of business: the experiment is intended to provide information as to whether additional investments of the new type might be profitable over the long run. It is less risky to conduct as a part of a closely controlled portfolio than in a portfolio of market securities, because the governance capabilities are greater in the former case.

The point is not that flexible governance structures are never used in managing a portfolio of marketable securities, but that in the latter case it is usually unnecessary to employ a high cost governance structure because the degree of asset specificity is minimal. By the same token, intermediated transactions typically involve a higher degree of asset specificity than do portfolio investments, as shown for example in the problems banks are currently having with Latin American debt. When the possibility of needing to make *ex post* adjustments is recognised at the outset, intermediaries attempt to set up governance structures with capabilities to handle the adjustments as and when they are needed.

Summary

This chapter examined the tasks of managing asset portfolios. Managing a portfolio of marketable securities principally involves selecting investment targets and trading assets to generate a target level of income while reducing risk as much as possible. These tasks

Managing portfolios

are addressed through diversification and the use of options, futures, and dynamic portfolio restructuring.

Managing the portfolios of non-marketable securities assembled by lending intermediaries principally involves screening new acquisitions, effecting *ex post* adjustments where necessary, and influencing the income pattern of the aggregate portfolio. All these tasks must be performed without relying on active trading to any significant extent. Loans or investments are characterised by intermediate degrees of asset specificity, and higher capability governance structures are needed to administer *ex post* adjustment needs.

Problems of asset specificity are at their greatest in managing portfolios of large, closely held investments. Both the problems posed by incomplete contracting, and the governance responses to these problems, were discussed in the context of a financial conglomerate, which in many ways represents the most effective governance structure for managing under uncertainty. The governance structures employed in such cases are high cost, but also have a high degree of capability for effecting *ex post* adjustments.

Notes
1 Asset specificity is a property of assets which are illiquid because they do not trade readily in a secondary market. As a result, such assets need close management by their owners in order to ensure that the owners receive the maximal worth from them.
2 Managers of marketable securities portfolios also trade derivative securities, but since their principal management activities already involve trading, the function is not as distinct. Moreover, a greater variety of means, both market and non-market, is used to manage the incomes of non-marketable securities portfolios.
3 On rare occasions, circumstances may require using special tactics for selling assets whose market value has declined. For example, in the event of a bankruptcy, portfolio managers may become involved in negotiations to realise some return on their investment. The processes in these cases are similar to the management processes used by lending intermediaries, as discussed below.
4 Orthodox portfolio selection theory does not distinguish between income and default risks, since for the theory's purposes both concepts can be incorporated satisfactorily in return distributions. As a practical matter, default risk becomes more important in the case of asset specific investments, as discussed below.
5 Portfolio theory recognises that not all asset combinations reduce risk. Indeed, it is possible to construct portfolios whose risk exceeds that of its individual components. For example, a security purchased on margin forms a portfolio with greater risk than the underlying security, even if the margin loan carries a riskless rate of interest.

The Economic Organisation of a Financial System

6   As an example of using options to increase risk, buying and holding stock options rather than the stocks themselves can be used to create a portfolio with both higher expected returns and a higher risk of achieving that return.
7   Securitisation is an exception (see pp. 72 and 117).
8   For simplicity, the discussion assumes that risk can be reduced without affecting the expected value of the revenue stream. Although the same principles apply in the case of reducing risk whilst not creating unfavourable reductions in expected revenue, these qualifications are ignored for ease of discussion.
9   Whether such transactions are privately negotiated or arranged in markets depends on transaction features discussed in Chapter 3.

Chapter eight

System organisation and performance

This chapter examines how individual financial transactions affect financial system organisation and performance. To provide a perspective, the chapter first considers relations between securities prices in a perfect financial market. The securities price effects of market incompleteness and of differing information are then discussed. The chapter next examines intermediary activity, focusing particularly on how informational conditions affect intermediaries' decisions to provide finance. Finally, the chapter considers the differences between governing routine and innovative transactions, and the effect of these differences on financial system structure.

Agents' experiences shape their ways of handling transactions. Frequently recurring transactions are usually standardised, so that an important proportion of the financings carried out within any financial system employs a standardised set of governance structures. These structures constitute a system's established features, and will persist so long as they remain cost-effective for both clients and financiers. While financial systems evolve continuously by developing new instruments and new forms of transacting, the rate of change is slow enough for established system features to persist over years or even decades. Thus it is useful to discuss financial system organisation and performance in terms of these features.

Neoclassical financial theory explains a number of system features: in particular, the equilibrium and efficiency properties of competitive markets. Moreover, the properties of public securities markets have been examined extensively using empirical techniques whose results offer considerable support for the theories. However, as pointed out previously, nearly all neoclassical theory applies to transacting under risk, and not all transactions are carried out under risk. This means that other kinds of financial markets may not have the same properties as active public securities markets.

Under uncertainty, neither agents' negotiations nor the nature of possible equilibria have been as thoroughly examined. The institutional economics on which this book is based both supplements the neoclassical theory and offer explanations which seem to accord with casual empiricism. However, none of the predictions of institutional theory has yet been tested as rigorously as some propositions of neoclassical theory. Moreover, testing the predictions of institutional economics is more difficult in at least one way: the time-scale of changes in financial practice seems to be much longer than the timescale of change normally examined in empirical studies of securities price determination (Merton, 1987).

The foregoing overview suggests that a combination of theoretical and empirical studies can be used to explain many prominent financial system features. This chapter organises such an explanation in the following way. Its first section surveys theories of equilibrium securities prices and the resulting efficiency properties of securities markets, contrasting theoretical predictions with observed phenomena. The predictions of these theories are premised on financial system completeness, a property which is unlikely to be attained in practice. Hence the second section contrasts the properties of a complete financial system with features commonly observed in practice, sketching how the theory needs to be modified to take these additional financial system properties into account. The third section discusses the effects of differing informational conditions on securities markets prices and equilibria, again comparing theory and practice wherever possible.

The fourth section examines intermediary activity, emphasising how intermediaries' capabilities for dealing with informational asymmetries and uncertainties affect the nature of a financial system, chiefly through the ways in which intermediaries decide to extend financing. The fifth section explains that routine transactions can usefully be regarded as occurring under risk, but that explanations of financial system change are likely to be more successful if they postulate uncertainty. For, the governance structures used for routine transactions are mainly capable of dealing with risk, while those used for experimental transactions have greater capabilities for dealing with uncertainty.

Perfect markets and securities prices

Clients choose among financing arrangements largely on the basis of perceived cost differences. While it has not traditionally done so, modern financial theory is beginning to recognise that such cost differences exist, and to explain why they do. To discuss these developments, it is useful first to review the equilibrium properties of a perfect market, where differences in financing costs do not occur.

Then, the analysis is expanded to indicate how differences in financing costs can arise from a variety of market imperfections.

Relations between securities prices

Beginning with the famous Modigliani–Miller conditions (1958, 1963), financial theory develops conditions under which differences in financing costs either cannot occur at all or if they do, are transient rather than equilibrium phenomena. Financing costs do not differ in a Modigliani–Miller world because costlessly repackaging a firm's securities (essentially, a costless form of arbitrage) can undo the effects of its capital structure decisions. Thus, if financing costs are found to differ in practice, one or more of the conditions under which the Modigliani–Miller possibilities for costless repackaging are established must not obtain: the conditions which create differences in financing costs are market imperfections of one type or another.[1] To see this, consider further the nature of a perfect capital market.

In a perfect capital market, numerous transactors take interest rates and hence securities prices as given. Transactors costlessly exchange funds for securities on the basis of equally distributed information, publicly available to all. Interest rates are adjusted for risk: higher risks bear higher equilibrium rates of return. The same interest rates apply to both borrowing and lending, and while most agree that unlimited borrowing can increase the probability of bankruptcy, if bankruptcy occurs, it is often assumed to be costless. Then, only risk and return matter, not the ways in which securities divide or recombine the risk–return combinations. For these reasons, differences in financing costs cannot be created by changing capital structures – the cost of funds to a firm depends on its underlying risk, not on how that risk is packaged.[2]

The perfect capital market also has other important properties. When securities of agreed quality are exchanged in markets between equally well-informed transactors, a transaction's unique features are completely reflected in its effective interest rate.[3] Moreover, there are no cost or institutional impediments to arbitraging, so that equilibrium interest rates conform to a risk–return relationship which holds across all securities. One form of this relationship is developed in capital asset pricing theory (CAPT).

In its most common form the CAPT explains how securities prices are determined in an equilibrium where all investors have the same expectations. The CAPT relates securities prices to the risk and return on a market portfolio which these investors would hold.[4] The market portfolio is efficient in the sense of offering a given expected return at lowest possible risk, the latter usually being measured by as

The Economic Organisation of a Financial System

the variance of portfolio return. The CAPT predicts that all investors hold combinations of the market portfolio and a risk free asset in a mix depending on individual attitudes toward risk. In conjunction with fixed supplies of securities, at equilibrium aggregate investor choices define a linear risk–return tradeoff called the Capital Market Line (CML). Along the CML, portfolio return increases with portfolio risk.

The return on an individual security is determined at equilibrium by assessing its contribution to the risk of the market portfolio. This relationship between individual security risk and return is given by another linear function called the security market line (SML). The SML relates each security's return to its individual risk, measured in terms of its contribution to the risk of the market portfolio; riskier securities bear higher interest rates.[5]

An alternative explanation of relations between securities prices and risks, the arbitrage pricing theory (APT, Ross, 1976) also argues that securities prices are related to each other, but uses a broader definition of risk than does the CAPT.[6] The APT says that securities promising the same payoff distribution should trade at the same market price, but defines risks in terms of underlying factors whose nature is to be determined empirically. APT emphasises arbitrage between all possible combinations of securities as the mechanism determining relative prices: if the same distributions do not trade at the same prices, arbitraging transactions will bring them back into line.

Although option pricing theory (OPT) was developed prior to the APT (Black and Scholes, 1973; Merton, 1973), it can be viewed as a specialised form of APT. In essence, OPT and other, subsequently developed theories of pricing derivative securities (e.g. futures pricing theory; see Chapter 4) rely on arbitraging to maintain price relationships between the derivative securities and the instruments against which they are written. Most theories of derivative securities pricing are developed in continuous time, meaning that trading to eliminate any emerging arbitrage opportuntities is also assumed to be continuous.

Other theories of financial market relationships are also based on arbitraging. The theory of the term structure of interest rates explains how interest rates on bonds with different terms to maturity but similar credit risk are related by arbitraging between bonds. In this case, however, more than just relative prices have been studied: the underlying determinants of the term structure are developed in a general equilibrium context by Cox, Ingersoll, and Ross (1981a, 1981b, 1985a).

Still other theories of how arbitrage determines relative prices can be found in the Fisher relation, in interest rate parity theory, and forward parity theory, as Chapter 4 pointed out. In practice, movements of funds between the markets contemplated are not always easy to effect, meaning that the arbitraging on which the theories rely can be impaired or take place only slowly. Accordingly, this group of theories generally holds less closely than those explaining relative securities prices.

All the foregoing theories say, in particular contexts, that the same arrangements will have the same equilibrium prices if arbitraging between them and close substitutes is not impeded. To reach these conclusions, the theories (sometimes implicitly) assume that arrangements offering the same return distributions are actually perceived by market transactors to be the same, and are then exchanged in a perfect market. In the case of all but the CAPT, most versions of the APT, and theories of the term structure, the theories describe only relative prices. In the exceptional cases the theories explain how securities prices are derived from such fundamentals as the underlying economy and the nature of agents' preferences.

Efficiency

A perfect, competitive financial market is both allocatively and operationally efficient. An allocatively efficient market is one in which equally risky propositions have equal access to funding. If an allocatively efficient market posts atypical interest rate differentials, they signal a profit opportunity to be exploited by arbitraging which should soon eliminate the anomaly.

An operationally efficient financial market is one in which transactions are carried out at least possible cost. Although the result is not usually stated explicitly, an operationally efficient market should quickly adopt any new technologies seen to offer net reductions in transaction costs. That is, any tensions between innovative and established ways of doing business should readily be resolved by calculating which alternative is the most profitable, and then adopting that method. On this interpretation, the theory of operationally efficient markets assumes that any costs of learning how to use new technologies can be readily assessed, and that there is no ambiguity about whether or not a new technology is available for adoption.

Practical considerations

In an allocatively efficient market, equilibrium prices incorporate any search, information production, and other transaction costs. However, an allocatively efficient market with positive transaction

The Economic Organisation of a Financial System

costs will not necessarily price securities exactly in accord with the CAPT or other theories discussed above under conditions of costless transacting. If arbitraging is costly, deviations from equilibrium interest rates will not stimulate offsetting trades unless the deviations are large enough to create a positive return net of those costs.

Hence for practical purposes allocative efficiency means that arbitraging removes any price or interest rate differences which are greater than the transactions costs incurred in carrying out the arbitrage. Thus, for example, in a CAPT with transaction costs the security market line is defined within bands defined by the magnitude of the costs. The risk–return relationship is defined more roughly than in the simpler version of the CAPT, but it still remains.

In practice, active markets seem likely to be competitive, and hence allocatively and operationally efficient in processing routine transactions, even if transactions costs are positive. However, not all markets exhibit equal degrees of operating efficiency. In particular, the smaller stock exchanges operate at higher unit costs than their larger counterparts. Similarly, smaller securities firms are less efficient than larger ones, again operating at higher unit costs than their larger counterparts.

As another practical matter, markets do not necessarily achieve the same efficiencies in handling new kinds of transactions as they do in consummating routine ones. For, new transactions involve experimenting, and it will not always be clear at the outset how to experiment cost-effectively, let alone efficiently. Nevertheless, cost-effective means of carrying out new transactions may be found after some trial and error, at least in those cases where the initial experiments do not prove unprofitable and are terminated.

Experimentation implies that financiers will sometimes enter new transactions without an objectively established profit rationale. For example, they may not be able to assess how much competition they might eventually face, and yet the degree of competition eventually manifest might be one of the most important influences on long-term profitability. Balanced against this unpredictability is another intangible – the first firm to enter a new form of business can gain cost advantages which help retard the entrance of competitors. Thus, if there are profits to be made by entering a market, fast action can sometimes prove as important as detailed profitability calculations. A financier may not know how profitable a venture will be, but can still hold the opinion that his likely future profits will be enhanced by experimenting rather than waiting. At the same time, he need not be willing or able to attach any precisely defined probability to this belief.[7]

If the foregoing view of financial experimentation is correct, some

System organisation and performance

experiments will prove to be unsuccessful. In practice, financiers do sometimes withdraw from certain lines of business after a trial period. Also in practice, the entry of numerous firms into a new market followed by a subsequent shakeout is typical, and illustrates the nature of experimentation. Some entrants experiment, some find successful means of remaining in business, while others are unable to do so and withdraw.

Completeness and incompleteness

A perfect financial market is a complete market, which again means that the neoclassical theory rules out certain practically important situations. To see this, consider first the properties of a complete market, after which incompleteness and the reasons for it will be examined. As a practical matter most financial systems exhibit at least a degree of incompleteness.

Properties of a complete market

A complete financial system is one in which the securities exchanged span all relevant states of the world; i.e. one which prices every relevant contingency. A financial system can be complete even though any given market or intermediary within it does not trade in all securities; what matters is that some combination of market traded securities and intermediary assets can be used to price each relevant state. In contrast, a financial system is incomplete if transactors define more states of the world than there are securities to span them.

Completeness is usually defined solely in terms of market traded securities. In some instances intermediaries create securities which help to span the states of the world, but even these securities will be related to market exchanges of some kind. Thus it suffices to discuss completeness in terms of market traded securities, and the present section does so.[8]

Complete and competitive financial markets are allocatively efficient under a relatively broad set of conditions, first outlined by Arrow (1964), and subsequently refined by other investigators. In addition, a complete market permits fully efficient risk sharing. The criteria to be used by firm management are also well defined: if markets are both complete and competitive shareholders unanimously prefer that firms select investment and production plans which maximise the market value of the firm's shares.

If financial markets are complete and in equilibrium, no agent with only publicly available information can profit from speculating against future price movements, since all future contingencies are appropriately priced relative to each other on the basis of the currently available information. However, an agent trading in such a market might still pay to acquire information everyone else had, because the information might permit the agent to gain greater utility from portfolio rebalancing at the equilibrium prices.

As a financial system develops, markets can become more nearly complete in a practical sense. For example, the recent development of index options, index futures and other similar derivative securities can be interpreted as tending to complete the set of tradable claims, because in some cases derivative instruments divide up risks differently than do the underlying securities. Indeed, the management oriented literature ascribes much financial innovation to increases in the risks associated with business, particularly international business.

These increases in risk have mainly developed since the first major OPEC oil price increase in 1974. They have received added impetus from the ensuing bursts of lending to Third World countries, and periods of world-wide inflation brought under control by stringently restrictive monetary policies in such countries as the USA and the UK. All these developments have contributed to increased volatility in world-wide financial markets. At the same time, world trade has expanded greatly, meaning that foreign exchange trading has expanded both because of trade flows and because of desires to hedge risks. In turn, all these devlopments have stimulated a revolution in financial markets' capabilities to trade more kinds of risks.

Incompleteness

Completeness has its greatest relevance in analysing decision making under risk. For under uncertainty, agents are not necessarily able to define the relevant states, let alone define securities to span them. In practice agents with limited reasoning powers and limited computational abilities may be unable to define the states which might obtain, unable to compute the consequences of dealing with a large number of states, or both. Thus, despite the possibility that increasingly sophisticated financial markets are becoming more nearly complete, it is unlikely that they will ever become wholly complete. Hence it becomes important to assess, as far as possible, the properties of incomplete markets.

In theory, the critical issues involved in assessing the performance of incomplete markets turn on the presence of trading constraints whose presence can prevent a market from being allocatively efficient. The actual presence of such constraints is more important than their source: removing constraints of one kind may remedy the effects caused by others. For example, removing constraints imposed by informational incompleteness can remedy constraints attributable to market incompleteness, and the reverse is also true (Ohlson, 1987). To see how either kind of trading constraint might be removed, consider a world in which all agents agree on the state definition and on the probabilities with which states occur; then suppose they all have the same information about all securities. As a result, if there are no other impediments to doing so, any existing trading constraints will create profit opportunities whose exploitation will remove the constraint.

Markets in information, or in new securities, will emerge as and when agents recognise the possibilities for mutual benefits from additional trading, at least so long as any costs associated with operating the governance structures needed to administer the incremental trades do not outweigh the benefits deriving from the trades. Incompleteness can thus be interpreted as evidence that neither exchange nor governance is costless. If claims against some states were not initially traded but there were no costs to doing so, the potential profits to be earned create incentives for new claims to be traded.

However, in many cases the nature of the costs which might prevent the emergence of new claims has not yet been explicated. For example, suppose a market's informational incompleteness is attributed solely to institutional restrictions. It may then be possible to introduce derivative securities or more frequent trading to complete the market. But without explaining the original source of such institutional restrictions, it is not clear how, or why, or with what effect the restriction is overcome.

Consequences of incompleteness

If a market is incomplete, some contingencies may not be competitively priced even if information is distributed symmetrically. Consequently incompleteness can lead to allocative inefficiency. In particular, risk sharing is not generally efficient in incomplete markets except under special circumstances. For example, if individuals' preferences are restricted appropriately, risk sharing can be efficient even in an incomplete market.

An incomplete market equilibrium (if it exists) need not have the same properties as a competitive equilibrium. For example, Grossman and Stiglitz (1977) observe that whenever markets are incomplete, the slope of consumers' budget lines can be altered by production decisions. As a result, efficient allocations cannot be attained without other conditions (such as one they term competitivity) being satisfied.

In practice, transactors' likely responses to incompleteness seem to depend on whether it seems profitable to remove it. For example, if it is not known how to trade claims against some states, but research into trading technology is cheap, expending research funds might be an initial response. If the research indicates a potential profit opportunity, and if the technology to overcome the incompleteness is available, transactors are likely to employ it. If these adjustment processes do not take place, there is presumptive evidence that removing the incompleteness is regarded as unprofitable. However, without further detailed investigation it will not be clear whether the conclusion should be attributed to a lack of demand for more securities, to the cost of creating new securities, or to incorrect assessments of the problem.

Dynamics of trading

A market with long-lived securities can be incomplete in a static sense but complete in a dynamic sense: it may be possible to complete the market dynamically by structuring portfolios whose composition changes through time. Indeed, the number of linearly independent, long-lived securities needed to achieve dynamic completion must only be as great as the largest number of events (partitions of possible future states) which can be distinguished at any point in time (Huang and Litzenberger, 1988).

It might further be conjectured that the possibilities of attaining dynamic completeness could be extended to situations where trading frequency increases. For example, if it became possible to trade more frequently than before, agents might find the number of relevant states reduced, meaning that fewer long-lived securities would be needed to achieve dynamic completeness. Such theoretical results have not yet been established rigorously. If they were, the conclusion that sophisticated financial systems, particularly those with much active trading, would suffer little from the problems of incompleteness might well follow.

Beja and Hakansson (1977) study aspects of disequilibrium trading in incomplete markets. They consider processes of both price and quantity adjustments, and ask: what will be communicated? what are communications worth? who benefits? How are the processes and any benefits affected by the passage of real time? These authors find that while disequilibrium trading can lead to allocatively efficient outcomes, the form of efficiency is defined, not with respect to initial endowments, but with respect to initial endowments plus wealth transfers. In such a setting, the trader who disturbs the equilibrium can benefit from the disequilibrium trading.

The Beja–Hakansson study is an important theoretical venture into a largely uncharted area. Nevertheless, it should be recognised that it remains a normative study in the neoclassical tradition. The existing theoretical results have limited applicability to positive studies aimed at describing real world trading dynamics. For, they do not take into account trading for the sake of creating new opportunities or trading on the basis of perceptual error (a result of bounded rationality) which might work against reaching an equilibrium. This is not to deny the value of theoretical work, which proceeds mainly by isolating phenomena and working out their implications one at a time. It is rather to recognise that the agenda for theoretical work incorporates many unanswered questions, and that neoclassical financial theory is not yet ready to answer all of them.

As one example, prices on even the major, active stock markets exhibit cycles which current theory does not explain. For example, the very sharp decline in US stock prices on 19 October 1987 was followed by similar declines in many other countries with very different economic statistics. As yet, no convincing explanations of why very different financial markets seem to be related in these ways have been offered, other than to postulate institutional impediments in some markets and a sort of contagion effect between markets. (For a pre-1987 discussion cf. Hogarth and Reder, 1986). The trading dynamics which lead to these effects are not yet well understood.

Securities markets and information

Informational asymmetries seem likely to have more profound effects on financial system organisation and performance than does market incompleteness. Neoclassical financial theory offers many results deriving from informational asymmetries, but as yet there have been few rigorous attempts to assess their importance using standard econometric techniques. On the other hand, this book has been able to show, with the help of institutional economics, that many structural differences in financial system organisation are explicable in terms of attempts to deal with informational asymmetries, particularly those arising under uncertainty rather than under risk. However, informational asymmetries have important effects on equilibrium even under risk.

Equilibrium with informational differences

Under asymmetric risk, securities price relationships do not always conform to the patterns discussed above. Consider first the questions related to differences in the depth of agents' information.[9] If securities are bought by more optimistic buyers, equilibrium prices can be higher than under symmetric information (E. Miller, 1977). On the other hand if enough securities are supplied so that at least some of them must be sold to pessimists, prices can be lower than if information were symmetrically distributed. Thus with asymmetric information there may be no single relationship between prices for the same risks, nor is there likely to be a market defined risk–return tradeoff. Rather, prices will be determined by a mix of prevailing views and the value of the trades effected by agents with differing views.

The equilibrium effects of informational asymmetries have been examined rigorously using rational expectations theory. A rational expectations equilibrium (REE) is one in which individuals form self-fulfilling conjectures about how events affect prices. One approach taken by rational expectations theorists to securities pricing recognises that investors may use the securities prices themselves as a source of information.[10]

The most fundamental question explored by rational expectations theories of securities price determination is whether differently informed agents will, through trading, be able to attain an equilibrium. A competitive equilibrium with complete markets will not exist in a world of asymmetrically informed individuals who do not learn from observing prices (cf. Huang and Litzenberger, 1988). With complete markets and asymmetric information, individuals must form some kind of rational expectations before an equilibrium can be attained.

In any REE with complete markets, equilibrium prices must reveal enough information to remove any initially prevailing differences. Such an equilibrium, in which prices reflect the collective information of all individuals taken together, is called a fully revealing REE. A fully revealing REE always exists in a world of perfectly competitive complete markets, and it is observationally indistinguishable from a competitive equilibrium in an artifical economy in which all individuals share the common information.

If markets are incomplete a REE need not exist, although there can still be a competitive equilibrium in which individuals ignore the informational content of the price system. If on the other hand individuals form rational expectations, a fully revealing REE will exist, and prices will be a sufficient statistic for conveying information. But then, given the equilibrium price, private information becomes redundant. This result is known as the Grossman–Stiglitz (1980) paradox, for if the information is costly, no one has an incentive to collect it. But without information collection, the equilibrium cannot exist.

The Grossman–Stiglitz paradox can be resolved if the REE is only partially revealing, meaning that securities prices only partially aggregate individual agents' information. A partially revealing REE exists if there is uncertainty about the aggregate supply of securities.[11] It is usually argued (cf. Huang and Litzenberger, 1988) that uncertainty of aggregate supply is unlikely to obtain in a share market economy, since the total supply of common shares (i.e. the number outstanding) is common knowledge. However, most discussions of share trading practices emphasise, at least in casual examinations, concepts of a float or available supply of uncertain magnitude. Accordingly, resolution of the Grossman–Stiglitz paradox by assuming uncertain securities supplies may be empirically less restrictive than is usually presumed.

A partially revealing REE offers a way of explaining why information is costly. Since information costs are as real as any other production costs, existence of a partially revealing REE does not necessarily imply market failure with respect to informational exchanges. Instead, the partially revealing REE means only that information is not freely produced by the workings of the marketplace. In a negative sense, then, conditions which define a partially revealing REE help to clarify the conditions under which some markets can exhibit costly information production.

Rational expectations equilibria have some peculiar properties. Milgrom and Stokey (1982) demonstrate that if an initial allocation is *ex ante* Pareto optimal the receipt of private information cannot create any incentives to trade, even though it can change prices. An agent's only motive for trading is the hope of finding an advantageous bet, but the willingness of other traders to accept such a bet means it cannot be advantageous to the first party. Trading can be consistent with more limited kinds of inference, but not with rational expectations. The Milgrom–Stokey results are based on the assumption that the agent receiving private information is not small in relation to the market: his actions are capable of affecting equilibrium prices. If the agent were small, he could benefit from private information production without affecting equilibrium prices. In addition, the Milgrom–Stokey results do not rule out that possibility that even an agent who is not small in relation to the market could still trade in situations where a Pareto optimal allocation did not obtain *ab initio*.

In summary, current theory recognises the importance of informational asymmetries to determining securities prices. It has not yet defined theoretical conditions under which asymmetries' effects can be ignored, either because they can somehow be offset or because they are inconsequential. Nor has there yet been substantial progress in assessing any effects of informational asymmetries empirically.[12] The tasks are important ones, because determining when asymmetries do not matter (or do not matter much) would also help to define the kinds of practical circumstances where informational differences might be significant. The further delineation of circumstances where the effects of asymmetries are material would in turn clarify any effects on securities prices.

Experimental studies at the level of individual markets offer some support for rational expectations models. Plott and Sunder (1982) simulate market trading with insider information, finding that in some cases the predictions of rational expectations models are attained, although they also find other experimental conditions under which rational expectations equilibria are not attained. Thus the results suggest that whether or not rational expectations equilibria might be attained in practice can depend rather delicately on information initially available to agents and possibly on the particular characteristics of markets in which they are traded. As yet there is little information as to when or to what extent such conditions are present in practice.

Differences in breadth of information

Merton (1987) examines the equilibrium effects of differences in the breadth of information using an index version of the CAPT. In essence, Merton postulates that agents only trade in securities about which they have information. For simplicity of analysis, all informed agents have the same information, but there are also agents who possess no information about certain securities. In the resulting equilibrium, securities prices depend on how knowledge regarding the securities is distributed among the agents.

Merton's results offer can explain a number of empirical phenomena. Merton finds that expected returns are lower on firms which are better known, a result consistent with security market line estimates which show the SML to be flatter than is predicted by capital asset pricing theory. Merton's findings are also consistent with the existence of small firm effects, and with observations that firms with larger specific variance have higher returns, even when adjusted for size. On the basis of his theory and a summary of others' empirical studies, Merton conjectures that a firm with a small investor base (relative to the value of its outstanding shares) might have shares whose returns offers a premium of some 3% over that predicted by the SML.

Merton's model explains still other phenomena: his theory holds that if firms are little-known, their securities will be underpriced, and

System organisation and performance

the firms' managers will face incentives to expand its investor base. This is consistent with the observation that some firms, or their agents, circulate well-known research reports to new investors. On Merton's theory, this could reduce a firm's cost of capital, as could listing the firm's shares on a larger stock exchange. In addition, informing investors might be more effective if publicity releases were bunched in time, as sometimes seems to occur.

Merton's theory may also explain the differing popularity of rights issues. It is well known that some firms use rights issues more than do others. The practice of using rights issues also shows substantial variation between countries. The theory indicates that firms with a small investor base, large specific variance, or both, might face more steeply sloping demand curves for their shares than other firms. Expansion of the investor base and increased investment expenditures would in these cases coincide more closely with negotiated underwritings than with rights issues to investors already familiar with the shares.

At this writing, Merton's results are preliminary, requiring both further theoretical investigation and detailed empirical study. Nevertheless, they are valuable for providing a setting which differs importantly from the traditional neoclassical predictions. Moreover, they provide these new insights without sacrificing either the clarity of standard neoclassical results or the ease with which they can be derived mathematically.

Effects of uncertainty

The effects of uncertainty on prices pose even greater theoretical challenges than do differences in estimated risks. At the theoretical level, Harrison and Kreps (1978) show that if agents trade speculatively, market equilibrium prices may not reflect any underlying fundamental values, but depend solely on agents' expectations. Speculative trading occurs when agents attempt to outguess each other, in effect trading on the basis of game theoretic considerations.

Conjectures regarding behavioural uncertainties (the reactions of other agents) importantly affect the prices at which securities trade, and the quantities in which they are exchanged. It is not obvious that agents with bounded rationality will make the self-fulfilling predictions assumed in rational expectations theories, and as a result it is not clear to what extent rational expectations theories can be regarded as descriptively realistic. Moreover, these questions are not likely to be resolved until negotiation processes under uncertainty have been modelled as explicitly, and investigated to the same extent, as have the negotiations of agents using rational expectations. Then, comparisons between the two approaches may be possible.

Even if negotiation processes under uncertainty can be more clearly structured in future theoretical research, they are likely to pose such problems as the existence of multiple equilibria, equilibria whose characteristics are highly sensitive to minor changes in the specification of the negotiation processes, or combinations of the two. Thus the problems of working out results analytically are considerably more difficult than the already difficult problems encountered in rational expectations theory.

In practice, securities sometimes seem to be exchanged without any explicit attempts at valuation. For example, equity positions in new ventures are sometimes demanded as a condition of providing financing, but neither party may have a objectively based notion of what the shares are worth. Financiers take such an equity position because they wish to share proportionately in the success of ventures if it should turn out to be highly profitable. However at the time of making the investment financiers may not be able to calculate the expected returns on their investments with any precision. Nor, for that matter, may the client.

Empirical findings

Some empirical studies suggest that stock prices vary about theoretically calculated fundamental values, sometimes remaining either overpriced or underpriced relative to these fundamentals for a period of several years (cf. Kleidon, 1986). The effects can be explained either by the workings of efficient markets and prices based only on fundamental values, or by hypotheses that prices are based on speculative assessments. At present it does not seem possible to discriminate between the two explanations. If the speculative hypotheses are correct, they may be interpreted in terms of expectations formed either under conditions of environmental uncertainty (games against a neutral nature) or under conditions of behavioural uncertainty regarding other traders' strategies (games against either cooperative or hostile opponents).

The explanations of relative prices provided by the CAPT, the APT, and other arbitrage-based theories fit the data relatively well in public markets where securities are actively traded, as has been shown by many careful empirical studies. However, arbitrage based theories do not apply equally well to all markets. The markets for smaller issues are not always allocatively efficient, as evidenced, for example, by the small firm effect.

Possible limits to the neoclassical explanations may also be indicated by differences in return on securities (of comparable risk) traded in different international markets. Arbitraging between different developed countries does not seem to take place to any appreciable extent, even in very active stock markets. It seems to be inhibited both by institutional and regulatory constraints on the one hand and lack of knowledge on the other, particularly the knowledge in breadth emphasised by Merton. In these cases, the implied interest rates on securities differ so substantially that few deny their existence. However, the factors contributing to the differences are not well understood, and require further study.

A related phenomenon has been noted by Mehra and Prescott (1985) in the context of an experimental study. Mehra and Prescott argue that even basic financial data seem to be inconsistent with macroeconomic data. They simulate an economy with crudely specified but nevertheless realistic parameters in which equity premiums (the difference in yields between shares and bonds) should be very much lower than the equity premiums reflected in US data. Since equity premiums are much lower in Japan than in the United States,[13] the Mehra–Prescott simulations may apply more closely to that country than to the US. But even so, the differences in equity premiums between the two countries then remain to be explained. At present, the only available explanations of the inter-country differences emphasise the differing natures of their institutions, and the governmental pressures which seem capable of impeding arbitraging between the markets.

Intermediation and finance

The ways in which intermediaries set securities prices, and the ways in which their operations affect the organisation of a financial system, are less completely worked out than are the theories of securities markets. Nevertheless, a number of results are available. Currently received neoclassical analyses explain why intermediaries diversify, and why they can realise scale economies from screening. Empirical studies estimate characteristics of intermediary cost functions. Institutional economics provides preliminary analyses of the economics of internal diversification or the costs of internal information processing.

On the other hand, many important aspects of financial intermediation have not yet been studied: for example, explanations of intermediaries' strategic behaviour, or of how decisions to experiment are reached, are not available. In part the number of unanswered questions is a function of the fact that while securities prices and market performance have been studied extensively, intermediary activity has only begun to be examined.

The Economic Organisation of a Financial System

Intermediary pricing practices

If intermediaries deal in competitive or contestable markets, competition will force them to offer market terms for the funds and the services they sell. While there is little empirical information about the extent to which intermediaries actually do operate in competitive or contestable markets,[14] the institutional economics of this book argues that individual financial markets can differ considerably in competitiveness. Non-competitive market conditions can persist where there are impediments to arbitraging or intermediary links with other markets, and where the market has barriers to direct entry.

In fact, since many of the markets in which intermediaries deal are not suited to arbitraging transactions, inter-market interest rate relationships depend mainly on competition between the intermediaries which assemble aggregate portfolios of these instruments.[15] Even so, it is not easy to assess the extent to which intermediaries have oligopolistic power to set their interest rates. Nor is it easy to determine the relationships which will obtain between the different markets served by such intermediaries.

Effects of asymmetric information

Current theory recognises that intermediaries generally have less information (in depth) about a transaction's risk than will the client.[16] Hence intermediaries must employ their governance capabilities intensively, both for intially screening risks and for dealing with clients on a continuing basis. Intermediaries deal with problems of asset specificity that do not arise in public securities markets transactions, but this also gives them advantages over markets. Their greater monitoring capabilities give them greater opportunties to learn about individual clients, and greater capabilities for effecting *ex post* adjustments. Hence, intermediaries can more readily entertain finnancings under conditions of asymmetric risk or of uncertainty. Even so, intermediary transactions show such effects of asymmetries as the credit rationing next discussed.

Asymmetries and credit rationing

Even if intermediaries charge competitive interest rates on the loans they extend, they cannot always equate the quantities of funds demanded with their supply (Stiglitz and Weiss, 1981). In some such cases, profit maximising intermediaries will find it optimal to use credit rationing, even at equilibrium.

When facing a pool of risks which it can only assess in terms of average quality, the profit maximising intermediary perceives loan profitability as a function of both the loans' interest rate and their average quality. Then, if interest rate increases induce clients to take greater risks than before, a rate increase can lower both average loan quality and the optimal amount the intermediary supplies. Moreover, the new combination can be less profitable than the originally chosen one. In these circumstances interest rate increases will not necessarily eliminate any excess demand for loans. Hence at any given interest rate and average loan quality there is no guarantee that the quantity demanded will be the same as that the intermediary finds it optimal to supply, and equilibrium credit rationing can result.

As yet, empirical estimates of the possible significance of equilibrium credit rationing are not available. But to determine its empirical importance, it is necessary to distinguish credit rationing from other, related phenomena. For example, market observers sometimes attribute (what they regard as) excessively high interest rates to credit rationing. What these observers seem to mean is that the supply curve for funds does not lie sufficiently far enough to the right. However, the apparently restricted supply can be due simply to different valuations based on different information. If financiers view risks more pessimistically than do their clients, and especially if the clients do not recognise the difference in views, interest rates will appear to clients as too high. There is no need to postulate an adverse selection effect for this phenomenon to occur, and if the adverse selection effect is not present, there need not be credit rationing in the technical sense discussed above.

Cycles and intermediary activity

Intermediaries sometimes enter new lines of business in a cyclical fashion, displaying an initial burst of intense activity, followed later by a decline in the volume of business. Profit rates on such new businesses are likely first to be negative, then rise rapidly to greater than competitive levels, and finally fall back to competitive levels. This profit cycle at first reflects the costs of learning a new business, then exploitation of a profit opportunity not subject to intense competition, followed finally by the entry or threatened entry of other firms which reduces profits to competitive levels.

Cycles in intermediary activity are at least partly attributable to adaptive learning processes, especially when learning occurs under uncertainty. New knowledge may be acquired in bursts rather than continuously, and acquiring the new knowledge may involve an outlay to cover fixed costs.[17] If the newly entered line of business is successful, it is likely to return high profit rates until competitors learn to emulate the innovator. Hence the pathbreaking activities of a given financier are likely to attract others to the business, increasing the volume of activity. Behavioural uncertainty regarding competitors' possible reactions can amplify this cyclicality. Many firms try to deal with uncertainty by emulation, which means that a number of them sometimes enter a new business at the same time. In some cases they may even terminate certain experiments more or less simultaneously.

Lending to Third World sovereign governments offers an example of a cycle in intermediary activity. International banks first believed such lending was highly lucrative, because they underestimated the risks involved. The international banks initially failed to recognise that repayment of sovereign loans depends on the taxing powers of the borrowing governments, and hence on the earning power of the economies they represent. They probably also failed to take into account the excesses of lending which followed as banks decided almost simultaneously to enter the developing Third World loan markets.

The international banks eventually realised the similarity between sovereign and corporate loans, after which they were able to specify countries' ability to pay more clearly. But by this time, many loans were already in arrears: recognition came too late to avoid difficulty. The arrears led in turn to disillusionment with the line of business, and new lending was sharply cut back by nearly all banks at the same time. Eventually the disillusionment was in turn transformed into today's increasingly realistic appraisals.

Intermediaries and new securities

Intermediaries handle different kinds of transactions than do markets, and thus perceive the needs for new securities differently. This difference in perception, combined with the fact that intermediary assets are less easily traded than are marketable securities, contributes to developing new instruments. As one example, interest rate swaps owe their existence at least partially to the intermediaries' own portfolio needs. Interest rate swaps were designed to help match individual intermediaries' patterns of interest revenues and interest costs, thus helping them to manage risk. As a second example, other portfolio management needs led to the development of securitisation. For instance, an intermediary which can originate many more residential mortgage loans than it can fund has an incentive to sell mortgage backed securities.

Routine and innovative transacting

In practice, routine transactions are often administered according to established rules of thumb. Under risk, the rules of thumb relate mainly to methods of estimating risk and to determining appropriate interest rates. For example, most firms with taxable income will regard debt as cheaper than equity because its interest is deductible from taxable income. They may use maximum gearing ratios to try to take account of informational asymmetries and any possible bankruptcy costs. These rules of thumb may restrict financing patterns: if a given transaction does not conform to conventional parameters, it may be avoided. What financiers regard as standard transactions are not always open to extended negotiation.

Risk, routine, and innovation

Established practices result from agents' using what they regard as the most efficient mechanisms currently available. Having learned how to perform some transactions quickly, easily, and efficiently, financiers come to regard the transactions as routine, involving only well-known risks. Although it is both a *non sequitur* and a conclusion not warranted by successful experience with a restricted set of transactions, the attitude that certain transactions can be handled routinely and efficiently is sometimes converted to a belief that the entire financial system is efficient. Agents holding these views are likely to regard proposals for innovation rather sceptically, and may be quite unwilling to consider new transaction forms. Fortunately, however, other agents realise that innovation can return profits above normal levels by creating, at least for a time, a degree of monopolistic advantage. As agents struggle to resolve the tension between the two opposing views, the system is sometimes innovative, sometimes not. Since the balance is usually an uncertain one, it exhibits cyclicality: bursts of innovative activity can be followed by periods in which relatively little innovation occurs.

Uncertainty and innovation

Under uncertainty, agents need to deal both with differences in information and with the possibility that their contracts are incomplete. Thus, incomplete contracts are likely to incorporate *ex post* adjustment mechanisms. As a result, governance under uncertainty is more costly than under risk, but it can also lead to more innovative transaction forms. For, under uncertainty it can be more difficult to evolve standard ways of doing business. The very fact that financiers recognise that they cannot stipulate all transaction circumstances at the outset indicates their willingness to experiment with new circumstances, at least so long as they believe the venture offers some chance of lucrative returns.

Clients offer terms they believe necessary to obtain financing. If they know of or can find alternative financing possibilities, clients will select the best available one. However, clients may have limited knowledge of alternatives, particularly if they deal with intermediaries, because they often complete a transaction with the first intermediary willing to finance their proposal. Information about alternative arrangements can be difficult to obtain, at least without expensive and time consuming negotiation. Thus client behaviour also depends on a balance of tensions, which again creates a tendency toward cyclicality. In this case bursts of search activity can be followed by periods in which clients generally use established financing arrangements. As with financiers, emulation affects the balance: if competitors are seen as innovative, a given client may be more tempted to engage in similar kinds of innovation.

Effects on system organisation

Agents are not only more likely to innovate under uncertainty, they are also more likely to perceive uncertainty whenever they attempt to innovate. In either case, innovative transactions may first be administered provisionally, using mechanisms which in subsequent transactions can be supplanted by others if new methods are discovered to be more cost-effective. Nevertheless, the economics of innovation is partly based on the same principles as the economics of handling routine transactions. Transactions are entered, and governance structures chosen, because they promise (on the basis of calculations made with varying degrees of precision, depending on the transaction's informational conditions) to generate incremental sources of net revenue. Governance structures are replaced or modified if new ones offering greater potential for reducing costs, or for handling transaction information more effectively, can be found.

Summary

This chapter examined how the aggregate effects of individual transactions determine a financial system's organisational structure and performance. It first considered theories of securities prices, examining the properties of a perfect market as well as the meaning and importance of financial market completeness. The effects of informational differences on equilibrium securities prices were next

System organisation and performance

addressed. Finally, some comments were offered regarding the impacts of uncertainty.

The chapter next examined how intermediaries affect system structure. The effects of asymmetric information and their implications for credit rationing were discussed, as were cycles in intermediary activity. The role of intermediaries in devising new securities was mentioned.

Finally, the chapter considered the kinds of governance structures most likely to be used with routine transacting on the one hand, with innovative transacting on the other. The choices of structures closely match the choices of structures to deal with risk and uncertainty respectively. Implications for system organisation and for bursts of innovation were drawn.

Notes

1 The value of this approach has recently been illustrated by Merton (1987), who uses neoclassical theory to introduce informational effects on securities prices and, consequently, on differences in financing costs.
2 The assumptions stated here were not, of course, in the original Modigliani–Miller development, which depended on risk classes and no bankruptcy. The version given here is based on both the original Modigliani–Miller propositions and subsequent further study.
3 Problems associated with externalities may still arise, but to consider them here would distract from the central theme of the discussion.
4 Chapter 7 discussed how the CAPT explains diversification.
5 In perfect markets, a firm cannot affect its cost of capital by issuing securities of different risks, even though the securities have different equilibrium rates. For, the weighted average of the different rates will equal the rate at which the firm's total cash flows are discounted. Dividing up a risk does not affect the discount rate applying it.
6 The conclusions of the APT can be derived without assuming that risks are viewed symmetrically by different agents.
7 Recall the comments in Chapter 2 regarding the Savage (1951) results.
8 Additional details regarding how intermediaries create new securities are, however, discussed on p. 144.
9 The important distinction between differences in depth and in breadth is due to Merton (1987), whose work on this topic is discussed in the next section.
10 The following summary is heavily indebted to Huang and Litzenberger (1988).
11 At the time of writing this book, little more is known about the properties of a partially revealing REE, particularly in multi-period economies. Indeed, even in a single period economy only one special case of a partially revealing REE has been studied in detail – that with negative exponential utility functions and normally distributed returns.

The Economic Organisation of a Financial System

12 The exceptional case of Merton's work on differences in the breadth of information (1987) is discussed in the next section.
13 How much lower depends on the way adjustments are made for different kinds of assets and for differences between the countries' accounting practices. Nevertheless, after such adjustments there still seem to be differences in prices for shares of similar risk.
14 Nathan and Neave (1989) provide some results for three Canadian financial industries.
15 Any competition between intermediaries and markets is limited by their differential governance capabilities.
16 In some cases they may have more, but as this would seem to occur much less frequently than the opposite situation, we emphasise the latter.
17 Merton (1987) suggests that new information may also be supplied in bursts.

Chapter nine

Financial system change and performance

This chapter examines the forces which stimulate financial system change and shows how they can be used to improve system performance. System change occurs as financiers search, in response to changing economic conditions and to changing knowledge, for new ways of increasing profits. To a lesser extent, system change also occurs as a response to regulatory change. Whatever its current form and nature of change, a financial system is unlikely to be free of performance problems and changes in regulation are usually intended to ameliorate such problems. Designing remedial regulation is best approached by recognising and taking advantage, as far as possible, of the forces which drive system change.

Performance problems arise in most financial systems. To explain how they arise and how to deal with them most effectively, it is useful first to review the economic forces underlying financial system change. Then, the chapter discusses remedies whose effectiveness can be enhanced by using these forces to advantage.

Forces of change

Financial system change occurs as financiers search for new ways of increasing profits, either through generating new revenues or through reducing costs. Change is manifest in the ways financial firms structure their organisations, enter new markets, and develop new products. The changes initiated by a profit seeking firm are intended to enhance its performance, and if a financial system is competitive, or if its markets are fully contestable, the benefits from successful changes will be passed on to the public. Hence in a competitive system, change will also enhance system efficiency.

The search for greater profits is conducted by financiers whose rationality is bounded. While experiments are intended to increase profitability, they represent attempts which are not certain to succeed. Financiers usually begin an experiment with only a rough idea of its likely profitability. As they learn more about the new activity financiers form new estimates, on the basis of which they may expand the line, continue the activity at present levels, or even abandon it. All outcomes are possible, particularly since profitability can depend importantly on competitor reactions or other forms of environmental change which are difficult to assess in advance.

Thus any explanation of financial system change should begin by examining the information available to the agents at the time they undertake the experiments, and continue by showing how that information changes over the course of the experiment. The possibility that actions might change in the light of new information does not mean they were originally taken irrationally, but rather that they were intendedly rational choices based on the information available at the time. Since not all experiments will be successful, a full explanation of the learning process should be able to account for failures as well as successes.

Underlying economics

The principal forces of change within modern financial systems are precipitous, long-term declines in the costs of computing and communications. These changes have radically altered the economics of financial activity, and will continue to affect it importantly for some time. The changes have created new profit opportunities by changing the costs of individual transactions and the costs of using existing organisational forms. The proliferation of new products and changes in organisational mechanisms are both economic responses to these kinds of changes.

One of the most important changes is manifest in client access. Retail clients can now deal with their domestic financial institutions using automated teller machines in many parts of the world. In some countries home banking is becoming a reality, as is increased access to securities markets through home computers. Corporations face similar changes in access: many businesses can now effect most financial transactions using their own in-house computers.

Lower computing and communications costs have stimulated a proliferation of new financial products and services. Computers can manipulate transaction parameters more cheaply and with lower error rates than can human beings, permitting financial firms to offer the precise tailoring of terms characteristic of many new products or services. At the same time, financiers are coming to understand more clearly what elements are common to different kinds of financial transactions, meaning that they can offer innovative products and services which are processed on the computer systems they already have in place.

The greater understanding of product commonality both lowers the costs of offering new products and affects the traditional boundaries of financial organisations: the new understanding of transaction commonality means that financiers are discovering new forms of scope economies. For example, banks, investment bankers, and insurance companies are becoming increasingly alike, conducting the same kinds of businesses using the same kinds of computing and distribution facilities. They are also learning to use computer-based expert systems to help overcome the staff training problems associated with offering a large variety of new products.

Changes in computing and communications capabilities have decreased the costs of many kinds of international financial transactions. At the same time, new forms of international finance were stimulated in the 1970s and early 1980s by oil price changes, new patterns of financing trade, more flexible exchange rates, and more volatile interest rates in many countries. All these changes combined to present new profit opportuntities in international banking, foreign currency and risk trading, and in the international securities business.

The new forms of business have stimulated much more active arbitraging between at least the larger and more active financial markets, both domestic and international. As a result, the world's financial sytem is becoming increasingly integrated, both between countries and within individual countries. While smaller domestic markets are unlikely to become as completely integrated as large international ones, integration of the financial system can be expected to continue for the foreseeable future.

Regulation

The 1970s' and 1980s' moves toward financial deregulation in many parts of the developed world are largely responses to the changes just discussed. As financial system activities have become more closely integrated, financiers have pressed for still greater freedom to combine activities in new ways, and these changes have created pressures for further deregulation. As one example, international financial business tends to move to the most benign (generally least restrictive) regulatory jurisdictions. Economies with restrictive, costly regulations thus tend to lose business to others, unless they adopt less stringent regulatory attitudes or can persuade others to maintain similarly high standards. Similarly, within domestic markets financial business tends to move toward jurisdictions with the least costly regulations.

Changes in regulation are sometimes followed by changes in

system organisation, but these changes can be simply formal responses rather than substantial innovations. The major forces of financial system change are economic, and much regulatory change consists of rewriting the rules as regulators perceive the effects of economic change. That is, regulatory changes are usually framed to recognise changes in existing business patterns. But it was changes in underlying economics which first stimulated development of the new business patterns.

As a general matter regulation does not usually and significantly affect market-intermediary boundaries or most of the types of business done by intermediaries, although it can influence the ownership arrangements used by financiers to conduct their businesses. In these cases, regulation is successful only in forcing the proscribed business on to the books of different legal entities rather than preventing it from taking place altogether.

The foregoing is not to claim that regulation is always and everywhere ineffective. On the contrary, some regulations have been effective over quite long periods. For example, in the United States, Britain, and Japan banks have been prevented from dealing in securities (apart from a few authorised exceptions such as trading in government bills and bonds) for many years. But these prohibitions have not usually prevented financiers from lobbying for permission to enter the securities business, or even in some cases from experimenting with new forms of actually doing so.

Towards an international currency?

Some observers believe the increasing integration of the world's financial system will lead eventually to the emergence of international currencies, possibly even to a single world currency. Proponents of the single currency view argue that arbitrage and international intermediation might well flourish even more vigorously in a world which used a common unit of account. If international business finds the attendant cost savings sufficiently important, the private sector may well initiate more frequent use of common units of account. For example, increasing amounts of international securities issues are being denominated in European Currency Units.

But whatever the responses of private sector constituencies, they are likely to be opposed by at least some national governments.[1] The reasons for government opposition are many, and a complete analysis of them is beyond the scope of this book. Accordingly, only one financial factor will be examined here: the possibility that increasing a country's money supply could sometimes be a cheap and convenient way of borrowing funds to finance a budgetary deficit.[2]

Financial system change and performance

Eventually, the government which resorts to the printing press to finance its operations pays a price in terms of inflation. In more extreme cases, the price can include loss of international confidence and possibly capital flight. All three outcomes can hinder prospects for economic growth, but over the near term the incentives facing a government can still favour financing a budgetary deficit by printing money. For, information regarding how much has been borrowed through monetary expansion can take a long time to be disseminated through financial markets. Thus the price to be paid can often be deferred long enough to make the initial monetary expansion politically attractive, especially to a relatively weak government.

The ability to expand the money supply without affecting the value of the currency adversely is now more tightly constrained than was formerly the case. In today's international currency markets with their modern computing and communications facilities, rapid monetary expansion is more quickly recognised and reflected in currency values than was the case, say, twenty years ago. Even so, the information standard (Wriston, 1988–89) does not yet remove entirely the possibility that sovereign governments can take independent action without immediately paying a price in changed currency values. This is particularly true of smaller countries whose monetary and fiscal actions do not receive the same intense international scrutiny as do those of the larger developed economies.

Accordingly, if they cannot find equally cheap, equally convenient substitute ways of borrowing, at least some countries' governments will be reluctant to surrender their powers of money creation. The argument has all the greater force when it is recognised that a great many countries face incentives to use the printing press episodically, even if they do not continuously resort to it. Under President Johnson, for example, the United States ran what were then relatively large federal deficits which were mainly financed by monetary expansion.

The foregoing argues that for financial reasons alone there is little likelihood of individual nations' universally agreeing on the desirability of a single currency, any more than a single type of indebtedness would likely serve the multitudinous purposes of all private sector borrowers. In the language of earlier chapters, borrowing through the printing press is financing which uses a particular type of governance mechanism,[3] while financing through debt issues is another.

Changing governance mechanisms can offer new advantages, but also the surrender of existing ones. If the loss of existing advantage is not to prevent change, the proponents of change must show that the existing advantages will either be retained or compensated for. If not, arguments for retaining the status quo may well prevail. Thus the principal question for analysis of the desirability of retaining the power to finance budgetary deficits by printing money is whether the proposed alternative governance offers net benefits to all involved parties. For the reasons outlined above, it is not obvious that this is presently so.

Performance problems

In a competitive or contestable financial system, the forces of change can increase allocative and operational efficiency. But whatever the resulting degree of efficiency attained in practice, a financial system will usually exhibit a spectrum of performance problems. For instance, many financial systems are imperfectly integrated, and exhibit gaps or fragmentation. In other cases externalities can mean that the mix of private sector activities differs from what is deemed to be socially optimal. Market failure can be a performance problem in that some transactions which would be desirable under symmetric information are prevented by informational asymmetries from occurring. Financiers can acquire market power, an outcome which is not usually judged to be socially optimal. Finally, episodic information release can create a variety of dynamic instabilities, with both private and societal effects. Each of these performance problems is discussed in turn.

Fragmentation and its causes

Fragmentation means that transactions in different parts of a financial system are not closely linked, either by arbitraging or by intermediation. A complete financial market with no transactions costs cannot exhibit fragmentation, but trading between incomplete markets can be inhibited by the factors contributing to the incompleteness, such as transactions costs and informational asymmetries. Since asymmetrically distributed information and transaction costs are ubiquitous real world phenomena, it becomes important to assess how and to what extent private sector financiers can cope with any fragmentation resulting from them. Not all factors are always present simultaneously: any single factor, or a combination, can explain a particular instance of fragmentation.

The main symptom of fragmentation is that the same risks bear different interest rates in different parts of the system: the law of one price does not apply because of impediments to transacting. In practice, the most important cause of fragmentation seems to be bounded rationality, for this can lead to estimates of high transactions costs or asymmetric views of profitability. As a consequence of bounded rationality, transactions do not occur, either because they are regarded as unprofitable, or because financiers do not know how to realise the profits which they believe might be present. To look at the same problem in another way, since new forms of arbitraging transactions develop quickly in competitive and sophisticated markets, fragmentation can also be regarded as a characteristic of underdevelopment.

At any point in time, it is possible to find situations where fragmentation is changing. Increasing integration has eliminated some kinds of fragmentation, as shown for example by the development of the interest rate swap market. This now highly active international market place saw only a few brokered transactions in the early 1970s when the idea of interest rate swaps was first being developed. As the profit opportunities in making such swaps came increasingly to be realised, new means to exploit them were developed. There are also situations in which fragmentation persists: the two-tier share markets in both the United Kingdom and the United States are instances. As mentioned earlier, arbitraging between the two tiers does not occur because institutions find it cost-effective to conduct research and to trade only in the larger issues.

The observed degree of system fragmentation depends on how a system is defined, and some discussions assume implicitly that financial systems are national or regional in scope. In such cases, the importance of fragmentation can be underemphasised. For example, if a financial system is examined on a national basis it will not appear to be fragmented even if it is not closely linked to the financial systems of other countries. However on a world scale, present day financial systems are only partly integrated. Even after taking into account the recent, rapid integration of some kinds of transactions, national financial systems are still largely fragmented from each other. Similarly, on a domestic scale parts of a regional system can still be fragmented from the rest of the national system.

Externalities

Externalities are third party effects created when interest rates do not fully reflect a transaction's net social benefits. Externalities can mean either that costs are imposed on society, or that social benefits are forgone. In the first case, interest rates charged to clients do not reflect a transaction's costs to society. In the second case, transactions are not entered because the rates on them are unattractive to financiers.

There are two conditions which, if satisfied, justify public sector intervention to deal with externalities. First, the private sector must not find it profitable to eliminate the problem on its own. Second, the costs of public sector intervention should not exceed its potential benefits. In such cases intervention can reap net social benefits.

As one example, externalities are suffered when very high volumes of public market trading overload exchange capabilities, slowing execution and delivery of trades. This situation occurred in October 1987, when trades between instruments sold on different exchanges – the futures, options, and stock exchanges – could be completed only after long delays. Worse still, settlement of the trades was sometimes delayed for even longer periods. In the future, such problems would prove less serious if cost-effective improvements to completing and settling trades could be found. One of the problems is that the different exchanges, operating under different regulatory jurisdictions, each settles separately with its trading clients. If the various regulatory bodies involved in supervising the different exchanges could devise effective net settlement procedures, traders could make more efficient use of their capital than is now possible, and an externality would be removed.

The effects of externalities can be observed in many different kinds of financial transactions. In export finance, improved financing arrangements can sometimes increase exports, benefiting society through increasing employment in both export-related and other industries. Government-provided export credit insurance covering the political risks that would otherwise be faced by private financiers is sometimes used to stimulate increases in export financing activity, thus capturing such benefits. As another example, additional financial and related businesses moved to London after the deregulatory actions known as the Big Bang. The more benign regulatory climate stimulated increases in financial activity. In turn, the additional activity led to employment increases, not just in financial services, but also in such industries as computing, communications, and office construction.

Some externalities can be eliminated by producing additional public information. There seem to be at least three instances of practical importance. First, additional information can sometimes improve production decisions: e.g. the educational activities of governments or of small business lenders can ultimately improve small business management. Second, increased information can expand the scope for risk sharing: e.g. increased knowledge about potential returns on smaller countries' stock exchanges can stimulate additional investment. Third, transactions which would be inhibited by *ex ante* informational asymmetries can sometimes be facilitated simply by ensuring that the information will be observed publicly *ex post*. For example, investors might be more willing to buy the securities of financial intermediaries whose portfolios were rated periodically by inspectors who publicly announced their findings.

Theory also argues that additional information can improve intertemporal allocations of wealth between savings and consumption. For example, more information about certain kinds of savings instruments can increase a nation's level of savings, and the increase can be a beneficial change under many (but not all) macroeconomic circumstances.

Market failure

Market failure occurs when transactors are unable to agree on terms, and are therefore unwilling to exchange funds[4] (Akerlof, 1970). For example, when there are informational asymmetries which financiers do not know how to resolve, they may be unwilling to advance any funds. In other cases a market can simply be too small to serve profitably using currently available technology. In still other cases market failure can result from a lack of confidence in either the financial system or the underlying economy. Financiers' confidence can be affected by the way a client conducts business, by such economic variables as the rate of inflation, and by domestic or international political developments.

Market power

If financiers possess or can acquire market power, they have an incentive to exercise it at their clients' expense. But financiers can only acquire such power in less than fully competitive markets which are also imperfectly contestable markets. Many observers assert that parts of a given financial system are not competitive, and while they are surely correct in at least some instances,[5] definitive empirical evidence to substantiate such claims does not seem to be available. Indeed, some empirical findings suggest that some financial markets are more competitive than is popularly believed (Nathan and Neave, 1989).

Market power is sometimes thought to arise from regulatory barriers to entry, but these barriers do not seem to be a very important source. History shows that regulations are usually ineffective in preventing profitable economic activity, particularly over longer time periods. This is not to claim that all regulation is ineffective, but to point out that many regulations are not as effective as popularly believed.

For example, regulation in many countries has successfully kept banking and the securities business in separately organised firms, at least until recently. On the other hand, regulation usually does not prevent informal cooperative arrangements or interlocking share arrangements from developing. As an example of ineffective regulation, United States unit banking laws have for many years been circumvented by using various forms of holding companies. Thus, regulatory barriers may be less of an obstacle to competition than they first appear, but this is still no argument to retain them if it can be shown that there are areas where they inhibit competition.

It is not clear that all natural barriers to entry can serve as a source of market power. Even if many financial firms exhibit increasing or constant returns to scale, scope economies can make competition between them active enough to create a contestable market. For, scope economies (which seem to have been enhanced by recent advances in computing and communications) raise the possibility of hit and run entry wherever profits above competitive levels are being earned. For example, banks' current entry into the securities business might well reduce the profit levels formerly enjoyed by securities firms. For these reasons, the threat of potential entry can constrain financiers from earning returns above competitive levels.

There is at least one form of natural barrier which does seem to be quite effective in preventing entry – that arising from informational asymmetries. Such informational asymmetries can persist for long periods of time. For example, even though emerging stock markets may adopt fairly stringent prohibitions against insider trading, the regulations are difficult to police and information can remain asymmetrically distributed despite concerted efforts by regulators.

Dynamic instabilities

Chapter 8 discussed how cycles arise in such businesses as property and casualty insurance. These cycles can be regarded as a form of dynamic instability, but the more extreme forms next discussed result from crises in confidence rather than from mere changes in profitability estimates. The effects of crises in confidence are considerably more important: they can be manifest as runs on banks or as stock market crashes.

Since crises of confidence represent sudden changes in expectations, it is important to examine how the changes occur. Whether expectations relate to securities prices or to the value of intermediary assets, they are usually formed by combining information from different sources. Indeed, expectations formation seems to represent a combination of intendedly objective economic analyses and assumptions regarding the stability of competitors' behaviour. A crisis results when the balance of these views changes, either because new information is released or because existing information is suddenly regarded differently.

For example, a run on a bank results when its loan portfolio is suspected to be worth less than originally anticipated. Since intermediaries transform illiquid assets, they can face dynamic problems if they are perceived to be illiquid (S. Williamson, 1983). Moreover, intermediaries with short histories can suffer more severely from sudden changes in confidence than firms with longer histories. In cases where short histories make it more costly for intermediaries to operate, they may be tempted to take greater risks than their more established competitors. These greater risks can make the newer intermediaries even more prone to failure. All these factors are taken into account when forming expectations of the worth of bank securities, but during a crisis the weighting of the different factors undergoes a sudden change.

Stock prices can also exhibit dynamic instabilities. A stock market crash can result when an apparently informed group of investors become suddenly unwilling to pay the kinds of prices they were previously willing to pay for the stocks, and other market participants treat this change in behaviour as indicating a change in underlying information. Uncertainty, and emulation of others' behaviour, seem jointly to contribute to the ways in which investor expectations change.

Remedial intervention

There are many different ways of attempting to ameliorate the performance problems just discussed. Some of the more effective seem to involve using fewer regulatory constraints, but greater information dissemination. Incentives can also be used to obtain improved system functioning, as the following discussion shows.[6] Effective intervention means both specifying goals and justifying the nature of the intervention.

Goals

A financial system should encourage informed risk taking. That is, the system should encourage undertaking those kinds of risks which seem to promise rewards commensurate with the risks. To foster these activities, it is important to design regulation and taxation so that financiers can reap rewards from intelligent risk bearing behaviour. On the other hand, regulation should not reward perverse forms of risk taking: costs such as deposit insurance premiums should rise, rather than remain the same as is now the case in most countries, if institutions take on greater asset risks.

Since many performance problems arise from obstacles to or restrictions on competition, one remedy is to frame regulations with a view to enhancing system competitiveness. Competitiveness can be enhanced by removing restrictive regulation, and further encouraged by ensuring that timely, accurate information regarding risk and profitability is at least potentially available to all. Unfortunately, most financial systems currently fail to produce timely and accurate information for all classes of transactions. One of the most important instances of informational asymmetries concerns the quality of various intermediaries' asset portfolios.

Justifying intervention

Remedial intervention can be justified if the social benefits realised from the intervention exceed the social costs of administering it. For example, subsidies to the private sector can be justified if the social benefit deriving from the increased business is worth more than the costs of the subsidy programme. However even when the net social benefits are positive, the benefits are only maximised if the most cost-effective form of intervention is chosen.

As with private sector governance mechanism choices, it is important to assess the conditions under which each possible choice of remedial form is likely to be effective. For example, discretionary rather than rule based governance mechanisms permit a financial system to adapt more readily to change. As a second instance, self regulation is likely to be effective if there is a small number of large firms with a history of continuing participation in an industry. It is less likely to be effective if many small firms can quickly enter, and equally quickly leave, the industry.

The form of regulation affects costs as well as effectiveness. For example, public sector intermediation can be theoretically justifiable, and yet deal with a performance problem less cost-effectively than would subsidised private sector firms. Witness the presence of government-owned financial intermediaries in the residential mortgage market, in agricultural credit, and small business loan markets. In more recent years, many countries have curtailed such activities, frequently by turning them over to the private sector.

The direct costs of intervention are usually those of administering a programme. Administrative costs depend on the type of programme chosen; for example, the cost of a subsidy programme is generally not much greater than the subsidies, while the costs of operating a government intermediary may also incorporate substantial administrative costs. Costs also depend on the manner in which the intervention is targeted. For example loans, investments and guarantees are instruments specific to a firm or individual whereas taxes, regulations, and tariffs usually affect all firms or individuals active in a market.

Actions and responses

Policy actions should be chosen with a view to financiers' likely responses. That is, regulatory governance mechanisms should be analysed in terms of the incentives they create, and of how these incentives will affect the mechanisms' likely effectiveness.

Regulatory choices

Competitiveness can be encouraged mainly by increasing freedom of entry, whether it is freedom to enter an industry such as banking or a particular market such as the market for consumer credit. Many countries still have restrictions on permitted types of business which constrain entry, at least unless financiers can find ways of technically avoiding regulatory prohibitions. Unless line of business restrictions can technically be avoided at low cost, they are likely to inhibit inter-industry competition.

On the same grounds, since it is difficult to predict the nature of future financial system change, any proposed regulation intended to fix the system into its current organisational form can later serve to inhibit its competitiveness. It is important, therefore, to take great care with such rule-based mechanisms as functional form regulations, a kind of regulation which many countries currently use.

New forms of networking are frequently experiments with new organisational forms, presumably undertaken with a view to realising either scale or scope economies. Sometimes networking and other experiments take the form of technically avoiding current regulatory restrictions. However, so long as competitiveness or safety are not obviously threatened by the experiments they should be encouraged. Attempts technically to circumvent existing regulation generally signal that profitable system operations are being restricted, and if the system is competitive this also means efficiency is impaired. In the absence of a clear threat to system safety or soundness, the best policy in such cases is to remove the constraint.

Ownership restrictions do not enhance system competitiveness. Indeed, small closely held firms can be more flexible, and better able to innovate, than their larger counterparts. Nor are ownership restrictions capable of effectively limiting self-dealing in larger financial firms. Thus most regulation restricting ownership should be avoided on the grounds that it at least potentially impairs competition without yielding offsetting benefits.

An exceptional instance in which ownership restrictions or other forms of close supervision are justified is when a closely held firm is set up to aggregate the small savings of numerous investors, which are then invested largely to serve the owners' own purposes with little or no regard to broader fiduciary responsibilities. Either firms using publicly raised funds should not be closely held or if so, their permitted investments should be restricted to obviate the conflict of interest that otherwise presents itself. Early public announcements regarding such activities would also reduce the incentives for abuse. Under a well-designed regulatory scheme, not only self-dealing managements, but also officials who failed to make appropriate public announcements, would be held accountable for their actions.

All financial firms, including market intermediaries such as securities brokers and dealers, should contribute to a public information base, reporting balance sheet and income statement data at the same time and as far as possible on the same basis. Intermediary assets should regularly be inspected by regulators whose quality assessments are then recorded in the public information base. Competition is enhanced by increasing the availability of information regarding both intermediary profitability and risk. In particular, publishing information about asset portfolios' quality will affect both intermediaries' ability to raise uninsured deposits and the value of any securities they issue.

If intermediaries change the risks of their asset portfolios, publicising the nature of the change ensures that the institutions will pay properly risk adjusted prices for (at least the uninsured) funds they raise. Thus, riskier institutions will not be subsidised by investors mistakenly placing lower cost funds with them. Riskier institutions will, as they should, have to pay more to attract public funds than will their safer counterparts.

Safety is better sought using incentives rather than constraints. A combination of publicity, graduated penalties and flexible rewards could be used to encourage intermediaries to evolve gradually over the medium term, entering new lines of business flexibly but slowly enough to allow regulators to assess the new developments' effects on system safety. For example, this principle could be used to allow financial intermediaries entry into the insurance business, and insurance firms into financial intermediation.

Deposit insurance premia should increase with insitutional risk, whether measured by leverage, asset quality, or in some other way. Then, institutions which increase their asset portfolio risk will face higher costs for doing so. If they still choose to assume the extra risks, they will have done so because they deem the additional prospective rewards more than compensate for the extra costs. A practical way of relating insurance premia to risk is to collect the same premia from all institutions in advance but with experience and the use of quality ratings to refund portions of the premia to institutions which appear to be operating most safely.

Regulators should make it clear in advance that uninsured depositors are to be left at risk in all cases. In this way riskier institutions will not benefit from the undiscerning placement of large deposits on their books, nor will they be able to suggest that they have the unofficial support of a government agency. Any changes in institutional quality ratings should be announced publicly and quickly.

Graduated disincentives to certain kinds of investments offer a more flexible approach to ensuring safety in operations while still encouraging and permitting institutions to evolve with changing conditions. Legislated capital requirements or guidelines such as those recently established by the Bank for International Settlements operate as relatively inflexible constraints and are therefore a less desirable way of pursuing system safety than publishing leverage ratios and flexibly increasing penalty costs such as deposit insurance premia charged against financial firms with high gearing (leverage) ratios.

Financial–industrial combinations may be able to realise both scale and scope economies by restructuring their organisations and their operations. Whether or not they can improve their cost-effectiveness through combining activities is a matter for the judgement of their managements; the public policy issue is whether or not such firms face incentives to pass on any efficiency benefits to the public. They will face such incentives in a competitive or contestable financial system, and hence in such circumstances would do no economic harm. Indeed, they might well create benefits.

Regulators need adequate resources to assess system operations and to administer an incentive programme flexibly. Despite political objections to it, centralised regulation is best suited to these purposes. Thus efforts should be directed toward harmonising regulations in different jurisdictions. The political and practical difficulties of taking further steps may partially be ameliorated by learning from the experiences of the European Community as it moves toward a common financial market in 1992.

Financiers' responses

Whenever regulation restricts profitability, financiers are motivated to circumvent the regulation, to seek changes in it, or both. For example, when the legislative environment differs for different inter-

The Economic Organisation of a Financial System

mediaries, the differences affect the legal form of organisation chosen to carry out a given kind of business.

If intervention attempts to prevent business from carrying out profitable activity, the usual response of business will be to find a substitute but technically different form of conducting the activity. One recent US example is a futures brokerage operation set up by Morgan Guaranty Trust. The bank takes the position that the financial futures brokerage business is a bank-related business and is therefore permitted by regulation. The appropriate regulatory authorities do not yet appear to have ruled on the matter. US banks' acquisition of discount brokerage firms constitutes another example, with the banks arguing that this is not the kind of underwriting activity prohibited by the (1933) Glass–Steagall act separating banking from the securities business.

If regulation can make an activity unprofitable, then the private sector will not engage in it, at least unless it can find ways to evade the restrictions profitably. Credit controls and foreign exchange controls are likely to prove unsuccessful, because they are too easy to avoid. Self-dealing is similarly difficult to control.

Summary

This chapter discussed financial system change, performance problems, and remedies. With respect to change, the chapter examined the economic forces which drive a financial system to evolve continuously. As one example illustrating the workings of change, the chapter considered some factors favouring and hindering the emergence of an international currency.

Financial system performance problems are created by the same underlying forces that drive system change. The chapter defined the most common performance problems – fragmentation, externalities, market failure, abuse of market power, and dynamic instabilities – and outlined the reasons for their emergence.

Effective remedies for performance problems must be based on understanding and dealing with the economic forces giving rise to them. The chapter outlined goals for remedial regulation and showed how it could effectively achieve these goals. Designing a regulatory mechanism poses the same problems of choosing a discriminating alignment between governance structure capabilities and transaction requirements as were discussed earlier in the book. Using these principles, regulatory alternatives and financiers' likely responses to them were examined.

The chapter argued that effectively tackling performance problems primarily means using discretionary, as opposed to rule-based, regulatory governance mechanisms. To encourage the further development of their financial systems, countries need to find ways of keeping their systems safe without reverting to restrictive regulation. They have an opportunity to achieve both these ends, by removing restrictive regulations which continue to inhibit competition, and by increasing the scope and stringency of inspection and reporting requirements to encourage an atmosphere of openness in the competition.

Notes

1 Witness, for example, Britain's opposition to entering the European Monetary System at the present time. Britain's opposition seems to be based both on an unwillingness to surrender of sovereign powers, and on a belief that the strains of maintaining fixed exchange rates might be too great. One of the factors which would contribute to such strains is examined below.
2 Flexible exchange rates also create greater independence for the conduct of monetary policy. Since this book's purpose is to explain financial system functions, the monetary policy arguments are not examined here.
3 Earlier chapters define a governance mechanism as a general purpose arrangement which when combined with particular transaction terms constitutes a governance structure. Since economic policies are usually framed with respect to transaction classes rather than with respect to individual transaction details, this chapter's use of the term 'mechanism' preserves the distinctions established earlier.
4 The capital rationing equilibrium of Chapter 8 is a partial market failure: complete failure means no transactions occur at all. In Chapter 8, a capital rationing equilibrium resulted from financiers' inability to screen different sorts of risks, but market failure can occur in any set of circumstances where financiers cannot see how to profit from a transaction.
5 For example, many Asian share markets currently have no prohibitions against insider trading, although in most cases this situation is changing as the markets become integrated with the rest of the world's financial system.
6 The rest of this chapter is largely based on Neave (1989).

Chapter ten

Finance and economic development

Finance affects economic development, either aiding or constraining capital formation according to the kinds of propositions financiers will entertain. A converse influence is also manifest: economic growth affects financial system change. Emerging demands for more or for new kinds of financing create profit opportunities which can stimulate financial system development.

Finance and economic development are interrelated. Any financial system which is not perfect is likely to direct funds preferentially to certain client groups. As a result, the decisions made by financiers influence the amount and kinds of capital formation which can take place. Capital formation activity in turn affects economic growth, both directly and indirectly. The direct effect of investment is to increase aggregate demand by a factor determined by the multiplier. The indirect effect of capital formation activity is its impact on the composition of an economy's capital stock. For, the nature of capital in place has an impact on the profitability of further investment.

The ways in which a financial system can affect an economy depend on client access to both domestic and international sources of finance. If a project is to be financed domestically, the financial system's governance structures must have the capability to administer the transaction. If these capabilities have not been developed, domestic finance is unlikely to be forthcoming.

If domestic finance is not forthcoming, it may still be possible to raise funds abroad. However, success in obtaining finance internationally depends first of all on whether clients have the knowledge and skills to approach international financiers successfully. It depends further on the reputation of the country in the eyes of the international financial community, and on whether the financiers approached have developed an expertise suitable for screening the proposal.

While finance affects economic development, the converse is also true. Economic development affects financial system evolution, chiefly through presenting new profit opportunities of which financiers can avail themselves. These effects are limited by the abilities of financiers to perceive the opportunities, by the impact of regulation on their ability to exploit new sources of profit, and by the political environment in which they function.

How domestic finance affects economic development

The question of how a domestic financial system can affect economic development has long attracted the attention of economic theorists.[1] Most early writers emphasise macroeconomic effects, particularly the relations between money supply and price levels. Until the mid-1970s, most analyses argue against excessively rapid monetary growth and the inflation consequent upon it. Such studies emphasise the pernicious effects of inflation, arguing that high and volatile inflation rates can retard economic growth through their negative effects on capital formation.

Early theory recognises two channels through which the negative effects of inflation are manifest. First, inflation can impair project profitability by altering the expected real rate of return on projects. Second, variable rates of inflation are a source of variation in real rates of return, and thus make projects more risky than they would otherwise be. The combination of changes in expected real returns and in their volatility has still further adverse effects. Not only do the changes make it more difficult to forecast the likely profits from a new project, but they can also make it more difficult to finance projects. In an inflationary environment, financing can be especially difficult to raise for longer-term projects, for the traditional sources of funding – long-term bonds with fixed nominal interest rates – are avoided by financiers.

In recent years some of the difficulties with fixed nominal rates of return have been circumvented through the use of floating rate instruments which shift some of the investors' risk to the client. If through floating rate arrangements both financiers and clients can insure themselves against the effects of inflation, the transaction is much more likely to be consummated. However, floating rate financing does not remove the uncertainty in the real rate of return on the project, and can even exacerbate the risks faced by clients who cannot further pass on the risk of changing financing costs to the buyers of their products.

Since they mainly discuss the impacts of monetary and fiscal policy on development, development theorists tend to ignore the detailed nature of the financial system, assuming in effect that one kind of finance is the same as another. Indeed, before the mid-1970s, the possibility that financiers' skills and financial system structure can affect economic development receives little explicit attention. However since then, theoretical and empirical studies have begun to distinguish different kinds of financing arrangements and to study the impact of these differences on economic development.

Theories from development economics

Early discussions of finance and economic activity emphasise the importance of liquidity preference. To Keynes, liquidity preference means that investors prefer the greater certainty of returns on liquid assets to the uncertainties of returns on productive capital assets (or titles to those assets). In the liquidity trap, interest rates will not fall below a floor level, but that floor is too high for full employment investment to occur. That is, liquid assets are too attractive in relation to more risky investments in real capital, and the demand for liquidity retards growth possibilities. Expansionary monetary policy will not help in the liquidity trap, because interest rates cannot be reduced below the minimum level defined by the trap.

Of course, increases in the money supply can expand economic activity whenever the economy is not in the liquidity trap. In these cases monetary expansion both satisfies the demand for liquidity and provides additional funds which encourage capital formation by lowering interest rates. This expansionary effect can even occur in the presence of interest rate ceilings, selective credit policies or other forms of what are sometimes called financial repression. For, once the demand for liquidity is satisfied, additional supplies of funds lower interest rates and hence stimulate capital formation.[2]

Risk–return tradeoffs do not enter the financial and economic literature until the mid-1960s. Keynesians discuss choices between liquid and illiquid assets, but do not recognise the existence of a risk–return tradeoff. Tobin (1965) first recognised that if returns are sufficiently high in relation to risk, investors will prefer to purchase risky assets rather than to hold liquid balances. Tobin's portfolio theory argues that households allocate their wealth between money and productive assets, holding larger ratios of capital assets (or titles to them) as the return to capital assets increases relative to the return to money.

One of the policy recommendations stemming from portfolio theory remains rooted in liquidity preference arguments. To Tobin and others, capital formation can be encouraged by increasing the opportunity cost of holding money (say by taxing returns on it) while keeping interest rates low. Another way to reduce the return on money is to increase the inflation rate, but this policy can create the difficulties mentioned above. For example, some writers point out

Finance and economic development

that as the rate or the variability of inflation increases, a shift from money to inflation hedges can occur, reducing productive investment and hence the rate of economic growth.

The development economics literature of the early 1970s stresses that financial liberalisation can enhance economic growth. Liberalisation means relaxing credit controls or removing restrictive regulation which inhibits certain kinds of financings. In essence, the proponents of liberalisation favour the use of market interest rates. For example, McKinnon (1973) and Shaw (1973) argue against interest rate ceilings or credit controls on the grounds of their likely adverse consequences. "Distortions of financial prices including interest rates and foreign exchange rates" reduce "the real rate of growth and the real size of the financial system relative to nonfinancial magnitudes," retarding the development process (Shaw, 1973).

McKinnon also considers the possibility that financial repression could lead to dualism: a developing economy may adopt both traditional techniques with low productivities and modern techniques with high productivities. Subsequent analysis shows that financial repression is not necessarily responsible for dualism: a two-technology economy can exist even with a freely functioning capital market (Fry 1988, 25–6). Nevertheless, the theoretical qualification does not deny the practicality of McKinnon's insight: economic growth can be enhanced by expanding capital market activities. For, expanding capital market activities can encourage growth by removing constraints on the availability of financing.

Neo-structuralists and types of finance

The neo-structuralist view emphasising the importance of alternative sources of finance also emerges in the mid-1970s. Neo-structuralist models stress the importance of two kinds of finance – one kind provided by markets, one by intermediaries. The neo-structuralists view market provided finance (which they call non-institutional or curb market finance) and intermediary finance as alternative ways of funding the same projects.

Neo-structuralist models have been used to analyse the effects of financial liberalisation. In these investigations, easing the terms on which intermediaries advance funds can enhance economic growth. The liberalising policies which bring about the easier terms involve removing credit constraints, removing interest rate ceilings, lowering reserve requirements or paying interest on required reserves. By lowering intermediary costs, the policies are viewed as lowering the cost of financing, and thus encouraging capital formation.

Neo-structuralists believe the effects of liberalisation depend on the terms according to which market provided and intermediary provided finance are assumed to be available. If intermediaries are more efficient at allocating investible funds than markets, and if households substitute mainly out of inflation hedges when real deposit rates increase, then liberalising the terms on which intermediaries can lend or invest raises the supply of credit, the quantity and quality of investment, and the rate of economic growth. If intermediaries are less efficient than markets, say because of the implicit tax on intermediaries posed by reserve requirements, other forms of liberalisation such as removing interest rate ceilings will have the opposite effects.

The neo-structuralists do not recognise that alternative sources of finance use different kinds of governance structures and might not therefore be perfect substitutes. Consider the neo-structuralist arguments regarding the costs of intermediated and curb market finance. Although liberalising the terms on which intermediaries can make loans or investments may increase their activity, it does not follow that the increase will occur wholly or even partially at the expense of market provided finance.

Consider an aggregate supply curve for financing, regarded as the sum of two supply curves – for intermediary finance and market provided finance respectively. Changing the cost conditions which affect the position of one of the supply curves will affect equilibrium interest rates, first for that type of financing, then for the other. But if the total quantity of financing is to remain more or less unchanged, there must be substitutions between the two individual types, and this substitution will not generally take place to any significant extent. Neither suppliers nor demanders of funds can switch readily between intermediated finance on the one hand, and market supplied finance on the other, because the two types use different governance structures and are therefore suitable for meeting transactions with different kinds of requirements. Moreover, in a world where both market agents and intermediaries can import additional funds from abroad, the substitution effect on which the neo-structuralist arguments depend is likely to be weaker still.

Relevance of institutional economics

Different governance mechanisms have relative advantages in effecting different kinds of transactions, meaning that any change in the operating costs of one governance mechanism is unlikely to lead to much substitution from the funds supplied through a different kind of mechanism. Consider again the differences between market and intermediated financing. Even if markets cannot overcome certain problems of informational asymmetries, intermediaries might still be able to do so. Where intermediation is needed to deal with informational asymmetries a change in the costs of markets will make little difference to how the intermediated transactions are arranged. However, the users of market provided finance would still benefit from the cost reductions, and their capital formation plans might be enhanced with consequent impacts on economic growth.

Fry's (1988) review of the development literature holds that by changing relative rates of return to different kinds of assets, ready availability of finance (shifts of the supply curve to the right) changes the desirability of investing in productive capital.

On the other hand, it is also possible that some projects cannot attract financing even at high interest rates: Fry recognises the equilibrium credit rationing possibilities developed by Stiglitz and Weiss (1981).

Institutional economics shows that certain kinds of adverse selection problems can be overcome with appropriate financing techniques, thus raising the possibility that the credit rationing arguments' applicability may be more limited than has so far been acknowledged. Institutional economics and financial theory show that the effects of credit rationing can sometimes be overcome by signalling, sometimes by switching to governance structures with greater capabilities. First, costless financial signalling equilibria can be designed to overcome what would otherwise be difficult screening problems (e.g. Brennan and Kraus, 1986). Second, the high-capability governance structures of earlier chapters can also sometimes ameliorate the Stiglitz–Weiss rationing possibilities (1981).

The theories outlined earlier in this book can also be used to reconsider development economics' view of layering. Since development economics does not recognise that the demand for financing represents an aggregate of demands arising from distinct types of transactions, it is unable to view layering as a possibly efficient response to the transactions' differing requirements. In the neo-structuralist models layering is regarded as increasing costs without gaining commensurate benefits. However, in both institutional economics and in practice clients usually view layering as valuable, either because it removes a constraint on their choices or because it offers them new, not otherwise available, possibilities for tailoring risks. Layering is a way of aligning governance structures with transaction requirements, and enhances the allocative efficiency of a financial system.

Moreover, the neo-structuralist assumptions that layering does nothing but increase financing costs are not sustained by theoretical analyses of market functioning. At least in competitive markets any recomposition of assets achieved by layering must be a valuable service. For any layering activity must cover its costs through the prices charged for the services provided thereby.[3] If a service cannot be priced to recover the costs of providing it, then the forces of competition will quickly eliminate the activity. If it plays no valuable role, layering will not survive except when, as indicated below, it is a creation of inappropriate policy.

Fry (1988) also emphasises that a well-developed and well-run financial system can foster confidence which itself enhances economic development. This confidence rests partially on the belief that the pernicious effects of inflation stressed by early theorists will not be permitted to ravage the real returns on existing financial arrangements and the capital formation they fund. Confidence also rests partially on the belief that the financial system operates within a legal and political infrastructure which ensures the stability of long-term contractual arrangements.

Not all financial systems foster such confidence. For example, a system lacking in strong financial management can exacerbate insolvency problems by making credit available to firms lacking the resources and capabilities to use it effectively. This would in turn result in a weakening of any pre-existing degree of confidence.

Empirical studies

Fry's (1988) summary of empirical studies suggests that financial conditions exert a modest impact on overall saving, but a considerable effect on allocative efficiency. In addition, some studies appear to support the McKinnon–Shaw arguments favouring liberalisation. Although their findings are based only on an examination of financial variables (rather than a combination of financial and real variables), the investigations suggest that financial systems are capable of influencing the rate and type of economic growth an economy can achieve.

Other evidence summarised by Fry (1988) suggests that a financial system can affect an economy's income distribution. Financial repression and the credit rationing which it can entail have been observed to worsen income distribution and increase industrial concentration. For example, some evidence suggests that subsidised credit policies discriminate against rather than favour small borrowers. Since small firms can be liquidity constrained and therefore unable to expand, their market prices are artificially low, making them attractive takeover targets. The situation is exacerbated if cheap subsidised credit is available to large firms, for the ready availability of funds then makes it easier for them to acquire the smaller firms. Such phenomena have been observed, for example, in Colombia and Korea.

Finance and economic development

Thus, selective credit policies can actually create more problems than they solve. Worse yet, efforts to avoid policy constraints, or to obtain subsidies for investments not directly targeted in the subsidy schemes, can lead to forms of layering which actually are unproductive, since they result from bad policy choices. These kinds of layering do, of course, contribute to higher transactions costs without corresponding benefits. The resulting distortions mean that the policies lower both overall investment and its efficiency. Fry concludes that the data support the notion that countries with selective credit policies do have low growth rates, and that their financial systems are more fragile.[4]

As yet, there is little empirical research regarding the comparative efficiency of intermediaries and markets, but the earlier chapters of this book argue that both intermediaries and markets are indeed likely to act as complementary suppliers of finance. Thus the effects on the economy of increasing the number of kinds of available financings merit considerable further investigation.

How external finance affects development

Whatever the constraints on capital formation posed by an underdeveloped domestic financial system, the availability of international finance also needs to be taken into account. Even if they cannot raise the funds at home, clients may be able to raise financing externally. The possibility of raising funds externally does not, however, extend to unlimited access.[5] Clients may have little knowledge of the different possible sources of international finance, meaning that their search costs are high enough to limit seeking out available sources.

On the supply side, international financiers can suffer from an inability to assess local conditions. They may or may not have a favourable perception of the country's political or economic climate. Threats of nationalisation, and the possibility of runaway inflation, are examples of the factors which discourage international finance. While a highly sophisticated international financial system can ameliorate some domestic financing constraints for some countries, it will not necessarily satisfy all of a given country's demands, and the extent to which it will satisfy any of them varies from country to country.

Effective development policies

The policy recommendations stemming from the development economics models are closely related to their assumptions. As Fry (1988) observes, both McKinnon and Shaw predict that an increase in the real deposit rate towards competitive equilibrium levels reduces inflation and increases growth. The neo-structuralist models predict the opposite because they emphasise that higher deposit rates will reduce returns to capital investment. The McKinnon–Shaw models thus assume that savings is interest elastic, while the neo-structuralist conclusions depend on an interest elastic demand for investment. If both domestic savings and investment demand are interest inelastic, the effect of higher interest rates will depend on whether the international supply of finance is interest elastic, as casual observation suggests it might be.

Other analyses presume that the aggregate supply of credit is relatively inelastic. Consider, for example, the effect of changing reserve requirements, an effect which depends on how the required reserves are used. Increases in required reserves reduce bank lending, but if the funds represented by the increased reserves are used by development banks, the total volume of loans could be increased. The relevant question for policy is not whether the analysis is correct within the confines it presumes, but whether such a policy change would have any significant impact on the aggregate supply of intermediary provided finance, particularly today in a world of at least partially integrated financial systems. The most likely effect of increased reserve requirements today is that business will be driven offshore or to nonbank intermediaries not facing the same requirements.

Indeed, in an open economy reserve or other regulatory policies can be more important than exchange rate policies, since inappropriate reserve policies or other forms of punitive or restrictive legislation can drive business offshore.[6] Thus, for example, foreign exchange and trade liberalisation in the presence of a high required reserve ratio can stimulate the development of offshore financial intermediation which avoids the imposition of the reserve tax. In addition, offshore financial centres may not be as likely as local financiers to put up funds for projects contributing to development, as mentioned above.

Desirability of market interest rates

The McKinnon–Shaw models of economic growth argue that the growth-maximising rate of deposit interest is the competitive market equilibrium rate. An increase in the equilibrium rate of deposit interest increases the real supply of credit and hence the rate of economic growth. The increase need not affect the competitive loan rate if either reserve requirements are lowered, or if the inflation rate (and hence the opportunity cost of holding non interest earning reserves) is lowered. The policy implications of these models are that interest rate ceilings should be abolished and the required reserve tax should be eliminated. In addition, new entry to the financial system should be made as easy as possible, so that the supply of finance becomes as interest elastic as possible.

Once different classes of financial assets are recognised, it becomes evident that the effects of institutional interest rates can be registered on portfolio composition rather than having the portfolio size effects discussed above. If households can be induced to substitute financial assets (representing claims on productive investment) for inflation hedges, the resulting portfolio reallocation can increase the average efficiency of investment and therefore economic growth rate in the medium run.

Financial liberalisation

Fry (1988) notes that financial repression has no benign effects in the McKinnon–Shaw models. On the other hand, there can be positive advantages to financial liberalisation; i.e. to removing constraints affecting private sector financiers. Unconstrained financiers are likely to be more forthcoming with financing arrangements. Moreover, liberalisation avoids or ameliorates the contractionary effects of deflation produced through monetary deceleration, mainly because it is more difficult to reduce the supply of credit in a liberalised economy.

Financial liberalisation is probably easier to achieve in open economies, both because vested interests have less to lose and because international pressures in favour of liberalisation are likely to be greater. Vested interests have less to lose in an open economy: even before liberalisation is implemented, external supplies of funds will have offset most domestic forms of market power. Countries which have already liberalised their financial systems exert pressures on those which have not yet done so: Japan and the European Community economies are examples of the late 1980s. In the case of Japan, much of the pressure emanates from the United States, while in the case of the European Community countries, much of the pressure emanates from the 1992 initiative.

Externally oriented policies

At present, not all policies capable of stimulating international financial development have been thoroughly analysed in the development economics literature. The main features of stimulative policies are to provide a taxation and regulatory environment no more costly than that of most other countries, as discussed above. But in addition, a free press and a democratic, financially conservative government are distinct assets from the point of view of international financiers, although the economic effects of encouraging these environmental conditions do not appear to have been assessed in any rigorous way.

Finally, on the grounds that well-informed financial markets do a better job of allocating scarce financial resources than their less well-informed counterparts, governments desiring to enhance their financial systems should consider seriously whether they could produce additional reliable information. If this were possible, the information could alert international financiers to profit opportunities they might not otherwise perceive. As one example of the possibilities, the International Finance Corporation provides public information regarding investment opportunities on Third World stock markets, information that individual countries themselves are not yet producing.

Policy comparisons

Some lessons can be derived from examining the policy mix in high growth developing economies. Some high growth economies have maintained interest rates below market equilibrium levels. The low rates appear to have stimulated relatively large quantities of capital formation, but the resulting capital stock has not always been efficient.

Rapid growth requires very high rates of investment and a financial system which promotes investment efficiency. These possibilities are probably best fostered by a regime which encourages the use of market rates of interest, and which implements relatively stable monetary and fiscal policies. In general, the Pacific Basin's developing economies have adopted such policies. At times, even the Pacific Basin economies have provided exceptions, however. Korea, Hong Kong, Taiwan, and Singapore have all on occasion implemented policies which caused real interest rates to move inversely with inflation.

Although the Pacific Basin developing economies are case studies of rapid economic growth, private sector behaviour in these economies does not seem to have differed significantly from that of other, less successful developing economies, such as in South America. Greater monetary discipline in the Pacific Basin countries seems at least partly responsible for their higher rates of economic growth, just as the early development theorists contended. Highly variable rates of monetary growth create shocks which seem to be negatively correlated with GNP growth. The Pacific Basin economies seem to have avoided these difficulties, but in many South American economies highly variable and often overly rapid monetary expansion has led to high rates of inflation, financial instabilities and crises.

Comparisons of fiscal policies are also informative. Shifts in the ratio of net government credit to total domestic credit affect output growth, at least in countries which do not have access to well-developed capital markets. Thus expansionary fiscal policy raises the ratio of net government credit to total domestic credit, and without developed capital markets these effects are more difficult to offset domestically. To the extent that international lenders use notions of borrowing capacity, governments' budgetary deficits may be more difficult to finance by borrowing from abroad. Thus in some countries it seems, contrary to the Ricardian equivalence hypothesis, that fiscal policy can lower output growth in the long run by starving the private sector of finance for productive investment. Comparisons of fiscal policies also appear to support the importance of increasing, as far as possible, the supply of domestic saving.

Finally, in recent years the amount of international debt outstanding seems to have affected capital formation in countries with debt repayment problems. Suppose a country has a relatively large debt in relation to its GNP, and its bankers are exerting pressure for more rapid repayment. Additional investment might well improve export earnings, but in the circumstances any earnings increases will likely be channelled into debt service payments. Thus, there are few or no short-term returns to capital formation; indeed, the outstanding debt can act as a disincentive to new capital formation. The effect seems to be of empirical significance: countries with the largest ratios of debt to GNP, and in difficulty with international lenders, have had lower rates of investment during the 1980s than countries not experiencing the same difficulties (*Economist*, 20 May 1989, p. 73).

How economic development encourages financial activity

Having seen some ways in which a financial system can contribute to economic development, it is now time to examine how economic development influences an economy's financial system. In essence, more business activity creates additional demands for financing, both of existing types and of new types. Growth in demand for output means growth in the derived demands for both capital formation and its financing, which in turn increase demands for financial services. There can also be supply effects: economic growth contributes to greater wealth, which in a stable economy can mean an increase in the supply of funds seeking profitable domestic investments.

Thus economic growth leads to demands both for more of the same kinds of financial services, and for innovative forms. With economic development, the ability to realise scale and scope economies in financial activities means the system can develop more specialised facilities for dealing with different kinds of financing demands.

How financial systems develop

Financial system development can be assessed in several ways. One way uses the volume of transactions in relation to national income. Financial development can also be measured by increases in the kind and sophistication of financial transactions, including increases in the degree of financial system integration. This discussion uses both measures, but emphasises the second.

Rybczynski (1984) argues that economic development affects the ways in which a system provides finance for business and other clients. Less-developed economies appear first to develop financial systems based mainly on bank financing, and with further development progress to using equity financing.[7] In developing countries, commercial banks usually dominate the financial sector,[8] and their performance has substantial influence on the overall efficiency of domestic resource mobilisation and allocation. In recent years, it has also become clear that increasing international economic activity stimulates the development of risk trading and risk management activities.

As economies develop further, the financial system becomes more complex, and the various forms of successive transactions referred to by development economists as financial layering emerge. As already noted, development economists do not regard layering favourably. Clearly, layering increases overall transactions costs. But by transforming and reallocating financial assets, layering can also improve the resource allocation process, either by creating new channels for funding or by creating new ways of managing risks. In particular, financial system development can increase the availability of finance to particular parts of an economy. In this way, the extra transaction costs can be more than offset by the additional benefits deriving from improvements to the resource allocation process.

Suppose, for example, regional intermediaries are more efficient at satisfying local needs than national institutions. On the other hand, local institutions are also usually more vulnerable, in that their assets are concentrated in the local economy. The benefits of regional knowledge can be gained without the costs of geographic specialisation if the regional institutions' assets can be securitised. With securitisation, transactions costs are higher than would otherwise be the case. Nevertheless, market directed selection of local institutions accompanied by securitisation is commonplace, and is also *prima facie* evidence of the efficiency of the layering activity from the participants' point of view.

The same arguments apply to the various forms of risk trading which have recently emerged in many highly developed capitalist economies. Despite frequent charges that much risk trading is simply casino-like activity, it can be argued that risk trading relaxes a constraint on the kinds of portfolios that financiers can construct. Interest rate swaps between financial intermediaries constitute an obvious example – the swaps remove a constraint on portfolio income risk. Creating synthetic insured portfolios with the use of index options and futures offer another example – the synthetic portfolios can be constructed at lower transactions costs than can portfolios using the underlying securities.

Development and regulation: some current issues

Financial system development is usually accompanied by changes in regulatory climate. Most developed systems exhibit similar growth patterns: from fragmented toward integrated markets, from an emphasis on accounting practice to the use of performance based incentives, from division of different functions to permitting their integration according to current perceptions of transaction economics.

Current World Bank policies attempt to gain the benefits of financial system development for the Bank's clients. The Bank's policies encourage developing a variety of financial institutions, a range of financial services, a reliable financial information system, a legal framework ensuring enforceability of contracts, and regulatory and supervisory systems which ensure stability. The Bank advocates developing curb markets to stimulate the development process further.

Cartelised or oligopolistic systems are viewed as jeopardising liberalisation: hence development programmes must address issues of market structure and management performance in order to succeed. Stiffer supervision is also advocated: the Bank sees many countries as having inadequate prudential supervision of financial institutions, and an inadequate legal system to enforce contract provisions.

As Chapter 9 argued, regulatory intervention can be justified in terms of perceived externalities, market failures, and impediments to transacting. But restrictive regulation can help vested interests to preserve entry barriers and to suppress competition. Hence intervention must be discriminating. Government ownership of financial institutions has sometimes led to high levels of nonperforming assets, and since the incentives facing government employees differ from those facing private sector employees, allocation of funds to appropriate risk categories may be done less efficiently by the public sector. Indeed, policies aimed at expanding the number of public sector specialised institutions have often produced disappointing results.

Fry (1988) suggests that when there is market failure because of informational asymmetries there may be a case for government intervention. To Fry, the recommended forms of intervention include taxing profitable investments and providing deposit insurance. The analysis of this book suggests first of all that the private sector has several means of overcoming the effects of informational asymmetries, ranging from using costless signalling to using more complex forms of governance structures. In the event that all these possibilities fail, an alternative to government intervention is to subsidise those activities of financiers which are currently unprofitable and which can also be shown to have sufficiently large positive externalities.

Summary

This chapter examined interrelations between economic and financial development. It first considered how finance, both domestic and international, affects development. Both theory and the lessons to be learned from examining various countries' policies were considered.

The chapter also considered how economic development affects finance, particularly noting that such financial developments as layering offer benefits as well as costs. Finally, some current issues regarding development and regulation were examined.

Notes

1 This chapter is heavily indebted to Fry (1988).
2 Keynes also emphasises the importance of expectations to investment demand, but many of his followers stress liquidity preference with little reference to expectational effects.
3 For example, the options and futures markets facilitate forms of risk management that would otherwise be much more costly to effect.
4 On the other hand, it is possible to find examples of planned economies which have, despite the selective credit policies they have employed, still posted high growth rates.
5 Merton's (1987) concept of breadth of knowledge is thus relevant to clients as well as financiers.
6 Moreover exchange rates may largely be determined by international capital flows over which domestic policy holds little sway.
7 The influence of the state may have important effects on the historical

Finance and economic development

proportion of bank versus market financing, but with increasing economic development different countries' proportions begin to converge, at least if they are influenced more by economics than by state decisions (Rybczynski, 1984).
8 Countries such as Germany and Japan have, of course, reached high stages of development with financial systems based much more heavily on banking than are those of such economies as Britain and the United States. Nevertheless, in recent years Germany's and, more especially, Japan's financial systems have approached the western model discussed here to a much greater degree. So far, the EEC 1992 initiative seems to be fostering further developments of this kind.

Chapter eleven

Conclusions

This chapter reiterates the book's purposes and summarises its findings. The book compares and contrasts an institutional economics theory of a financial system with more commonly accepted, neoclassical financial theory, offering a synthesis of the two based on Williamson's notions of aligning transaction requirements with governance structure capabilities. The book argues that while neoclassical theory has helped to define important properties of financial transactions and their aggregate effects, its normative orientation leaves aspects of financial activity unexplained. As a result, neoclassical financial theory has less descriptive applicability: less power to explain the details of financing transactions and the financial system's resulting features. Institutional economics is therefore used to elaborate a descriptive theory of financial system activity, explaining a number of additional transaction and system features.

Further progress toward a more nearly complete theory of financial system organisation and performance will, it is hoped, benefit from the tensions that a comparison and contrast of normative and descriptive theories inevitably creates. The integration attempted here recognises that the appropriateness of normative and descriptive theories usually depends on the purpose of the theoretical investigation, and consequently on the emphasis it employs. Neoclassical financial theory is concerned mainly with underlying economics when agents act as if they are so competent they can solve even the most difficult decision problems, and obtain all the necessary data to do so. On the other hand, institutional theory addresses situations where agents' competence is limited by conceptual or computational considerations.

One way of reflecting a disparity between competence and the difficulty of decision making is through the nature of financial transactions' informational conditions. The neoclassical theory's view of unlimited competence is reflected in its assumptions of decision making under risk, while the institutional theory's view of limited competence is reflected in the assumption of decision making under uncertainty. The distinction between risk and uncertainty helps to show that many routine decisions and financial system practices are well explained with neoclassical theory, but many changes in existing practice are more easily analysed using an institutional approach.

The details of the argument are developed along the following lines. Chapter 2 defines the important dimensions of financial system functions and organisation: the nature of agents, their goals and the conditions under which they pursue these goals. Agents' intendedly rational goal pursuit constitutes the system's most basic driving force. However, the nature of any informational differences between agents and the costs of processing information profoundly affect the means agents choose to carry out individual transactions. Then, since a financial system is defined by the aggregate effects of individual transactions, information processing and transaction cost considerations affect the system's form (i.e. the combination of institutions, markets, and practices it employs) through the governance structures employed to administer the various transaction classes.

The three basic mechanisms for governing financial transactions – markets, intermediaries, and internal arrangements – were first distinguished by Oliver Williamson. In this book, as in Williamson, each type is seen as having specialised capabilities which give it advantages in administering some, but not all kinds of transactions. Since the mechanisms' respective advantages can best be explained by elaborating each type's most important costs and capabilities, Chapter 3 examines their costs and capabilities in detail, thus showing how and why the different mechanisms play complementary roles in a financial system.

Chapter 4 explains that the competitive advantage of a governance mechanism can be enhanced by specialisation. Specialisation is mainly intended to sharpen competitive advantage through realising economies from focussing on particular kinds of transactions. Understanding the costs and benefits of specialisation further explains different mechanisms' complementary roles. The economics of specialisation also helps to explain how the mechanisms adapt in response to clients' changing demands.

Chapter 5 examines the choices made in aligning transaction requirements with the capabilities of alternative governance mechanisms. Agents' purposes inform their choices of both transaction types and the mechanisms to govern the requirements the transactions pose. With regard to financing demands, system clients choose between alternative sources mainly on the basis of perceived financing costs. Financiers premise decisions to supply funds on their ability to govern transaction requirements, and on the most effective ways of realising these capabilities.

Transacting parties' views of the informational conditions they each face constitute one of the most important transaction requirements. Agents' perceptions can differ in both kind and degree, and they may receive new information at different times during the course of a transaction. These matters were elaborated using two prototypical situations: mergers and acquisitions on the one hand, intermediary crises on the other. Mergers and acquisitions illustrate the need for using flexible governance structures; financial crises show how the transition from less to more flexible governance structures is effected when the need to do so is recognised after the transaction origination.

Chapter 6 considers the choices of transaction details which complete a governance structure. Many of these choices represent attempts to manage informational differences through using incentive schemes and setting up processes to effect *ex post* adjustments of contract terms. These choices can mitigate any unfavourable impacts of realised outcomes, but they can also increase transaction costs, even to the point of preventing some transactions from occurring.

Chapter 7 points out that while financiers set up transactions individually, they also manage transactions in the aggregate. Managers of marketable securities portfolios are principally concerned with trading assets to generate a target level of income while managing risk effectively. On the other hand, agents managing portfolios composed mainly of illiquid assets (the managers of intermediaries or of portfolios of closely held investments) must work to influence the income pattern and default risks of their assets without relying heavily, or perhaps even at all, on active trading. In some illiquid portfolios, returns are better regarded as uncertain rather than risky. Whether returns are risky or uncertain, however, the main task of portfolio management is to assemble and to manage assets which yield a return appropriate to the risks or uncertainties they entail.

Chapter 8 examines how agents' combined actions define financial system properties. The chapter first considers how the system's markets determine securities prices, then how intermediaries affect financing availability. Institutional theory is compared with neoclassical theory and an overview of empirical findings in attempts to note which system properties are presently well explained, which currently appear anomalous.

Chapter 9 considers the manner in which financial systems evolve and the kinds of performance problems frequently associated with highly evolved systems. The effects of regulation on system organisa-

Conclusions

tion and the likely prospects of ameliorating performance difficulties through using regulation are both examined.

Chapter 10 considers how finance and economic development are interrelated. A financial system shapes its own domestic economy, and can influence other economies' development as well. For, financial availability can either promote or constrain economic growth. In turn, economies shape financial systems, since economic growth usually leads to further development of a financial system. The chapter also shows that development economics does not yet recognise important differences between governance structures, differences which mean that intermediary and market provided finance are substitutes only to a limited degree. Differing transaction requirements also mean that layering is not always unproductive. Indeed, the new kinds of transactions which have emerged in the 1970s and 1980s perform highly valuable resource allocation and risk management roles.

In sum, this book strives to synthesise neoclassical and institutional theories of finance to explain a financial system's manifest form. It uses neoclassical and institutional economics to complement each other; the latter is particularly useful for explaining many transaction details which the neoclassical theory does not address. In addition, the book provides theories of financial decision making under uncertainty, and financial system change, still other matters which are not addressed by neoclassical theory. The theme of aligning governance mechanism capabilities with transaction requirements provides a means of synthesising the different theories currently available.

References

Admati, Anat R., "A Noisy Rational Expectations Equilibrium for Multi-Asset Securities Markets", *Econometrica* (1985), 629–56.

Akerlof, George A., "The Market for 'Lemons': Qualitative Uncertainty and the Market Mechanism, *Quarterly Journal of Economics* **84**, (1970), 488–500.

Altman, Edward I., and Subrahmanyam, Marti G., eds., *Recent Advances in Corporate Finance*, Homewood, Ill.: Irwin, 1984.

Arrow, Kenneth J., "Control in Large Organizations", *Management Science* **10**, (1964), 397–408.

Arrow, Kenneth J., "The Role of Securities in the Optimal Allocation of Risk Bearing", *Rev. Ec. Studies*, (April 1964).

Arrow, Kenneth J., *The Economics of Organization*, New York: Norton, 1972.

Atkinson, A.A. and Edwin H. Neave, *An Incentive Scheme with Desirable Multiperiod Properties*, INFOR21, (1983), 76–83.

Baltensperger, E., "Alternative Approaches to the Theory of the Banking Firm", *Journal of Monetary Economics* **6**, (1980), 1–36.

Barnea, Amir, Haugen, Robert A., and Senbet, Lemma W., *Agency Problems and Financial Contracting*, Englewood Cliffs, N.J.: Prentice-Hall, 1984.

Barney, Jay B., and Ouchi, William G., eds., *Organizational Economics*, San Francisco: Jossey-Bass, 1986.

Barry, Christopher, and Brown, Stephen, "Limited Information as a Source of Risk", *Journal of Portfolio Management* **12**, (Winter 1986), 66–72.

Beja, Avraham and Hakansson, Nils H., "Dynamic Market Processes and the Rewards to Up-to-Date Information", *Journal of Finance* **32**, (1977), 291.

Benson, E.D. "The Search for Information by Underwriters and its Impact on Municipal Interest Cost", *Journal of Finance* **34**, (1979), 871–85.

Bhattacharya, Sudipto and Constantinides, George, eds., *Frontiers of Financial Theory*, Totowa, N.J.: Littlefield and Adams, 1987.

Bhattacharya, Sudipto and Pfleiderer, Paul, "Delegated Portfolio Management" *Journal of Economic Theory* **36**, (1985), 1–24.

Black, Fischer, and Myron Scholes, "The Pricing of Options and Corporate Liabilities", *Journal of Political Economy* **81**, (1973), 637–59.

Boyd, John H. and Prescott, Edward C., "Financial Intermediary-Coalitions", *Journal of Economic Theory* **38**(2), (1986), 211–36.

References

Breeden, D., "Futures Markets and Commodity Options: Hedging and Optimality in Incomplete Markets", *Journal of Economic Theory* **32**, (1984), 275-300.

Breeden and Litzenberger, "Prices of State Contingent Claims Implicit in Option Prices", *Journal of Business* (October 1978).

Brennan, M., and Kraus, A., "Efficient Financing under Asymmetric Information", *Journal of Finance* 42, (1987), 1225-44.

Brennan, M., and Schwartz, E., "The Pricing of Equity-Linked Life Insurance Policies with an Asset Guarantee", *Journal of Financial Economics* 3, (1976), 195-213.

Brennan, M. J., and Schwartz, E. S., "Optimal Financial Policy and Firm Valuation", *Journal of Finance* **39**(3), (1984), 593-605.

Chan, Y., "On the Positive Role of Financial Intermediation in the Allocation of Venture Capital in a Market with Imperfect Information", *Journal of Finance* **38**, (1983), 1543-67.

Chan, Yuk-Shee and King-Tim Nak, "Depositors' Welfare, Deposit Insurance, and Deregulation", *Journal of Finance* **40**(3), (1985), 959-73.

Constantinides, George, and Bruce Grundy, "Optimal Investment with Stock Repurchase and Financing as Signals", University of Chicago Graduate School of Business Working Paper, 1986.

Cooper, S. Kerry, and Fraser, Donald R., *Banking Deregulation and the New Competition in Financial Services*, New York: Harper and Row, 1983.

Cox, John C., Jonathon Ingersoll, and Stephen A. Ross, "A Reexamination of Traditional Hypotheses About the Term Structure of Interest Rates", *Journal of Finance* **36**, (1981a), 769-800.

Cox, John C., Jonathon Ingersoll, and Stephen A. Ross, "The Relation between Forward Prices and Futures Prices", *Journal of Financial Economics* **9**, (1981b), 321-46.

Cox, John C., Jonathon Ingersoll and Stephen A. Ross, "A Theory of the Term Structure of Interest Rates", *Econometrica* 53 (1985), 385-406.

Cox, John C. and Mark Rubinstein, *Options Markets*, Englewood Cliffs, N.J.: Prentice-Hall, 1986.

Crawford, V., and J. Sobel, "Strategic Information Transmission", *Econometrica* **50**, (1982), 1431-51.

Cyert, Richard M. and James G. March, *A Behavioral Theory of the Firm*, Englewood Cliffs, N.J.: Prentice-Hall, 1965.

Diamond, Douglas W., "Asset Services and Financial Intermediation", University of Chicago Graduate School of Business Working Paper 182, July 1986.

Diamond, Douglas W., "Financial Intermediation and Delegated Monitoring", *Review of Economic Studies* (1984), 393-413.

Diamond, Douglas W., "Optimal Release of Information by Firms", *Journal of Finance* **40**(4), (1985), 1071-93.

Diamond, Douglas W., "Reputation Acquisition in Debt Markets", University of Chicago Graduate School of Business Working Paper, May 1985.

Diamond, D., and R. Verecchia, "Information Aggregation in a Noisy Rational Expectations Economy", *Journal of Financial Economics* **9**, (1981), 221-34.

References

Diamond, D. W., and Dybvig, P. H., "Bank Runs, Deposit Insurance, and Liquidity", *Journal of Political Economy* **91**, (1983), 401–18.

Diamond, Peter A., "The Role of a Stock Market in a General Equilibrium Model with Technological Uncertainty", *American Economic Review* **57**, (1967), 759–76.

Dotan, Amihud, and Ravid, S. Abraham, "On the Interaction of Real and Financial Decisions of the Firm Under Uncertainty", *Journal of Finance* **40**, (1985), 501–17.

Economist, The, "Debtors' Hangover", 20 May 1989, p. 73.

Fama, Eugene F., "The Information in the Term Structure", *Journal of Financial Economics* **13**, (1984), 509–27.

Fama, Eugene F., "Term Premiums in Bond Returns", *Journal of Financial Economics* **13**, (1984), 529–45.

Fama, Eugene F., "What's Different about Banks?" *Journal of Monetary Economics* **15**, (1985), 29–39.

Fama, Eugene F., and Jensen, Michael C., "Agency Problems and Residual Claims", *Journal of Law and Economics* **26**, (1983), 327–48.

Fama, Eugene F., and Jensen, Michael C., "Organizational Forms and Investment Decisions", *Journal of Financial Economics* **14**, (1985), 101–19.

Fellingham, John C., Newman D. Paul, and Suk, Yoon S., "Contracts without Memory in Multiperiod Agency Models", *Journal of Economic Theory* **37**(2), 340–54.

Figlewski, S., "Market 'Efficiency' in a Market with Heterogeneous Information", *Journal of Political Economy* (1978), 581–97.

Flannery, Mark J., "Asymmetric Information and Risky Debt Maturity Choice", *Journal of Finance* **41**(19), (1986), 19–36.

Fry, Maxwell J., *Money, Interest, and Banking in Economic Development*, Baltimore: Johns Hopkins University Press, 1988.

Gale, Douglas and Martin Hellwig, "Incentive-Compatible Debt Contracts: The One-Period Problem", Working Paper London School of Economics, International Centre for Economics and Related Disciplines, 1983.

Gatto, Mary Ann, Robert Geske, Robert Litzenberger, and Howard Sosin, "Mutual Fund Insurance", *Journal of Financial Economics* **8**, (1980), 283–317.

Geske, Robert, and Johnson, Herb E., "The American Put Option Valued Analytically", *Journal of Finance* **39**, (1984), 1293–139.

Glosten, Lawrence and Milgrom, Paul, "Bid Ask and Transaction Prices in a Specialist Market with Heterogeneously Informed Traders", *Journal of Financial Economics* (1985), 71–98.

Grinblatt, Mark S. and Stephen A. Ross, "Market Power in a Securities Market with Endogenous Information", *Quarterly Journal of Economics* (1985), 1143–67.

Grossman, Sanford J., "On the Efficiency of Competitive Stock Markets Where Traders have Diverse Information", *Journal of Finance* **81**, (1976), 573–84.

Grossman, Sanford J., "The Existence of Futures Markets, Noisy Rational Expectations, and Information Externalities", *Review of Economic Studies* (1977), 431–48.

References

Grossman, Sanford J., "A Characterization of the Optimality of Equilibrium in Incomplete Markets", *Journal of Economic Theory* 17, (1977).

Grossman, Sanford J., "Further Results on the Informational Efficiency of Competitive Stock Markets", *Journal of Economic Theory* 18, (1978), 81–101.

Grossman, Sanford J., "An Introduction to the Theory of Rational Expectations Under Asymmetric Information", *Review of Economic Studies* (1981), 541–58.

Grossman, Sanford J., and Hart, Oliver D., "The Allocational Role of Takeover Bids in Situations with Asymmetric Information", *Journal of Finance* 36, (1981), 253–70.

Grossman, Sanford J., and Hart, Oliver D., "An Analysis of the Principal–Agent Problem", *Econometrica* 51, (1983), 7–44.

Grossman, Sanford J., and Hart, Oliver D., "One Share/One Vote and the Market for Corporate Control,' MIT Department of Economics Working Paper 440, February 1987.

Grossman, Sanford, and Stiglitz, J. E., "On Value Maximization and the Alternative Objectives of the Firm", *Journal of Finance* 32, (1977), 389–402.

Grossman, Sanford J., and Stiglitz, Joseph E., "On the Impossibility of Informationally Efficient Markets", *American Economic Review* 70, (1980), 393–407.

Hadar, Joseph, and W. R. Russell (1969), "Rules for Ordering Uncertain Prospects", *American Economic Review* 59, 25–34.

Hancock, Diana, "The Financial Firm: Production with Monetary and Non Monetary Goods", *Journal of Political Economy* 93, (1985), 859–80.

Hansen, L., and Singleton, K., "Stochastic Consumption, Risk Aversion, and the Temporal Behaviour of Asset Prices", *Journal of Political Economy* 91, (1983), 249–64.

Hansen, Robert G., "A Theory for the Choice of Exchange Medium in Mergers and Acquisitions", *Journal of Business* 60, (1987), 75–95.

Harris, Milton, and Raviv, Artur, "A Sequential Signalling Model of Convertible Debt Policy", *Journal of Finance* 40, (1985), 1263–82.

Harrison, J.M. and David M. Kreps "Speculative Investor Behaviour in a Stock Market with Heterogeneous Expectations", *Quarterly Journal of Economics* (1978), 323–36

Harrison, J., and Kreps, D., "Martingales and Arbitrage in Multiperiod Securities Markets", *Journal of Economic Theory* 20, (1979), 381–407.

Haubrich, J. G., and King, R. G., "Banking and Insurance", National Bureau of Economic Research Working Paper, 1983.

Heiner, Ronald A., "The Origin of Predictable Behavior", *American Economic Review* 73, (1983), 560–95.

Heinkel, Robert, "A Theory of Capital Structure Relevance under Imperfect Information", *Journal of Finance*, December, 1982.

Heinkel, Robert and Schwatrz, Eduardo S., "Rights versus Underwritten Offerings: An Asymmetric Information Approach", *Journal of Finance* 41, (1), (1986), 1–17.

Hogarth, Robin, and Reder, Melvin, eds., "The Behavioural Foundations of Economic Theory", *Journal of Business* 59, Part 2, October 1986.

References

Huang, Chi-fu, and Robert H. Litzenberger, *Foundations for Financial Economics*, New York: North Holland, 1988.

Huberman, G., "A Simple Approach to Arbitrage Pricing Theory", *Journal of Economic Theory* 28 (1982), 183-91.

Hurwicz, L., R. Radner, and S. Reiter, "A Stochastic Decentralized Resource Allocation Process", *Econometrica*, March and May, 1975.

Ingersoll, Jonathon, "A Contingent-Claim Valuation of Convertible Securities", *Journal of Financial Economics*, May, 1976.

Jagannathan, Ravi, "Call Options and the Risk of Underlying Securities", *Journal of Financial Economics* 13, (1984), 425-33.

Jensen, Michael C., and W. Meckling, "Theory of the Firm: Managerial Behavior, Agency Costs, and Ownership Structure", *Journal of Financial Economics* 5, (1976), 305-60.

John, Kose, and Nachman, David C., "Risky Debt, Investment Incentives, and Reputation in a Sequential Equilibrium", *Journal of Finance* 40, (1985), 863-76.

John, Kose, and Williams, Joseph, "Dividends, Dilution, and Taxes: A Signalling Equilibrium", *Journal of Finance* 40, (1985), 1053-70.

Kim, Wi Saeng and Eric H. Sorenson, "Evidence of the Impact of the Agency Costs of Debt on Corporate Debt Policy", *Journal of Financial and Quantitative Analysis* 21(2), (1986), 131-44.

Kleidon, Allan W., "Anomalies in Financial Economics: Blueprint for Change?", in Robin M. Hogarth and Melvin W. Reder, *Rational Choice*, Chicago: University of Chicago Press, 1986.

Knight, Frank H., *Risk, Uncertainty, and Profit*, Chicago: University of Chicago Press, 1971. (Originally published 1933).

Kyle, Albert S., "Continuous Auctions and Insider Trading", *Econometrica* (1985), 1315-34.

Leland, Hayne and David Pyle, "Information Asymmetrics, Financial Structure and Financial Intermediation", *Journal of Finance* 32, (1977), 371-87.

Langlois, Richard N., ed., *Economics as a Process*, Cambridge: Cambridge University Press, 1986.

Litzenberger, Robert, H. and H. B. Sosin, "The Theory of Recapitalizations and the Evidence of Dual Purpose Funds", *Journal of Finance* 32, (1977), 1433-56.

Littlechild, Stephen C., "Three Types of Market Process", in Richard N. Langlois, ed., *Economics as Process*, Cambridge: Cambridge University Press.

Marcus, Alan J., and Shaked, Israel, "The Valuation of FDIC Deposit Insurance using Option Pricing Estimates", *Journal of Money, Credit, and Banking* 16, (1984), 446-60.

Marshall, J. M., "Private Incentives and Public Information", *American Economic Review* 64, June 1974, 373-90.

Mayers, David and Smith, Clifford W. Jr., "Ownership, Structure, and Control: The Mutualization of Stock Life Insurance Companies", *Journal of Financial Economics* 16(1), (1986), 41-72.

McLeod, Alex N., *The Principles of Financial Intermediation*, University Presses of America, 1983. (Reviewed JEL June 1985, p. 636.)

References

McKinnon, Ronald, I., *Money and Capital in Economic Development*, Washington, D.C.: Brookings Institution, 1973.

Mehra, R., and Prescott, E., "The equity premium: a puzzle", *Journal of Monetary Economics* **15**, (1985), 145–61.

Mendelson, Haim, "Market Behavior in a Clearing House", *Econometrica* (1982), 1505–23.

Merton, Robert C., "Theory of Rational Option Pricing", *Bell Journal of Economics and Management Science* **4**, (1973), 141–83.

Merton, Robert C., "On the Pricing of Corporate Debt", *Journal of Finance* (May 1974).

Merton, Robert C., "An Analytic Derivation of the Cost of Deposit Insurance and Loan Guarantees", *Journal of Banking and Finance* **1**, (1977), 3–10.

Merton, Robert C., "On the Cost of Deposit Insurance When there are Surveillance Costs", *Journal of Business* **51**, (1978), 439–52.

Merton, Robert C., "A Simple Model of Capital Market Equilibrium with Incomplete Information", *Journal of Finance* **42**, (1987), 483–510.

Milgrom, P., and Stokey, N., "Information, Trade, and Common Knowledge", *Journal of Economic Theory* **26**, (1982), 17–26.

Miller, Edward M., "Risk Uncertainty and the Divergence of Opinion" *Journal of Finance* **32**, (1977), 1151–67.

Miller, Merton H., "Financial Innovation: the Last Twenty Years and the Next", *Journal of Financial and Quantitative Analysis* **21**, (1986), 459–71.

Millon, Marcia H., and Thakor, Anjan, "Moral Hazard and Information Sharing: A Model of Financial Information Gathering Agencies", *Journal of Finance* **40**, (1985), 1403–22.

Modigliani, Franco, and Merton H. Miller, "The Cost of Capital, Corporation Finance, and the Theory of Investment", *American Economic Review* **48**, (1958), 261–97.

Modigliani, Franco, and Merton H. Miller, "Corporate Income Taxes and the Cost of Capital", *American Economic Review* **53**, (1963), 433–43.

Mookherjee, D., "Optimal Incentive Schemes with Many Agents", *Review of Economic Studies* **51**, (1984), 433–46.

Myers, Stewart C., "The Capital Structure Puzzle", *Journal of Finance* **39**, (1984), 575–92.

Nathan, Alli, and Neave, Edwin H., "Competitiveness and Contestability in Canada's Financial System: Empirical Results", Canadian *Journal of Economics* **23**, (1989), 574–91.

Neave, Edwin H. "An Approach to Canada's Financial Regulation, *Canadian Public Policy* **10**, 1989, 1–11.

Neave, Edwin H., "Competitiveness and Contestability in Canada's Financial System", Queen's University Working Paper, 1984.

Neave, Edwin H. "Options, Informational Asymmetries and New Financings", Proceedings, Ninth International Financial Conference, University of Paris – Dauphine, Paris, 1989.

O'Hara, Maureen, "Property Rights and the Financial Firm", *Journal of Law and Economics* **24**, (1981), 317–32.

Ohlson, James A., *The Theory of Financial Markets and Information*, New York: North-Holland, 1987.

References

Plott, Charles R., and Sunder, Shyam, "Efficiency of Experimental Security Markets with Insider Information: An Application of Rational Expectations Models", *Journal of Political Economy* 90, (1982), 663–97.

Ramakrishnan, T. S., and Thakor, A. V., "Information Reliability and a Theory of Financial Intermediation", *Review of Economic Studies* 51, (1984), 415–32.

Riley, J., "Informational Equilibrium", *Econometrica* 47, (1979), 331–58.

Ross, S. A., "The Arbitrage Theory of Capital Asset Pricing", *Journal of Economic Theory* 13, (1976), 341–60.

Ross, S. A., "The Determination of Financial Structure: the Incentive Signalling Approach", *Bell Jnl* 8, 1977, 371–86.

Rothschild, M., and J. Stiglitz (1971), "Increasing Risk II: Its Economic Consequences", *Journal of Economic Theory* 3, 66–91.

Rubinstein, M., "An Aggregation Theorem for Securities Markets", *J. Fin. Economics* (Sept. 1974).

Rybczynski, Tad M., "Industrial Finance System in Europe, US and Japan", *Journal of Economic Behavior and Organization* 5, (1984), 275–86.

Savage, Leonard J. *The Foundations of Statistics*, New York: Wiley, 1951.

Samuelson, W., "Bargaining under Asymmetric Information", *Econometrica* 52, (1984), 995–1005.

Shaw, Edward, S., *Financial Deepening in Economic Development*, New York: Oxford University Press, 1973.

Simon, Herbert A., *Administrative Behavior*, New York: Wiley, 1961.

Smirlock, Michael, "Evidence on the (Non) Relationship between Concentration and Profitability in Banking", *Journal of Money, Credit and Banking* 17, (1985), 69–83.

Smith, C. W., "Investment Banking and the Capital Acquisition Process", *Journal of Financial Economics* 15(1/2), (1986), 3–28.

Smith, C. W., "Option Pricing: A Review", *Journal of Financial Economics* 3, (1976), 3–51.

Smith, C. W., and Warner, J. B., "On Financial Contracting: An Analysis of Bond Covenants", *Journal of Financial Economics* 7, (1979), 117–61.

Stapleton, R. C., and Subrahmanyan, M.G., "The Valuation of Multivariate Contingent Claims in Discrete Time Models", *Journal of Finance* 39, (1984), 207–27.

Stapleton, Richard C., and Subrahmanyam, Marti G., "The Valuation of Options when Asset Returns are Generated by a Binomial Process", *Journal of Finance* 39, (1984), 1525–38.

Stiglitz, Joseph E., and Weiss, Andrew, "Credit Rationing in Markets with Imperfect Information", *American Economic Review* (1981), June, 393–49.

Thakor, Anjan V., "An Exploration of Competitive Signalling Equilibria with 'Third Party' Information Production: The Case of Debt Insurance", *Journal of Finance* 37, (1982), 717–38.

Tobin, "Money and Economic Growth", *Econometrica* 33, (1965), 671–84.

Townsend, R. M., "Theories of Intermediated Structures", in *Carnegie-Rochester Conference Series on Public Policy* 18, 221–72.

Weitzman, Martin, "The New Soviet Incentive Scheme", *Bell Journal of*

References

Economics and Management Science, (1977).
Werner, Jan, "Equilibrium in Economies with Incomplete Financial Markets", *Journal of Economic Theory* **36** (1985), 110–18.
Williamson, Oliver E., *Markets and Hierarchies*, New York: Free Press, 1972.
Williamson, Oliver E., *The Economic Institutions of Capitalism*, New York: Free Press, 1985.
Williamson, Oliver E., *The Economic Organization of Capitalist Institutions*, London: Wheatsheaf, 1986.
Williamson, Oliver E., "Corporate Finance and Corporate Governance", *Journal of Finance* **43** (1988), 567–91.
Williamson, Stephen D., "Costly Monitoring, Financial Monitoring, and Equilibrium Credit Rationing", Queen's Unversity Department of Economics Discussion Paper 583, 1983.
Wilson, Robert, "Theory of Syndicates", *Econometrica* **36**, (1968), 119–32.
Wriston, Walter B., "Technology and Sovereignty", *Foreign Affairs* **67**, (1988–89), 45–62.

Index

accounting services 61
adverse selection 106–7
affiliated organisations 64, 82
agency effects 82–4
allocative efficiency 129–30, 131, 133–4
arbitrage: between markets 67, 68–70, 88; and option pricing 57–8; and portfolio management 114; and securities prices 128–9, 140–1
arbitrage pricing theory (APT) 1, 68, 128
Arrow, Kenneth J. 131
asset services 60
asset specificity: and contracts 26
Austrian view of transactor criteria 22–4

Beja, Avraham 134–5
Benson, E.D. 100
Bhattacharya, Sudipto 44, 83–4
bonding 79–80, 84
Boyd, John H. 43
bridging finance 86–7
broker markets 54–5
budgetary deficit, financing of 152–4

capital asset pricing theory (CAPT) 68–9, 97, 127–8, 130, 138
capital market line 128
Chan, Y. 43
change *see* financial system change
client access 150
closely held investments, portfolio of 111, 121-2

competence, transactor 6, 21–2, 24–5; and transaction frequency 26–7
completeness and incompleteness: of contracts *see under* contract terms; of markets 131–5
contingency planning 101
contract terms 5–6, 14–15, 21, 39: completeness or incompleteness 25–6, 38–9, 84–5, 94–109; (and innovation 145–6; in portfolio management 111, 114, 115, 118, 121–2; and signalling 80, 99–101, 106)
corporate control *see* mergers and acquisitions
costs 27; and governance mechanisms 35–6, 37, 47; (intermediaries 42, 65; markets 50–1, 52, 53); in perfect market 126–7; and portfolio management 112–13; and risk 27–9; and uncertainty 29–30
covenants, restrictive 103, 106
credit rationing 142–3, 169, 171, 172–3
credit risk 116
crises of confidence 89–90, 158–9
criteria, transactor 22–5
currency: single international 152–4; swap market 60; trading 55, 58–9, 60, 70, 132

dealer markets 54–5
debt financing 26, 78–9, 99
default risk 82, 115–16, 117–18

194

Index

deposit insurance premiums 159–60, 162–3
derivative securities *see* futures; options
development economics 3, 6, 168–9, 171, 173–7
Diamond, Douglas W. 44, 99
disclosure requirements 53, 54
disequilibrium trading 134–5
diversification: of intermediaries 43–4, 63–4; in portfolio management 111, 112–13, 117–18, 121–2
divided signal 100
domestic financial system: and economic development 167–73
dynamic instability 158–9
dynamic portfolio management 113–15

economic development 3, 166–80
effectiveness: and governance mechanisms 34–5; and information conditions 36–9
efficiency 12; and governance mechanisms 34–5; and market completedness 131, 133–4; and securities prices 129–30; *see also* performance problems
equity financing 26, 78–9, 99
European Currency Unit 152
evolution *see* financial system change
export finance 156
externalities 155–7

Fama, Eugene F. 77, 100
financial system change 5, 6, 72–3, 130–1, 149–54
Fisher relation 69, 129
Flannery, Mark J. 101
foreign exchange markets 55, 58–9, 60, 70, 132
forward contracts 58
forward parity theorem 70, 129
fragmentation 70, 154–5
frequency, transaction 26–7
Fry, Maxwell J. 171, 172, 173, 175, 180

fundamental transformation 26, 111
funds: demands for 76–81; supply of 13, 81–5
futures contracts 58, 59–60; and complete market 132; interest rate 120–1; and portfolio management 113, 114, 120–1

geographical diversification 63–4
governance mechanisms 5–6; 13, 32–49; capabilities of 32–9; combination of 71–2; and economic development 169–71, 173; specialisation of 35–6, 50–75; *see also* intermediaries; internal financings; market(s)
governance structure 5–6, 12, 13
Grossman, Sanford J. 80, 83, 87–8, 133, 136–7

Hakansson, Nils H. 134–5
Harris, Milton 101
Harrison, J.M. 139
Hart, Oliver D. 80, 83
hedging 57, 58
Heiner, Ronald A. 25
Heinkel, Robert 99–100
hyperrationality 4

incentive schemes 21, 42, 83, 99, 106
income risk 115–16, 118; intermediary income management 119–21
index futures and options 113, 114, 132
inflation 167, 168–9, 170, 172, 174–5
information, production of: by intermediaries 45, 62–3; for public consumption 156–7, 162, 176
informational conditions 4, 6; differences 20–1, 23; (as barrier to entry 158; in breadth 138–9); and effectiveness 36–9; and securities prices 135–41, 142; *see also* risk; uncertainty
innovation 2, 145–6
insider knowledge 41, 99, 138

195

Index

institutional economics 2–3, 5, 170–2
insurance 56, 57, 72; in portfolio management 113, 114–15
interest rate(s): and credit rationing 142–3; differentials 67–8, 69–70; and economic development 168, 170, 174–5, 176; futures 120–1; swaps 60, 120, 144, 155, 179
interest parity theory 69–70, 129
intermediaries, financial 1, 2, 5, 37, 42–6, 48; cycles of activity of 143–4; and economic development 169–71, 173; financing from 79, 82; liabilities of 88–91; portfolio management by 111–12, 116–21; and securities prices 141–4; specialisation of 50, 51, 60–7, 70–1
internal financings 5, 37, 46–8; specialisation of 50, 51
international financial transactions 151, 166, 173, 175–6, 177; and common currency 152–4

Jensen, Michael C. 77
John, Kose 100, 101
junk bonds 87, 88

Kim, Wi Saeng 84
Knight, Frank H. 4, 16, 19, 73
Kreps, David M. 139

layering, financial 171–2, 178–9
learning 15–16, 21–2, 108; and costs 28, 36
Leland, Hayne 44
lender of last resort 91
Levi, Leon 73
liability services 60
liberalisation, financial 169–70, 172, 175
linkages 67–8, 88
liquidity preference 168
listing requirements 54
Littlechild, Stephen C. 22

McKinnon, Ronald L. 169, 172, 173–4, 175

market(s), financial 2, 3, 5, 37, 39–42, 48; and economic development 169–71, 173; financing from 78–9; specialisation of 50, 52–60
market failure 157, 180
market power 157–8
market risk 115–16
marketable securities, portfolio of 110, 111–15
matching 119
Mayers, David 77
Mehra, R. 141
mergers and acquisitions: losses from 116; takeover financing 85–8
Merton, Robert C. 68, 138–9, 141
Milgrom, P. 137
Millon, Marcia H. 45
misrepresentation penalties 79–80
Modigliani–Miller conditions 127
money supply: and budgetary deficit 152–4; and economic policy 167, 168
monitoring 33; and contract terms 84–5, 107–8; by intermediaries 44, 45
moral hazard 89, 106–7

Nachman, David C. 101
Neave, Edwin H. 40
neoclassical financial theory 1–2, 3–5; and transactor criteria 22–4
neo-structuralist models 169–70, 171, 174
networking, new forms of 161
non-marketable securities, portfolio of 110–11, 115–18

operational efficiency 29, 129, 130
opportunism 14, 21, 41
option(s) 57–8, 59–60; and complete market 132; and portfolio management 113, 114
option pricing theory 89, 128
ownership restrictions 161–2

Pacific Basin 176–7
perfect capital market 125–31

Index

performance problems 154–9; remedies for 159–64
Pfleiderer, Paul 44, 83–4
Plott, Charles R. 138
portfolio management 110–24, 179
Prescott, Edward C. 43, 141
prices *see* securities prices
primary market transactions 52–4, 56
private markets 53–4
project substitution 107
public markets 53–4
Pyle, David 44

radical subjectivist view of transactor criteria 22–4
Ramakrishnan, T.S. 45–6
rational expectations theories 136–7, 138, 139–40
rationality, bounded and unbounded 21–2, 24–5, 37–8, 84–5, 97; and fragmentation 154–5
Raviv, Artur 101
regulation 3, 151–2, 156, 157–8, 159–64; and economic development 179–80; *see also* credit rationing; liberalisation
reinsurance 72
resolution 98–9
rights issues 80, 100, 139
risk 4, 16, 17–18, 22, 125; and competence 6, 24; and contract terms 25, 94–101, 107, and costs 27–9; and economic development 167, 169–9; and governance mechanisms 33, 37; (intermediaries 45; markets 40–2); and portfolio management 115–16, 117–18, 119–21; and securities prices 127–8, 135–8; and supply of funds 81; symmetric and asymmetric views of 19–20
risk trading 55–60, 66–7, 179
Ross, S.A. 79
routine transactions 145
Rybczynski, Tad M. 178

satisficing 35, 37, 38
Savage, Leonard J. 17
Schwartz, Eduardo S. 100
screening 81–2; costs of 36, 47; by intermediaries 43–4, 45, 66, 82; by internal governance 47; by markets 54; and portfolio management 111, 113, 115, 116
secondary market transactions 52–4, 56
securities prices 1, 2, 3, 67; and information 135–41; and perfect market 126–31
securitisation 48, 63, 72, 117–18, 178–9
security market line 128, 138
self-interest 13–14, 21, 42
Shaw, Edward S. 169, 172, 173–4, 175
signalling 79–80; and contract terms 80, 99–101, 106; and credit rationing 171; and crisis of confidence 90; during takeovers 86
Smith, Clifford W., Jr 77, 80
Sorenson, Eric H. 84
specialisation: of governance mechanisms 35–6, 50–75
speculation 56, 57, 58; in complete market 131–2; *see also* risk trading
Stiglitz, Joseph E. 87–8, 133, 136–7, 171
Stokey, N. 137
Sunder, Shyam 138
supermarkets, financial 61
supervision *see* monitoring
symmetric versus asymmetric views of transactions 19–20
syndicated loans 71–2
synthetic insured portfolios 114, 179

takeovers *see* mergers and acquisitions
technological change 5, 15, 29, 36, 129, 150, 151; and governance mechanisms 50, 65
term structure theory 68, 128

197

Index

Thakor, Anjan 45–6, 100
third parties: effects of 155–7; signals from 101; uncertainty and 103
Third World countries 105, 132, 144
Tobin 168
treasury bill futures 120–1

uncertainty 2, 4–5, 16–17, 18–19, 22, 125–6; and competence 6, 24; and contract terms 25, 38–9; 94–7, 101–6, 107; (in portfolio management 111, 114, 115, 118, 121–2); and costs 29–30; and governance mechanisms 33–4, 37–9; (intermediaries 45; markets 40–2); and innovation 145–6; and securities prices 139–40; and supply of funds 81, 84–5; symmetric and asymmetric views of 19–20

voting rights of shareholders 80–1

Weiss, Andrew 171
Williams, Joseph 100
Williamson, Oliver 2–3, 4, 26, 46, 78–9, 80, 84, 85, 96, 104
World Bank 179